Knowledge resistance

Manchester University Press

Knowledge resistance

How we avoid insight from others

Mikael Klintman

Manchester University Press

Published by Manchester University Press
Altrincham Street, Manchester M1 7JA
www.manchesteruniversitypress.co.uk

British Library Cataloguing-in-Publication Data
A catalogue record for this book is available from the British Library

ISBN 978 1 5261 3520 9 hardback

ISBN 978 1 5261 5174 2 paperback

First published 2019

Typeset by Servis Filmsetting Ltd, Stockport, Cheshire
Printed in Great Britain by TJ Books Limited, Padstow

Contents

Acknowledgements

A lot of people deserve my warm thanks for providing me with encouragement, help, and inspiration for this book.

I'm especially indebted to my wife, Jenny, and our boys, Leo, Bruno, Fred and Matti. Many things they did were crucial to this book project. Here I should particularly mention how Jenny initiated the plans for our two-year visit to Oxford and London (2016–18). In the process she patiently helped me to recognise my own initial knowledge resistance (read: I was a ramrod) to the great opportunities that our two-year visit to Oxford and London would offer us all: medical research for Jenny, British school experiences for the boys, research about knowledge resistance for me, and the accumulation of lots of character-building family memories. It turned out to be these two years that made it possible for me to conduct all the interviews and have all the informal discussions with UK scholars; dialogues on which this book is partly built. Lots of love to you all!

I began preparing for this book at Oxford University. I'd like to thank Dominic Johnson for inviting me to St Antony's College, where I spent a year as an academic visitor. Roman Frigg, Director of the Centre for Philosophy of Natural and Social Science (CPNSS) at London School of Economics and Political Science deserves my warm thanks for inviting me to join this research community as a visiting scholar for the second year. Laura O'Keefe and Mehrun Absar gave me a lot of practical help at CPNSS, and I very much enjoyed our chats. The CPNSS became my research hub for openly and informally exchanging ideas about knowledge resistance, and a place to analyse the many series of interviews that I conducted with human scientists at various universities.

Special thanks go to the directors of the sociology department at Lund University in Sweden, where I have my position as a professor. Without the help and flexibility of the directors – Britt-Marie Johansson and, later, Åsa Lundquist – I wouldn't have been able to spend the concentrated, extended period abroad writing this book. The sociology department at Lund is a very friendly and stimulating workplace that has been great to come back to, finishing the writing of this book in parallel with teaching and discussions with my Swedish colleagues.

Several other people have provided me with additional help, ideas, or inspiration, or have kindly agreed to be interviewed for this book. Here are a few of them, in alphabetical order: Aaron Reeves, Allan Dafoe, Andreas Olsson, Anna-Lisa Lindén, Avner Offer, Bent Flyvbjerg, Björn Ulvaeus, Catharina Landström, Christofer Edling, David Stainforth, Fredrike Otto, George Gaskell, Jacquelyn Pless, Javier Lezaun, Jerry Ravitz, Joan Costa-Font, Martin Bauer, Mohammad Mortazavi, Oliver Scott, Olle Frödin, Peter Sosue, Peter Walton, Ragnar Löfstedt, Rebecca Elliot, Rob Bellamy, Robin Dunbar, Sarah Darby, Thomas Hale, Thomas Lunderquist, Tim Schwanen, and Val Compton.

The research for and writing of this book was made financially possible by generous contributions from a few Swedish research foundations. The Swedish Research Council (VR: 2017-02885) has funded parts of the research for and publication of this book. Furthermore, The Foundation for Humanities and Social Sciences (RJ, FSK15:108:1) has provided financial support for the research behind this book that deals with knowledge collaboration. The coordinator, Anna Jonsson, and our co-researcher, Maria Grafström, deserve particular thanks for our exciting research and lively discussions, partly on how knowledge collaboration can help to prevent or reduce problematic knowledge resistance. Mistra Sustainable Consumption (Mistra SC) is an extensive research programme that has supported specific case studies of how consumers reason and process information – or resist such information – about the sustainability record of various goods and services. The programme coordinators, Åsa Svenfelt and Karin Bradley, have been very helpful in giving me time to integrate specific findings from Mistra SC into this book. The financial contributions from the Magnus Bergvall Foundation (Dnr. 2015-00973 & Dnr. 2016-01456) and the Åke Wiberg Foundation (H16-0142) have been much appreciated, covering some of the additional costs for the research visit to the UK.

Additional thanks go to Senior Commissioning Editor Tom Dark, David Appleyard, Robert Byron, and the rest of the staff at Manchester University Press involved in the production of this book, along with the exemplary copy-editor, Joe Haining.

Finally, I'd like to extend my warm thanks to my parents – Lillemor and Holger – for trying to teach me how to think with integrity. I guess a good dose of integrity is indispensable for minimising problematic knowledge resistance among ourselves and others, let alone for writing a thought-provoking book about knowledge resistance. I leave it to you readers to judge how well I listened to them.

Introduction

Knowledge has infinite time even if our lifespan is short. That's always the problem.

> Robin Dunbar, evolutionary psychologist, in an interview for
> this book, 13 February 2018

Stories and reality

Her tiny hand makes his sweaty. This doesn't alarm him. During recovery it's common to be hot. Sitting next to her bed, he tries to cheer her up. This time he shows her how to make little animals out of pipe-cleaners. Cheering people up, or at least making their hearts smile, particularly through storytelling, is his area of expertise. His stories usually begin with unpleasant adults who make children's lives miserable: there are the parents who ignore Matilda's interest in books and learning, instead making her spend all day watching soap operas and eating fast food in front of the TV; we have the unfriendly giants trying to capture the orphan child Sophie for no apparent reason; or the influential adults whose actions indirectly leave 11-year-old Charlie with few other life ambitions than keeping warm – he spends much of his time lying in a huge bed shared with his kind, but impoverished, parents and grandparents.

Now it's the man's own daughter who is lying in bed. Like most of the children that he is to write about in the years following this November morning in 1962, Olivia will be fine, he thinks. One thing puzzles him, however. When she tries to fashion a pipe-cleaner animal, her hands don't obey her mind. She cannot do it.

'Are you feeling alright?' he asks her.

'I feel all sleepy,' she says.

In an hour, Olivia is in a coma. In twelve hours, she is dead.[1]

The Norwegian-British author Roald Dahl probably identified more with the adults who help to save the children in his stories: Matilda's teacher, Miss Honey, who gives her books, stimulates her talents, and creates a loving home for her; the Big Friendly Giant, who uses his small brain and big heart to save Sophie from the evil giants; Willy Wonka, who puts an end to Charlie's and his family's poverty by crowning Charlie the winner and inheritor of the chocolate factory. But unlike these benevolent adults, Dahl had no chance of saving his daughter. She died from measles one year before a reliable vaccine was available. He didn't tell us more precisely how Olivia died. That's none of our business, of course. The most frequent complication with measles is pneumonia. Swelling of the brain is another complication, as are convulsions, blindness, and loss of hearing. Extensive knowledge resistance among the public about the measles vaccine is the reason Roald Dahl wrote an article about his daughter in the mid-1980s, sharing his family tragedy with the world.

A few years after he had published this piece (and after ambitious information dissemination and vaccination programmes), the effects of the measles vaccine became a story of scientific success. A dramatic reduction in the number of cases of measles followed. By the turn of the millennium, the disease was declared eliminated in several countries. Among them was the US. Deciding to have one's child vaccinated could mean the difference between life and death, not only for that child – it also reduces risks for other people, such as vulnerable people who cannot get vaccinated for medical reasons.

However, this didn't turn out to be the end of the measles story. In 1998, Andrew Wakefield, a medical doctor, claimed that the measles, mumps, and rubella (MMR) vaccine caused autism. According to him, the virus in the vaccine leads to inflammation in children's guts, impeding normal development of the brain. He published this idea in the

2

prestigious journal *The Lancet*.[2] A few years after he had published this study, the vaccination rates in the UK against measles dropped below 80 per cent.[3] Similar reductions in vaccination rates were found in other countries. As a result, the frequency of measles incidents was on the rise again.

Soon, other scientists began to scrutinise the message that Wakefield and several others had spread through outreach campaigns and public lectures. It didn't take long before numerous studies appeared that showed Wakefield's idea was entirely false. A wide range of methods were employed and groups of people with autism were examined. Nowhere was the correlation between the MMR vaccination and autism confirmed. When looking at Wakefield's own original 'study', scientists concluded that his research method, sample, and interpretation of data had been flawed.[4] It also turned out he had financial interests behind his false claim. In 2004 a journalist revealed these interests: Wakefield was a paid consultant to lawyers of parents claiming the autism of their children had been caused by the MMR vaccine. He and several other anti-vaccine lobbyists tried to convince the public in the US and else-where about the link between the MMR vaccine and autism. As a result of the new findings, he lost his medical licence and the scientific journal retracted his article.

When insight makes no difference

Scandals such as this happen from time to time, as most people will have observed from daily news. The media love such scandals since they sell papers. It isn't that strange that single individuals, like Wakefield, develop their own scientific claims. Nor is it particularly odd that Wakefield continued to preach his claims even after a number of scientists had rejected them. Much prestige and money are at stake. The practices of such *enfants terribles* might even be said to benefit society in some ways. This might seem bizarre to argue in a case that might very well have resulted in deaths, but deviants in science and society can sometimes force the mainstream to scrutinise, refine, or change its own beliefs for the better.

A more intriguing issue is how the surrounding public – people like you and me – handle instances where scientific claims are twisted. It turns out that myths like the one about a link between the MMR vaccination and autism are persistent among the public. Measles was officially declared eradicated in the US in 2000. However, parental refusal to have their children vaccinated led to more than six hundred reported cases of this potentially deadly disease in 2014.[5] Two years later, a study found that up to 41 per cent of the public in Europe and Russia still believed that vaccines have harmful side effects that outweigh their benefits.[6] Even after the scientific debunking of the myth, many people held on to it. To investigate what impact additional, relevant information has on beliefs about vaccines, psychologists divided people into several groups. The psychologists tested various strategies that might affect people's beliefs about the measles vaccine. What impact did factual and understandable information that dispels the myth have on people's knowledge beliefs? It had *no* impact. Among those who had a firm belief that the measles vaccine is linked to autism, the myth-busting information didn't change their position of refusal. In fact, the information didn't change the negative view among this group any more than among groups that had received information unrelated to vaccination. People who believed the measles vaccine to be safe used the additional information merely to confirm their beliefs.[7]

In some situations we are almost immune to information that challenges our assumptions. Many of us resist well-substantiated claims about vast improvements that have taken place in most places in the world – reduced violence, better health, and better conditions for women and children.[8] Such claims even provoke some of us, as if they imply that no further improvements need to take place. We resist acting on information about unspectacular but relatively high-risk situations around us in our communities, for instance the unhealthy air quality in many cities, road traffic accidents, accidental falls in the home, extensive sunbathing, excessive use of antibiotics in the world, and loneliness. On the other hand, we are like sponges absorbing news about sensational risks that are immensely tragic on the few occasions they materialise in the world, but that are nonetheless extremely unlikely at any given point

4

in time. These include aeroplane crashes, suicide bombings, kidnapping, and lethal encounters with snakes.

The typical complaints about what is usually called 'fact resistance' point to the absurdity of clinging to apparent myths, lies, and disproportionate worries: if people could only pull themselves together and be more reasonable, if they could only use some healthy scepticism and embrace all of the accurate facts, these complaints contend, imagine how many misconceptions and problems the world would overcome! Still, such reactions – although most of us might spontaneously echo them – are indicative of the naive reactions to fact resistance, reactions that I here call 'common-sense complaints' about fact resistance. Their philosophical roots can be traced back millennia in history, although their most famous rebirth took place in the Enlightenment period of the eighteenth century. The positive side of the Enlightenment in those early days and up until the early twenty-first century can hardly be exaggerated. Enlightenment culture's stressing of the value of observable facts and reasoned argument as opposed to myths, speculation, and excessive respect for the knowledge claims of charismatic authorities has been an indispensable part of the subsequent centuries of progress – from medicine to democracy and welfare. Still, despite their honourable roots in early Enlightenment thinking, the common-sense complaints about fact resistance of recent years have turned out to be of little use. There are even scientific findings indicating how the 'let's be more reasonable' approach to fact resistance can be harmful and counter-productive. This I will explain later this book, before suggesting an alternative approach that demands some update of Enlightenment thinking.

One of the reasons that common-sense complaints about fact resistance are naive is how deeply this resistance runs in us. The human sciences show that we are highly motivated – nonconsciously – to absorb and trust much of the false information that is spread about groups other than our own. In times when computers are programmed to spread false information to impact public opinion, this is not just about spreading lies. It is something more profound: to accurately tailor misleading or false information to people's current worries and prejudice. Such tailoring is sufficient to trigger people's hardwired processes of confirmation.[9] It is not only the busy general public who are inclined to confirm their previous beliefs and to resist challenging claims; it also happens in academia. In my discipline, sociology, a survey was conducted some years ago in the US regarding sociologists' positions concerning the role of evolution and biology in certain behavioural traits. Among the 155 academic sociologists who responded, 28.6 per cent identified themselves as radical, 56.7 per cent as liberal (in the US, social liberal sense), and 4.8 per cent as conservative. Less than half – 44 per cent – of all these highly educated people found it plausible that 'feelings of sexual jealousy have a significant evolutionary biological component'.[10] This differs starkly from research done by, for instance, the evolutionary psychologist David Buss along with other scholars. Buss maintains that sexual jealousy is an 'evolved solution [an adaptation] to the recurrent problem of survival or reproduction'.[11] Sexual jealousy is a manifestation of your genetic interest in your partner staying faithful.

As we'll see later, the claim that a human trait has evolutionary and biological roots is certainly not an excuse for any violation of norms. Nor is it a statement that we shouldn't fight the expressions of that trait: of course we should if the expression of the trait causes harm. This is the case when traits such as jealousy are turned into men's violence or control over women.[12] Yet, fighting presupposes recognising. Thus, fighting the expressions of those traits becomes impossible if we – like some of the sociologists in the study described above – resist insights from evolutionary science. It isn't a proven fact in the strictest sense that jealousy decreases the risk of having one's partner cheat. Nor is it a proven fact that jealousy increases the reproductive chances of the jealous person. No one has been able to divide thousands of generations of hominids based on their degree of jealousy. It has not been possible to calculate the difference in reproductive success between two such groups. Still, there seem to be no equally plausible or better explanations available. The researchers responsible for the survey, Mark Horowitz and his colleagues, conclude that they 'find the mechanical dismissal of the adaptiveness hypothesis dogmatic'.[13]

Another commonly used example that affects the general population is climate change. The tendency towards mechanical dismissal is particularly striking in light of the increasing amounts of data pointing towards human-made climate change. The evidence of human-made climate change has become more sophisticated. Still, knowledge beliefs about the reality or falsehood of climate change have become even more polarised since the 1990s. How confident in their doubts are the more scientifically literate and knowledgeable who contest human-made climate change? They are very confident, on average. In fact, their high scientific literacy and knowledge make them more confident that human-made climate change isn't happening than less knowledgeable people.[14] The discipline of geoengineering has proposed a set of large-scale technological measures that might – if we are lucky – reduce the effects of climate change. Such technologies include using plastic polymers in order to pull gas from the atmosphere or sending thousands of mirrors into space between the earth and the sun to reflect the sun's rays away from the earth. Climate sceptics presented with such measures have in several instances been converted to climate change believers.[15] How this can be possible will be discussed further on.

The point of this book

People and groups that seem so reasonable still block some of what appears to be overwhelming evidence or logical arguments. They sometimes avoid insights into anything from trivial matters to serious ones. During the 2010s, journalists and scholars have expressed increasing resentment as well as puzzlement with what they identify as fact resistance or denial among the general public, politicians, public thinkers, religious leaders, and even some scientists.[16] Ambitious attempts at reducing fact resistance have been made by the late Swedish physician and public speaker Hans Rosling, among others.[17] Their approach has been to provide additional facts and smart heuristics to dispel myths, for instance about health issues around the globe. Such efforts are immensely valuable, to be sure, as part of the old Enlightenment thinking that is continuously needed for identifying and demystifying dubious knowledge claims. While these efforts are important – necessary, even – they remain part of the common-sense complaints about fact resistance. In this book, I will show many ways in which they are insufficient if our goal is to gain a thorough and broad understanding of fact resistance. Such an understanding will be needed in order to do something more substantial about such resistance in areas where it is problematic. For now, it suffices to mention the peculiarity of trying to reduce fact resistance only by supplying more facts about the phenomenon resisted. To simply add facts might affect some people but not others; some are even likely to become increasingly fact resistant the more facts they are given in a particular area. For example, try to calm your travelling companion who suffers from a fear of flying by reading them statistics about how minuscule the risk is that a plane will go down. Even if they are a statistician, the statistics will probably not calm them. This is a less than perfect comparison, of course. Fear of flying is in many cases a specific individual's mental issue, whereas fact resistance is a much broader societal phenomenon. Nevertheless, fear of flying and fact resistance have one thing in common: they run deeply in us. This often makes it insufficient to try to reduce them using more and better facts alone. In addition, some serious rethinking about fact resistance is needed, as has been done concerning the fear of flying. Having said this, it's time to leave the comparison behind us.

The point of this book is to move beyond common-sense complaints about fact resistance. A few of the observations and questions that are common in such complaints will be discussed here as well. For instance, people and groups still block some of what appears to be overwhelming evidence or logical arguments. They sometimes avoid insights into anything from trivial matters to serious issues. Why, and what could be done about it in areas where it seems problematic?

In contrast to several contemporary books about fake news and alternative facts, this volume isn't interested in unveiling new details about a corrupt media culture, political liars, religious demagogues, or scientific charlatans. Prospective readers who are hoping to find one or a few reasons – ideally personified – for fact resistance that are unique to current society should probably consult some of the earlier works instead. This book has another goal: to rethink what is often simplistically called 'fact resistance'. To understand, and in turn find ways of handling, problematic – even dangerous – cases of how people resist the insights of others, we need to consider treating such resistance as the multifaceted and profoundly human phenomenon it is. This demands that we introduce a more comprehensive and less black-and-white term than fact resistance. I have used it several times above already: knowledge resistance (I will return to the distinction between the two terms in Chapter 1).

Such rethinking requires that we do at least two things differently. We have to allow ourselves to gain insights from what the broadest range of human sciences have to say about knowledge resistance – not just psychology or political science or economics or sociology or evolutionary thought, but all of it. Moreover, we have to leave some of our – usually negative – preconceptions about knowledge resistance aside. Why? Because in order to understand knowledge resistance – or anything else for that matter – it's necessary to search for the possible functions, rationales, and even benefits of that thing. This meant that I, in my research interviews for this book, had to add a question that might seem at odds with the love of knowledge (the Greek *philosophia* comes from the root words for 'love' and 'wisdom') that most of us probably believe that we harbour: 'Tell me about *the benefits* of knowledge resistance?' That question clearly caused at least some of my renowned scientific interviewees some unease. Still, it had to be asked; and they had to admit that the benefits of knowledge resistance are many. It is not until we thoroughly understand the benefits and beneficiaries of knowledge resistance that we can develop multifaceted tools to get to grips with its negative sides.

I've had the privilege of spending a quarter of a century studying and teaching about the intriguing ways in which people deal with sometimes uncomfortable knowledge. The main issues have been health, environment, and social wellbeing. Regardless of what sector or group of actors

I've researched, my work almost always ends up revolving around ways in which people handle knowledge. How people handle, and why they sometimes resist, knowledge is subject to intensive research within several academic disciplines. In this book, I crudely call the relevant disciplines the social, economic, and evolutionary sciences. Certain collaboration takes place between them; however, they also show a significant degree of mutual rivalry. There's an obvious irony here: scholars in disciplines that study knowledge resistance resist insights from rival disciplines concerning knowledge resistance. A term apt for parts of this phenomenon has been coined by the sociologist Pierre van den Berghe: 'proud ignorance'.[18]

It would be terribly unfair to call all, or most, scholars who do research on knowledge resistance proudly ignorant. Still, it's all the fairer to note that most writings – often excellent ones – on how scholars handle, and sometimes resist, insights stick to their own specific area.[19] There are both pros and cons of sticking safely to one's mother discipline, of course. One possible advantage is that one's writings will comfortably fit the curricula of these disciplines. The fact that each discipline often has its own storyline that the author can build on also makes it easier to stick to that story. In traditional economics, one story is that people are entirely rational, even in their knowledge resistance and inattention. People make active choices. They are fully aware of what knowledge they resist, and avoid that knowledge in order to reach a given goal.[20] Social science, particularly sociology, has other storylines. One is that it is people's social position and the norms in their culture that steer what knowledge is considered valuable. This often results in people in the lower socio-economic classes moving towards false beliefs. Such false beliefs contend, for instance, that if they just work really hard they can climb the social ladder to the top. False beliefs might trigger increased self-esteem and reduce deviant behaviour in young people. Children aged 11–12 have been a particular research focus. Over time, however, these false beliefs change. By the time children are a couple of years older, the realisation that some of the beliefs they held may in fact be false can lead to low self-esteem. Part of the reason is that they begin to see the gap between the belief concerned and their own experiences.[21]

To give a third example, the story of behavioural economics would suggest that individuals are irrational. They act based on various simplifying heuristics and biases. People interpret and avoid knowledge in ways that hinder them from reaching their true, individual, and often long-term goals. Issues that behavioural economists are particularly interested in are usually specific. The topics typically concern how people often distort knowledge about money and healthy living by failing to plan appropriately for their golden years.[22]

In this book, I take the liberty of bringing up findings from most, if not all, disciplines that focus on knowledge resistance. This is necessary in order to give you a fuller picture of why knowledge resistance works the way it does. It also enables us to see how knowledge resistance could be dealt with, both by the individual and society. Another reason is that it would be odd to avoid insights from neighbouring disciplines in a book examining how people avoid insights from others. When working on contemporary problems related to the environment and health it seems strange not to collaborate across disciplines and beliefs. Relevant actors to collaborate with include people from any field from physics to religious studies. There are at least as many relevant people in governmental and nongovernmental organisations and companies, as well as households. Creating bonds of mutual learning lengthwise and crosswise is both exciting and frustrating, with all the challenges and opportunities of understanding people that think differently. In any case, I don't see any better alternatives.

Contemporary problems, such as how people navigate between conflicting knowledge claims about health, the environment, and social wellbeing, need contemporary ways of understanding and handling. That is the 'undisciplined' approach, if you will, taken in this book. The term 'undisciplined' is stolen from Steven Rayner, the great Oxford University scholar with a focus on science in society. Based on my own and my colleagues' research across the human sciences, we will see why, and in what contexts, people and informal groups resist knowledge. We'll look at numerous examples that concern social wellbeing, health, and the environment, as well as other widespread issues that are particularly illustrative. This will help us see what can be done – in organisations, informal groups, and by you as a reader – to prevent or manage knowledge resistance where it can be problematic.

What this book will cover

The next chapter is intended to establish a basic, unpedantic order where knowledge resistance – including knowledge, as such – can be placed at the appropriate distance to neighbouring phenomena. We will bring order to the tangle of words and notions that relate to knowledge resistance, using conceptual tools and ideas, in order to begin our journey towards creating a better understanding of what knowledge resistance is. This will make it easier to avoid unnecessary confusion in subsequent chapters.

Chapter 2 will begin with a personal experience I had in my teens when I spent a year in the US staying with an evangelical Christian host family in Colorado. This example will help us see a central pattern for how groups acquire certain knowledge and resist other claims. It concerns how people mark a clear distinction between what people in their own group, 'we', believe is valid and true, and what other groups, 'they', believe. We'll learn how the shaping of knowledge beliefs among some communities obeys the following principle: if 'they' believe that a certain type of food is unacceptable to eat, 'we' must shape our knowledge beliefs in a way that makes it acceptable to eat that type of food. This can be seen in the establishment of monotheism millennia ago. We can also see it today where dedicated carnivores – with categorical knowledge claims about health and ecology – have reacted to the increasing popularity of veganism by becoming ever more entrenched in their desire to eat meat.[23] A similar cultural distinction can be found in contemporary reactions to the notion in parts of the psychological community about the benefits of positive thinking. Positive thinking has become partially challenged by a battery of countering knowledge claims. These are made by communities of risk researchers and beyond, emphasising the benefits of the very opposite state of mind: chronic unease.[24]

In Chapter 3, the picture will be broadened from descriptions of how community-based knowledge resistance takes place to why such patterns are so prevalent. This demands that we think in evolutionary terms. What – if anything – could be the 'adaptive value' of the knowledge resistance of groups? Could different chances of survival and reproduction throughout the long history of humanity be associated with differences in people's inclination to conform to the knowledge beliefs of their community? Community-based knowledge conformity will be illustrated in religious and scientific groups. We'll also look at such conformity in male-dominated audiophile communities in their passionate pursuit of the perfect sound (to be explained later).

In Chapter 4, we'll move from the community level to individuals. The chapter will show how we shape our knowledge beliefs, how we make use of our fast, Dionysian intuitions about the world, and where slow, Apollonian reasoning comes in. This chapter challenges much common-sense thinking about the point of human intuition, reasoning, and the infected term 'intelligence'.

In Chapter 5, we'll examine an idea found among some economists: knowledge resistance might be something that people consciously and actively engage in to pursue their goals more efficiently. There are a few different and intriguing versions of this idea that help us challenge the notion that knowledge resistance is an entirely irrational phenomenon.

From views in economics of how we sometimes resist knowledge to save money, time, and effort, Chapter 6 will move to social scientific perspectives on some direct benefits of ignorance. Here we'll find a school of thought called 'ignorance studies'. It sheds light on how knowledge resistance may affect a sense of responsibility, freedom, and a strong potential to learn more.

In Chapter 7, I intend to show a powerful factor in making sense of concrete cases of knowledge resistance. That factor is people's concern about what would happen in culture and politics at large if we don't resist specific knowledge claims.

Examining the role of people's fears of the broader consequences of changing their views of reality is the focus of Chapter 8. It addresses what could or should be done – if anything – about knowledge resistance. We'll look at examples of how knowledge resistance has been handled and reduced in various cases. The chapter will outline additional ways you as a reader may manage and minimise knowledge resistance in areas where it becomes problematic.

The final chapter will conclude and discuss the findings. By using a question-and-answer format, we'll tie the findings to the central premise of this book about the universality of knowledge resistance, yet with ample room for managing and reducing knowledge resistance wherever needed. At the same time, we will be reminded of exceptions. There might be specific areas in which knowledge resistance doesn't harm anyone and might even do some good. In such cases, we would possibly do best ignoring it.

1

What knowledge resistance isn't and a hint at what it is

When you started reading this book, you brought with you terms, associations, and experiences that relate to knowledge resistance. This chapter fleshes out some phenomena that in one way or another are typically discussed in the same breath as the topic of knowledge resistance. Here I challenge some things that most of us take for granted: what knowledge is, and whether or not knowledge resistance is merely letting our passion override our reason. Some important things that are typically ignored about knowledge resistance – in the media, public debate, and even scholarly writings – are also highlighted.

Sceptical – the opposite of knowledge resistant

Whereas fact resistance overlaps with knowledge resistance, scepticism is the opposite. We have all witnessed – and perhaps felt – the infuriation expressed in media worldwide about disrespect of knowledge. Most of us might agree that scepticism regarding claims of having the most reliable knowledge is a good thing; this can be referred to as 'sound scepticism'. It seems right, for instance, that other scientists were sceptical of Andrew Wakefield's proposed link between the measles vaccine and autism, discussed in the Introduction. Scientific scepticism doesn't emerge only when a research claim appears particularly dubious, such as in the Wakefield case. The other scientists simply did what science is supposed to do, annoying as that may be to the one who has presented a knowledge claim. Researchers test, retest, reject, or modify knowledge claims. Scepticism is the essence of science.

At the same time, we may get frustrated when someone expresses stern scepticism to what we're saying. Being sceptical can annoy, to be sure, and not only in the field of science. At the same time, there is a certain admiration of sceptics. Doubting Thomas in the New Testament makes the other disciples (as well as readers) frustrated. He has to see for himself the wounds of Jesus before believing Christ has been resurrected. Nonetheless, or maybe actually for this reason, millions of Christians have since named their baby boys Thomas. Resolutions to scepticism can often be found nearby in straightforward cases. Once Thomas sees and feels Jesus's wounds for himself, his doubts are over. Scepticism can be eased with substantial evidence, good arguments, and with a trust that the one making a claim is a reliable person. Knowledge resistance is different. To resist knowledge is to be almost immune to evidence, arguments, or the experiences of others. Even following the publication of extensive evidence confirming that Wakefield's claim was flawed, many people categorically resisted recognising the validity or relevance of this evidence. Unlike with scepticism, their knowledge resistance works to fool them. Whereas scepticism can be said to be the opposite of knowledge resistance, gullibility is a sibling of such resistance. The nineteenth-century philosopher Søren Kierkegaard put it much more eloquently:

> We can be decieved by believing what is untrue, but we certainly are also deceived by not believing what is true.[1]

A case in point was when in 1912 an amateur archaeologist in the UK, Charles Dawson, caused something of a stir in the Geological Society of London. He presented a skull, including jaw bones, which he'd found near Piltdown in Sussex. *The Times* of London reported his finding, given the Latin name *Eoanthropus dawsoni*, as 'First Evidence of a New Human Type'. The Geological Society, along with *The Times*, and echoed by the *New York Times Magazine*, was instantly and blindly convinced that the earliest known human was not African, Asian, Australasian, or from the Americas, nor did they come from another European country. The earliest human was British. They instantly believed this hoax, since it fitted perfectly with their cultural values and worldview. Still, it ought to have been extremely easy to recognise a few-hundred-year-old human skull combined with a chimpanzee's teeth and an orangutan's jaw bones.[2] Moreover, the numerous authentic prehistoric skulls found in Africa in the nineteenth century should have made the Society hesitant to draw their Anglo-centric conclusion.

Contemporary terms such as 'post-truth', 'alternative facts', and 'fake news' only add to decades of concerns among large groups that knowledge resistance appears to have become a pandemic. Matters such as these are typically connected to the increase in the number of self-confirming and tribal Internet groups. Do knowledge and competence even matter anymore? What happened to respect for good old analytical expertise or practical skills? Various voices raise such concerns when problems regarding health and the environment are relativised and neglected with no serious counter-evidence.

Knowledge resistance: wider and deeper than fact resistance

I mentioned in the Introduction that the term fact resistance is actually not ideal as the principal term for this book. Throughout my process of *rethinking* fact resistance, that term has turned out to be insufficient, too limited. What are the similarities and differences between fact resistance and the term preferred here – knowledge resistance? Knowledge resistance and fact resistance have this in common: both refer to how people or groups avoid acquiring and accepting specific information that the informant claims to refer to something real in the world. However, there is a fundamental difference between the two terms. Briefly put, fact resistance implies that it would be a simple and often black-and-white phenomenon. To speak in terms of knowledge resistance is to conceive of the phenomenon as multifaceted. Not that fact resistance would be easy to reduce in society. Stubborn resistance to unambiguous facts about the prevention of HIV, as well as other diseases, where there is sufficient and straightforward information available is immensely complicated and challenging, of course.[3] It involves cultural, religious, political, economic, psychological, and many other parameters. Yet, the core of what people label fact resistance is simple. When people and groups identify others as being fact resistant, the view of the former is the following: clear and indisputable facts are available about the cause of a problem and what is needed to solve that problem. Still, some people and groups resist accepting these facts as valid or relevant.

Resistance to evident and indisputable facts is no doubt a pressing problem in society, not least in areas of health, the environment, and other aspects of the human condition. Indeed, this book will discuss several cases that in the media often fall under the label fact resistance. However, fact resistance is far from the whole story when people and groups seem to avoid crucial insights about the climate, vaccination, crime prevention, or social wellbeing. To fully understand and handle the stubborn avoidance of insight shown in key problem areas, knowledge resistance is a far more useful concept. I will try to convince you of this through numerous – hopefully engaging – examples in this book.

Knowledge resistance includes fact resistance, but the former is more extensive, more profound, and less categorical – in other words, more complicated but immensely important to recognise. Here are a couple of examples. The first is as common among people who identify themselves as liberal or progressive as among people with other ideologies. It refers to people and organisations being factually correct but at the same time knowledge resistant concerning the risks and safety of genetic engineering in food production.[4] Genetic engineering, sometimes called genetic manipulation, is when scientists alter the genetic composition of something, for instance of plants so that they can become better adapted to grow in some areas. There are different views between different groups of scientists regarding the possible risks and benefits of such practices.[5] Sometimes opponents point out in the media that it cannot be stated with 100 per cent certainty that genetic engineering does not carry long-term risks of any kind. This is indeed a valid fact. Science in general doesn't deal in absolutes, only with probabilities.[6] The context of the fact here is the context of how knowledge and science works: it's futile to demand full certainty.

Here's another example of how it's possible to use correct facts in misleading ways that can be associated with knowledge resistance. In some countries in Europe it's common to make the claim that refugees that have immigrated to European countries in the first decades of the twenty-first century are over-represented in cases of violent crime. This claim is sometimes followed by supporting statistics. A government-commissioned study in Lower Saxony, for example, indicated that asylum seekers altered the decreasing trend of violent crimes between 2007 and 2014. Asylum seekers were said to have accounted for 92.1 per cent of the incidents that resulted in a 10.4 per cent increase in solved crime cases by early 2017.[7] Let's assume that these conspicuous data are correct, for the sake of argument. Even if they are valid, it would be misleading to make the factual claim that asylum seekers have caused a rise in violent crime without discussing a valid way to interpret the data. To be sure, believing in those facts doesn't make you fact resistant. After all, the claim is valid (again, for the sake of argument in this book). However, treating this fact as the single defining feature of the problematic situation would make you knowledge resistant. How? By avoiding recognising or caring about the more comprehensive, explanatory picture. It would be misleading to compare refugees with the average of well-established, integrated groups in a country; refugees who have immigrated to that country are in an entirely different position. A higher proportion of refugees than of the general population are marginalised. They have lower social status and lower chances of getting a job. Recently arrived refugees have little chance of participating in society on equal terms with more integrated people, often for many years afterwards. Moreover, in many areas the cohort of refugees between 2015 and 2017 consisted of a much higher proportion of young males in their late teens than are found among the general population. This is a category that in every culture and every period of history has committed more violent crimes than other groups on average.[8] Sociology and criminology – including the cited report – teaches us that all these factors increase the risks dramatically for being involved in violent crime. If we introduce controls for all these factors, there might be very little, if any, explanatory power left for the specific ethnicity of the refugees in question. Still, the possibly valid fact about refugees being over-represented in incidents of violent crime does something to many of us. It makes us draw a rapid, erroneous conclusion, unless we are careful: that committing violent crimes is an intrinsic part of this ethnicity, culturally or even genetically.

Beyond passion v. reason

The risk of the false conclusion regarding proclivity towards violent crime among certain ethnic groups is high because it points to an 'us' (the established part of a society) and 'them' (refugees). This deeply rooted impulse of separating us from them is an example of what the psychologist Daniel Kahneman calls 'fast' thinking.[9] In order to translate Kahneman into the collective, cultural level, this book uses ideas about the characters of two half-brother gods in Greek mythology: Dionysus and Apollo. The German philosopher Friedrich Nietzsche famously used the images of these gods when analysing theatre.[10] To him, Dionysus represented human drunkenness and passion, for instance, whereas Apollo stood for dreaming and reason. Although I will leave out the main part of Nietzsche's brilliant analysis, a few things are quite helpful to learn from him as well as from pre-Nietzschean ideas about these two gods. Dionysus will here represent fast, impulsive thinking. Like Kahneman's 'fast' thinking, Dionysian characteristics are spontaneity, impulsiveness, rapidness, and partial nonconsciousness. Yet, Kahneman and others who use the concept of fast thinking often fail to mention a key feature, a feature that becomes clear when we think about Dionysus and his intoxicated orgies (which had less erotic associations in Ancient Greece than today): a strong group orientation, where the individual dissolves into the group, or at least where integrity and separateness is reduced. Our Dionysian group orientation, inherent in all of us – largely in the older parts of our brains – provides us with an inclination to quickly and unreflectively define 'them' more negatively than 'us'. We attribute good things that 'we' do to our inherent characteristics and disposition, whereas we attribute bad things that we do to unfortunate circumstances. What the others do is interpreted in the reverse way, a biased interpretation known as the fundamental attribution error.[11]

Whether or not people accept the fact that refugees on average commit far more crimes than others is an insignificant piece of the problem. To avoid knowledge resistance in this case, we'd need to make more use of what Kahneman calls 'slow' thinking. I associate this slow thinking with Dionysus's half-brother, the god Apollo. He is well known for being self-controlled, engaging in long-term planning, slow, well informed, visionary, and with high individual integrity.[12] Both the Dionysian and Apollonian dimensions are in our brains. The Dionysian activates particularly the older parts of our brains, and the Apollonian activates more of our more recently developed parts, such as the prefrontal cortex. However, as Nietzsche noted in his cultural analysis, it would be a mistake, of which Kahneman has sometimes been accused, to portray these two modes of thinking as operating in full separation.[13] Our Dionysian, passionate, fast mode and our Apollonian, reason-oriented, slow mode are always operating in our brains and culture, intertwined, although the two modes are not equally active all the time.[14] This intertwining of the Dionysian and Apollonian within ourselves and in society becomes evident in many concrete situations. Kahneman emphasises how the Apollonian side may help us question our spontaneous, Dionysus-like inclinations, such as a preference for moving out of a residential area where an increasing share of people have a different ethnicity from ourselves. Such Apollonian, reasoned questioning could include checking the statistics of violence and theft, sometimes resulting in a conclusion that our multi-ethnic neighbourhood is at least as safe as more homogeneous neighbourhoods. To be sure, this type of reasoning is sometimes possible. Still, more often, there seems to be this intertwining between the two gods: the Dionysus-like, urgent inclination to move is amplified by subsequent Apollonian reasoning that confirms our Dionysian impulse. Even self-ascribed multiculturalists seek solid, culturally accepted reasons to move from more colourful neighbourhoods: that its traffic seems more dangerous, that property values might not increase at the same pace as elsewhere, that the neighbourhood might become more dangerous in the near future, and so forth. This book will illustrate this constant interaction, which will make the phenomenon of knowledge resistance clearer in its many forms and situations.

If we are to take facts seriously, we need to see them in context, otherwise we risk misleading others and sometimes ourselves. We fall into the trap of knowledge resistance. This is a salient issue that, for some strange reason, is often missing in books, articles, and the public debate about fact resistance. An additional point is typically missing in the common-sense complaints about fact resistance: that facts and knowledge should always be open for renewed scrutiny; they need to be revised over time. When facts are presented, the implication is that they are absolute and undebatable. However, this is not the case. Both facts and knowledge claims are partly uncertain, fallible, and dependent on context. However, this is easier to recognise when we talk about knowledge claims than about facts. There is also another side that facts and knowledge share, but is most obvious concerning knowledge claims. Despite their imperfection, it is often possible to compare and rank knowledge claims in terms of quality, sophistication, and usefulness. This two-sided view of knowledge claims will help us identify the shades and nuances of knowledge resistance throughout this book.

Good and bad knowledge claims

There is still another way in which knowledge resistance is more complicated than if we simply narrowed the scope and discussed fact resistance. A situation that is commonly labelled one of fact resistance is where individuals or groups reject or ignore factual claims that mainstream science perceives as valid and relevant. The basic assertions 'measles vaccines don't cause autism' and 'human activities have an impact on the global climate' are such factual statements. They are subject to broad consensus in mainstream scientific communities. However, knowledge is more than just such facts. Knowledge comes in different shapes and colours: through systematic laboratory experiments and modelling, but also through daily experiences. Think about the knowledge preschool teachers, farmers, social workers, fishers, construction workers, and others acquire through years of experience. To resist what they have to say is not fact resistance, as long as their claims aren't grounded in scientifically acquired data. Nonetheless, ignoring what they say in areas where they have years of experience could qualify as knowledge resistance.

There is a significant challenge in broadening the topic from fact resistance to knowledge resistance. In some cultures, finding a dead bird is a bad omen. You might think that you should cancel the flight you had planned to take to that boring business meeting in light of this warning sign. This would be a case of fact resistance: mainstream science conceives it as an obvious fact that seeing a dead bird will not impact the probability that your plane will go down later in the day. You will have to admit that you have, for some irrational reason, resisted a simple fact that is accepted widely in contemporary society. If we widen the concept from facts to knowledge, isn't there a risk that all kinds of claims – including superstitious beliefs about dead birds and air travel safety – although not 'factual' (since there's no scientific basis for them) will have to be taken seriously? Isn't there a risk that unreliable knowledge claims will be treated as equally valid as any good or better knowledge claims that science may ever produce? How about the knowledge claims of shamans, apocalyptic preachers, astrologists, or any of us, even when we don't really know what we are talking about? Outside of science, such knowledge is often called a gut feeling, higher truth, or even wisdom.

What happens if no criteria are in place to define what qualifies as knowledge? We then run the risk of ending up in a type of relativism that I very much wish to avoid in this book. I call it 'hardcore relativism'. Although the philosopher Roy Bhaskar does not use that term, he describes it perfectly, defining it as the stance that 'all beliefs are equally valid in the sense that there are no rational [read: cognitive] grounds for preferring one to another'.[15] In hardcore relativism, knowledge claims are reducible to what I call 'knowledge tastes' between which no judgement could or should be made. Luckily, there is another type of relativism. I label it 'softcore relativism'. It is the understanding that knowledge claims and beliefs are created in and influenced by the social context where the people who make the assertions come from. Believers or non-believers have had their views shaped in different social milieus. That type of knowledge stems from research questions raised through value judgements, priorities, assumptions about what is important, opportunities for research funding, and so forth. The sociology of science has convincingly shown how even science is relative in this soft sense.

One of my interviewees, the social scientist Javier Lezaun, describes his own softcore relativism as follows:

> I'm for the most part a big fan of scientific research. It has for the most part a robust set of criteria to determine what should count as accepted knowledge for the time being. I think it's also often a much more reflexive form of practice than other practices that also generate knowledge. If I had to choose, I would choose the scientific process to determine facts. But I would understand that process and the criteria driving it as socially and historically contingent. But to me that doesn't detract from the value of those claims.[16]

There is nothing strange about this, although parts of the scientific community are unwilling to admit it. A sign that the natural sciences are also softly relative is the alternative prize for unusual or trivial achievements in science, the so-called Ig Nobel Prize. Among the methodologically authoritative studies that have received the award we have, for instance, James Heathcote's medical research study 'Why Do Old Men Have Big Ears?'[17] There is also the linguistic study by Juan Toro and his colleagues, which discovered that rats sometimes can't distinguish between Dutch spoken backwards and Japanese spoken backwards.[18] Then there is my personal Ig Nobel Prize favourite: the physicist Robert Matthews and his research asserting that slices of buttered toast that fall to the ground more often end up with the buttered side down than up.[19] The scientific articles that are awarded the Ig Nobel Prize are often grounded in impeccable, scientific procedures. What is it that makes people – scientists and non-scientists alike – chuckle when we hear about them? I would argue it's that the scholars behind them have tried – sometimes for comic effect and sometimes not – to leave aside the social values and soft relativity that otherwise steers what appears to be 'meaningful' research. The studies seem to be motivated at random – by 'the view from nowhere' – rather than from socially embedded people in search of meaningful knowledge. The scientists have avoided the crucial question that is vital to ask when searching for insight: 'so what?' This is the implicit question that researchers and funding institutions often test before they become involved in a new study. The test is founded on the value judgement that some knowledge is more interesting and valuable than other knowledge.

Softcore relativism is an inevitable part of most knowledge production. By recognising this, we can see how various conflicting knowledge claims have a point based on the perspective of from where the knowledge claim stems. What I instead seek to avoid is portraying knowledge resistance as a phenomenon caught in hardcore relativism. In a culture where hardcore relativism rules, everyone who makes a knowledge claim even without substantial evidence and sophisticated arguments can accuse others of being knowledge resistant. They may begin their accusation as soon as anyone refuses to accept their claims. On the other hand, it could be argued that all alternative knowledge claims that are supported by rich evidence and sophisticated arguments should be taken seriously. They should be given a fair chance before being rejected. In the interviews with human scientists about knowledge resistance that I conducted for this book, I came across numerous intriguing examples of alternative claims that nevertheless appeared to deserve serious attention. For instance, one of my respondents, a science and technology scholar from Israel, made a knowledge claim that I'd never heard before: he maintained that *not* wearing a bicycle helmet in traffic is significantly safer than wearing one. Counter-intuitive, and seemingly against common sense, of course! Still, he had scrutinised existing data thoroughly and had produced some of his own data rigorously. Overall, he had worked with great scientific intensity to examine whether his claim was defendable. If we gave this claim a chance, we wouldn't have fallen into hardcore relativism. In fact, we'd be obliged to give his proposition a chance if we were not to commit knowledge resistance just because his claim differed from the conventional one concerning safe cycling.

The gaps between knowledge, affects, and behaviour

As all of us have experienced the feeling that there often seems to be a gap between what we know and what we do. Why did we just buy that grotesque SUV? We know that this vehicle has an awful environmental performance and is plain vulgar. We know some people even go to the extreme of vandalising the paintwork of such cars for these reasons. Or why do we keep bringing up political topics during Sunday dinners with the in-laws when we know that it will only cause tension?

Gaps of these kinds where we don't appear to act coherently with our knowledge have several names, including the affect, behaviour, cognition (ABC) gap,[20] the value–action gap,[21] and the intention–behaviour gap.[22] Beneath studies of such gaps – not least those concerning environmental and health-related knowledge – often lies a frustration. Why can't people be more consistent, translating their knowledge into action, so that, for instance, they smoke and drink less, and buy a bicycle instead of an SUV? The frustrations and assumptions about an ideal consistency between what people know and do are based on a misunderstanding of what matters most to them – and all of us – as a social species.[23] This is a significant research area in social psychology as well as in so-called environmental sociology, an area in which I incidentally do much of my work. My colleagues and I have written extensively about such gaps elsewhere.

Although this topic deserves to be mentioned here, since many people associate knowledge-related challenges with such gaps, strictly speaking it is beyond the scope of this book. The reason is that the issue when there seems to be a gap between knowing and doing is not necessarily ignorance. People do know, for instance, that bringing up political views at those Sunday dinners will cause unnecessary tension. Nor is it that SUV buyers have resisted the validity of the claim that their vehicles are bad for the environment (at least compared to having no car at all). They know it, but they just choose not to turn their knowledge into practice.

Instead, knowledge resistance concerns what knowledge and information we treat as valid and relevant in the first place, shaping our knowledge beliefs. Indeed, I will provide examples that illustrate some intriguing ways in which people distort their knowledge beliefs in order to make sense of their behaviours. The social psychologist Leon Festinger broke new ground in the 1950s with his term 'cognitive dissonance', through which he reversed the relationship between knowledge and behaviour.[24] In order to reduce the unpleasant tensions that he claimed emerge when knowledge, affects, and behaviour are dissonant, we often don't change our behaviour. Instead, we change something else: our knowledge beliefs. This can happen when we, for instance, consider buying an SUV. We know the harm it causes. Moreover, we have emotions that make us care about these problems to which we would contribute by running such a vehicle. In order to feel better, we can resist or downplay knowledge about the total amount of energy and materials needed to produce that car. We can also resist or downplay stories about large vehicles increasing traffic risks for children biking or walking to school. Instead, we may focus on the level of emissions from our new SUV, which might be lower than our previous, smaller car. Beyond those knowledge–behaviour gaps that shed direct light on knowledge resistance, you may wish to consult the publications referred to here to read more about other gaps.

What is often ignored about knowledge resistance

So far, I have mainly tried to narrow down the definition of knowledge resistance by pointing at what it is not. Now it's time to spell out the general premise of the book, its overarching argument, if you will. It turns out to be two-fold. As you will see throughout the book, this two-fold premise differs from most other writings about the puzzling ways in which people and groups handle knowledge.

Knowledge resistance is everywhere, but not all the time

The first thing that struck me when I began collecting material for this book was that discussions about knowledge resistance are routinely formulated in 'us v. them' fashion. Depending on who is talking, 'they' can be those who have been indoctrinated into what some argue to be medieval reasoning. Or 'they' can be those who allow themselves to be deceived by liberal elitism and special interests within the science community. If you find the examples on the following pages overly neat and polarised, this is a good sign that your own experience with people and groups is far more intricate and nuanced. The reason that I present these examples in such a divided way is that this is how the media usually delineate the current political and cultural climate in several countries. Moreover, at our deepest human level, our thoughts and feelings lean towards binarity – between them and us.

The US is a country where this polarisation is particularly evident. By 'polarisation' I mean the binary view of 'us' versus 'them' in the public debate about ideology and politics. Surveys show that knowledge beliefs are not clear-cut. Some liberals (in the US, social liberal sense) are dismissive of the idea that humans are a result of biological evolution; some conservatives embrace the evolutionary explanation.[25] In many cases, differences in knowledge beliefs don't follow a perfect, ideological line. Still, public debates and media coverage often try to draw such a perfect line. There is, for instance, the article by the *New York Times* bestselling comic author Andy Borowitz, entitled 'Earth Endangered by a New Strain of Fact-Resistant Humans'. He refers to conservative groups of climate change deniers, describing their psychological condition as follows:

> The normal functions of human consciousness have been completely nullified.[26]

Borowitz and other liberals (in the US sense) who mock what they see as the knowledge resistance of 'others' might have in mind statements such as this one that Mike Pence gave in the US House of Representatives:

> Even though my training is in the law and in history, it has ever been an avocation of mine to contemplate and *to study* the origins of man and of life here on Earth ... only the theory of intelligent design provides even a remotely rational explanation for the known universe.[27] (My emphasis)

Pence made this statement several years before he became the vice-president of the US. By the time he was elected vice-president, in 2016, he had not rejected this claim. To anyone who has absorbed the most basic findings of biology, the quote is a mind-blowing example of knowledge resistance. Pence must have resisted acrobatically the basic biology lessons which every privileged person in a free democracy experiences from time to time from junior high school and for decades afterwards. Pence maintains that studying the origins of man has always been an 'avocation' of his. This means he must have had all the opportunities in the world to recognise the sophistication with which science explains the origin of humans. That explanation contends that human life can be explained best as a gradual evolution through random, natural selection. It rejects the notion of a personal, father-like God's purposive creation of a man and later a woman as finished and complete beings. Pence has effectively resisted recognising the value of the most central findings that mainstream science has produced ever since Darwin.[28] This is viewed with amazement among many liberals as well as some conservatives who perceive themselves as enlightened and pro-science. Those at the other pole who identify themselves as conservatives seem puzzled by the reaction of the leftist, liberal elite, which they conceive as a form of knowledge resistance. One of the most intriguing expressions of this comes from the former US president Ronald Reagan:

> The trouble with our liberal friends is not that they are ignorant. It's just that they know so much that isn't so.[29]

The argument that conservatives use is that liberals seem immune to fundamental, human experiences related to our own traditions, ethics, and community. Liberals, leftists, and also greens accordingly refuse to make use of lessons about what seemed to work for previous generations. This includes the 'naturalness' of traditional family values and the dignity and sacredness of human life – including foetuses. The so-called progressives also ignore the hazards of trying to 'play God' by using gene therapy to cure human diseases. From a conservative perspective, liberals, leftists, and greens are anti-science and anti-technology in certain specific issues. Accordingly, they see a resistance among greens, leftists, and liberals to apply scientific and technological advances in areas where they should be applied, such as genetic engineering in agriculture. It's unreasonable, some conservatives contend, to postpone the use of advances in food production through more sophisticated pesticides and genetically modi-fied crops. They argue that we can't wait until we are 100 per cent certain that they are safe for the environment. Such certainty, they correctly remark, is never possible to reach in any case. And it's unreasonable, they argue, to abandon or place hard regulations on fossil-based fuel technologies and other technologies that have been proven to drive pros-perity in the past.

This resistance goes far beyond 'their' tendencies, whoever 'they' are. A study by Jeremy Frimer and his colleagues showed that liberals and conservatives are equally inclined to avoid learning about the other side's opinion, and the knowledge claims behind their views. The researchers compared how likely it was that people on opposing sides of 'Culture War' issues – gun control, abortion, same-sex marriage, and legalising marijuana – would be willing to learn more than they already knew about the arguments of the other side. Participants in the study were offered cost-free entry in a lottery in exchange for listening to the knowledge beliefs and belief-confirming statements of the others, an offer which two-thirds of the people on each ideological side declined.[30] Instead, both sides preferred to engage in a dull and meaningless task that took the same amount of time as the knowledge exchange would have taken.

Knowledge resistance is in all of us. It's not just 'they' who have a conscious and nonconscious selectivity that sometimes amounts to knowledge resistance.[31] Extensive research has indicated that also sci-entists have this inclination under certain circumstances.[32] Despite the fact – yes, fact – that knowledge resistance is universal, it's something which we accuse others of and rarely recognise in ourselves as individuals or groups. This is true not only in public debate and private life. Parts of the scientific community and science writers often come close to this us–them view of people and groups. For example, the respected science writer Michael Shermer divides people into sceptics (who don't believe in unusual things) and non-sceptics (who do). The title of one of his books is *Why People Believe Weird Things*, so you can perhaps guess where he places himself.[33] His mission is important: helping people think critically and avoid charlatans and charismatic authorities who try to make us blind to our potential for rational thinking. Aside from this welcome mission, some aspects of his approach are problematic. The first issue is that his either/or perspective mainly works in extreme cases. These include, for instance, cases where people and groups let their religious faith blind them to solid facts and scientific findings. Other relevant examples are where individuals and groups let their post-modern beliefs cloud their judgement in situations where some knowledge claims are far better than others. But aside from such obvious cases, the usefulness of the division between sceptics and non-sceptics is far from clear. In many parts of our lives, we deal with knowledge assumptions that are uncertain. Am I a sceptic or a non-sceptic, or both, if I believe that the assessments by various experts about the risks of nuclear power are exaggerated or underestimated? Or should I, to be a good Shermerian sceptic, take expert assessments as 'the truth', as long as these assessments are said to be based on science? Am I a sceptic or non-sceptic, or both, if I pay more in order to give my children an expensive, organic diet? After all, science has shown there to be no significant difference in health impact between the two types of diet (and I leave the environmental impact aside here). I would argue that it's simplistic, and misguided, to distinguish between sceptical and non-sceptical people, and between their respective approaches to life.

The second way in which Shermer's approach is problematic concerns 'weird things'. He defines weird things as notions such as spiritual beliefs, superstition, religion, or unfounded risk perceptions. However, from most well-established human scientific perspectives, it isn't these things that are weird. On the contrary, these are the kinds of things that *Homo sapiens* has successfully evolved *not* to find weird. Try lying in the grass and looking up at the clouds; see how long it takes before you see a face. Or to take a similar example, on a hike in the mountains, my family and I once competed to see who could find the most faces (human-like and animal-like) on the rocks. We all saw a lot, and so would you. Imagine that you lived in a community far away from strong scientific or established religious convictions; in such a community there is more room for a more basic human intuition – where you imagine, for instance, that the rock creatures you saw impact the life of you and your group.[34] Soon you have an existential belief that you share with others in your community. From the perspective of human perception, seeing faces and creatures in rocks and clouds, and believing that they impact our lives, is far less weird than, for instance, climate change; evolution by random, natural selection; or black holes, antimatter, and parallel universes. These things are truly weird to most of us, psychologically. Shermer well knows this. Still, his definition of weirdness portrays the idea of an entirely sober human being who always handles his or her impressions in a nonbiased way. This ideal person filters all input correctly, resisting false knowledge claims and absorbing the valid ones. The problem with this isn't just that it sounds boring to be such a person, there is a deeper problem here. If humans had always functioned like this, they wouldn't have been able to survive and reproduce from the beginning of humanity until today.[35] This is why knowledge resistance, in its various shapes and degrees – is a universal phenomenon.

In this book, I will show why the ability to – consciously and nonconsciously – avoid seeing the knowledge resistance in ourselves is a necessary human trait. However, we shouldn't forget the point made earlier about avoiding hardcore relativism. Certainly, we should fully recognise that social groups differ in how open they are to the knowledge that challenges their previous beliefs. Membership of fundamentalist religious groups, for instance, implies – by definition – a far lower openness to particular types of knowledge claims and scientific findings.

We haven't primarily evolved as truth-seekers who sometimes fail

The second part of this book's premise is actually an explanation of the first part, which is the universality of knowledge resistance. My research for this book made clear how people in and outside of academia discuss knowledge resistance as something that is always bad. Exceptions can be found in economics (about 'rational ignorance') and the sociology of science (about the benefits of being humble about what one doesn't know: one's 'nonknowledge'). True, I have also treated it as quite bad so far. However, the premise of this book is that there must be some point in knowledge resistance – a function, an adaptation, or suchlike. Numerous books challenge the view that we are inherently ultimate knowledge-seekers. Absent are, however, discussions of in which contexts, and for whom, knowledge resistance is likely to entail problems or benefits.

People – including many scientists – overlook one thing when they complain about the knowledge resistance of others: we – *Homo sapiens* – haven't evolved to be knowledge- and truth-maximising machines. Instead, we have evolved and still dance on this earth, since our ancestors became genetically adapted to learn how to manoeuvre and collaborate in our social and physical environments, mainly as hunters and gatherers. In such societies, and also agrarian as well as modern urban societies, it wouldn't be adaptive (meaning that it wouldn't increase our chances of survival and reproduction) to be truth-maximising machines. What has been adaptive, and still is, is to be *social* survival machines. This means, for example, that most of us have a high capacity to cooperate, develop ties to others, avoid being exploited, and get away with some exploitation of others. This is a genetic adaptation. Higher social capacities have been particularly significant in increasing our chances of survival, reproduction, and successfully taking care of our young ones. These social capabilities have, on average, been far more useful than a capacity for always identifying and sharing the best possible knowledge.

As I demonstrated in a previous book, knowledge refinement and truth-seeking should be understood as subordinate to deeply social interests.[36] This doesn't mean that individuals and groups are not interested in getting their knowledge right. It's wonderful to be proven correct while others have to admit that they were wrong. However, it means that when deeply social interests and knowledge claims are in conflict, we should expect people more often to prioritise the satisfaction of their social interests, particularly if knowledge resistance is more likely to strengthen their social interests. These include interests in strengthening social bonds and maintaining or increasing status. In a conflict between sticking to the seemingly most accurate knowledge claim and social interests, people should be expected to resist information that would entail more accurate knowledge. In such cases, it is 'socially rational' for people, groups, and organisations to take the route that helps them strengthen or maintain their social position. I will show how this is the case whether it concerns academic disciplines (why scientists usually stick with the central beliefs of their discipline), religious communities, or other communities.

In search of hidden common-sense thinking

One of my research areas is people's views about the possible negative environmental or health-related impact of practices in their daily lives. These practices include how they travel, heat their homes, and to what extent they recycle their waste. Other examples are what it takes for consumers to boycott products that are produced in ways that exploit workers or harm animals, for instance.[37]

As a postdoctoral student, I travelled around to people's homes, first in Sweden and some years later in the US, conducting interviews about how people had chosen their specific type of heating system. I also compared statistics of what people said and did about various risks to health and the environment. Fortunately, I've often had colleagues in other countries undertaking similar collection of interviews and additional information, enabling us to compare. Many times I've had to revise my previous assumptions about how people's knowledge about health and the environment are related to their values, opinions, and daily practices. Contrary to what I had assumed, several people who said that they didn't know or care much about the environment turned out to be the most ambitious in recycling their waste. Many of them were engaged in thorough, time-consuming composting, and they made the effort to get the 'cleanest' smoke out of their chimneys. My colleagues and I have also interviewed people who labelled themselves as 'voluntary simplifiers' – they aim to minimise their consumption and negative environmental impact. These voluntary simplifiers share a passionate interest in learning about how this can be done. Some of them had certainly managed to reduce their energy use and greenhouse gas emissions, for example. Others – not least some of those living in the countryside – were not quite as successful. These findings are supported by numerous other studies on lifestyles and environmental impact. Such studies have found that many of those who neither know or care much about environmental issues – and who live in multi-apartment homes in towns and cities – have a better environmental track record than those living in more rural settings. To add to this list of counter-intuitive findings, there was the study we made about how people viewed the risks of nuclear power plants in Lithuania and Sweden. One preliminary result was that people found nuclear power plants riskier the further away they lived from a plant.

These seemingly strange findings are particularly puzzling if you think that there is a clear and straight line between what people know, claim to care about, and do. However, if there is no such straight line, does people's knowledge even matter? This was a question that I began to ask after I had been an active researcher in the first few studies. Now I can say with full certainty that yes, people's knowledge matters – and very much so – for themselves as well as for what type of society we decide to have. But it took quite a bit of additional research and analysis of a broad range of human sciences before I could explain how knowledge matters in various situations. I did this by diving into perhaps the most fundamental question of them all: what are people's deepest interests anyway? Do they desire a better, cleaner, and more peaceful world? Or prosperity and comfort? Or something else? Some of the answers will be given in this book, in cases where those answers directly concern knowledge. After oceans of time and effort on this deceptively simple issue, I had laid the necessary basis for preparing for this book on knowledge resistance.

In the course of these preparations it became clear that I had some earlier experiences that had triggered my interest in what role knowledge beliefs have in our lives. When I was 17 years old, I was sent as an exchange student from my liberal and religiously agnostic home in Sweden to a family in Colorado Springs in the US. For one year they hosted me like a family member. During the term time I went to high school with my host 'brother'. On Sundays I went to church with the rest of the family. A couple of days a week there were youth groups in the church that I also participated in. The church was conservative and evangelical, and turned out to be one of the fastest growing in the US. Once, before going on a road trip, we laid our hands on the silver Toyota sedan, praying that God's angels would literally and concretely position themselves around the car and join us for the whole trip in order to make it a safe one. On another occasion, my host 'father', Bill, who was a hobby pilot, asked me if I'd like to see four US states in one day – that same day. I was excited, and before I knew it, he and I were in a tiny, four-person propeller aeroplane that he had rented. It felt like a VW Beetle with wings. After twenty minutes or so in the air there was a terrible noise coming from the engine. Bill couldn't help but notice that my nails were ruining the fake leather seat. He asked me very calmly if I wanted us to complete our mission and see those four states, or head back immediately. 'But before you make up your mind', he said, 'you should know that we will be okay even if we do the whole flight the way we had planned. When I turned 50 [two years earlier], God told me that I would live to be 100. You can trust me, and God of course, that we'll be safe.' In that moment I identified strongly with Doubting Thomas. I immediately responded as calmly as I could something along these lines: 'Well, good for you, Bill, that God told you that, but let's go back – right now – please!' So we did, making it back safe and sound. Bill, a generous person who meant so much to me, sadly passed away three decades later, aged 83, through natural causes.

My experiences from that high school year made me concretely aware of what a contested 'resource' knowledge is. By recognising this in the evangelical Christian community in Colorado, it also became apparent in my Swedish, secular one. I will share more additional (true) stories from that year throughout this book. These stories will help us better understand how people and groups, regardless of religion and ideology, handle and sometimes resist knowledge.

Conclusion

In sum, I've been lucky to be able to collect a vast arrange of experiences and research for this book. In addition to the Colorado year, there are the many years of research on households, authorities, agencies, and non-governmental organisations and how they acquire, produce, and share knowledge. In the latter part of my career I've been given the opportunity to further add to the richness of insights about knowledge resistance. In the space of two years I was a visiting scholar first at Oxford University and later at the London School of Economics. In the UK, a number other social, economic, and evolutionary scientists told me about their experiences of knowledge resistance. Their input through interviews has not only generated additional, valuable examples, it has also helped this book to provide well-grounded ideas on how to understand and explain knowledge resistance. This, in turn, has made it possible for me to make substantial claims about what could be done about knowledge resistance in areas where it could be viewed as problematic. It's been important to remain consistent with one of the central notions in this book: that knowledge resistance is a ubiquitous phenomenon. Thus, the interviews haven't been spared from my reflections about knowledge resistance among these human scientists or within myself.

I hope that the experiences across the human sciences along with my research and experiences will stimulate your recognition of knowledge resistance where you hadn't thought about it before. The book will help you see situations where you – and all of us – are likely to be gullible, either by being overly resistant to alternative claims or excessively non-sceptical. It will also show how vague terms such as 'structure' and 'social norms', on which we often blame knowledge resistance, can often be translated to situations in daily life. In some of these situations there is room for doing something about knowledge resistance. It is possible to introduce measures, not least in workplaces and other organisational settings, to minimise the knowledge resistance of ourselves and others where it becomes problematic. By recognising structural and evolutionary rooted factors, the book will give practical suggestions that have a solid scientific anchoring.

2

If you're with us, don't believe them

Shallow curiosity

'Slap, slap, slap!'

The sound bounced around the small room. The man tried to slow his breathing by staring through a window at the distant mountains. He held up his small, muscular hand towards the window to compare his palm with the remote, reddish mountains. The hair hanging down over his forehead was wet. His cheeks were wet too. It might have been tears. In the Rockies, I saw men cry more openly than back home in Sweden.

I'd joined my host family at this house for brunch after the Sunday service at the New Life Evangelical Church a few miles away. 'How did I end up sitting here during this private moment?' I remember thinking while tossing a little boy's egg-shaped football back and forth between my hands. Was it even a private moment? The boy's bottom – with two large, burning marks on each cheek – was fully exposed. His ironed, marine-blue chinos were pulled down to the ankles. The boy lay across his father's knees. While the man had been hitting the boy ten times with his right hand, hard and loud, he'd been patting his son tenderly on the head with the other. I couldn't see any of the evil, or even sadistic, drive behind this routine that they'd told me about back in Sweden. Unlike the a triumphant ritardando at the end of a piece of music, the man had accelerated the last slaps so as to get it over with as rapidly as possible. With no visible anger, he had completed one of his household chores.

My eyes had been closed during part of the spanking. During the split-seconds when I'd watched, I'd noticed how the man also closed his eyes now and then. The boy, who'd been mostly quiet during this paternal rite, was now retching. Had his pain been delayed? And if it had, which pain? The one felt on his body or in his mind? Or both? I moved closer to the boy to comfort him. But the father was quicker and took him in his arms. The boy was given the warmest, most loving hug a child could receive. His pants were still down.

'Your mom has told you several times that you should never play with her car keys. Now we can't find the keys, and it will take us a lot of time and money to get new ones – do you understand? Don't ever do that again, Josh – never, okay?'

'Okay, Dad,' the boy almost whispered, the pitch of his voice high even though he tried to make it low.

Surprised at myself, I said to the man, with the most authoritarian voice that my 17-year-old body could produce, 'In Sweden, parents don't hit their kids.'

'Really?'

'It can be dangerous!'

'In what way could this be dangerous to Josh?'

He spoke gently, but his voice was a bit louder than necessary in that tiny room.

'I've heard that kids who have been beaten up a lot by their parents are at higher risk in all kinds of ways,' I explained.

'Beaten up?'

'Sorry, "spanked".'

'How?'

'They can become violent when they grow up. Or become alcoholics, or nervous wrecks.'

I was getting worried that I'd gone too far in my know-it-all assessment of what had taken place. At the moment I stated all these knowledge claims they sounded very mature; but a second later, they seemed to me far less sophisticated than when adults back home in Sweden had spoken on the same subject. Oddly enough, the man didn't seem annoyed. He was a friend of my American host family in Colorado Springs (who I introduced in Chapter 1). Maybe he didn't want to turn this into a big argument about my teenage attitude. Or he was just playing with me, curious to see how this cultural clash between rival knowledge beliefs would further unfold.

'Let me tell you something, Mike,' the man continued. 'The psychologists, those scholars who do those studies, they already know what they wish to prove beforehand. And – big surprise – they get the result they want: "Spanking is bad". Because, you know, almost all who study those things are liberals or left wing. They just follow their ideology.'

We threw glances at each other in silence, the man and I. A curiosity had unfolded between us, but it was a shallow one. There were no signs that either of us had any interest in truly learning the position of 'the best available knowledge' concerning child-rearing. We weren't truly interested in the experiences and detailed knowledge beliefs of the other either. If anything sincerely interested us at that moment, it was the further strengthening of the defence of our respective culture's knowledge beliefs. The main benefit both of us probably saw in our 'cultural exchange' was the golden opportunity of telling an excellent story to our respective communities about the weird beliefs of that other, exotic culture.

Studies have suggested that it was not just this Colorado father and I who were unusually narrow-minded. If translating our shallow curiosity into how conservatives and liberals relate to each other's knowledge beliefs, studies indicate that people of neither side are overly interested in learning more about the experiences behind the other's knowledge claims. As described in Chapter 1, the moral psychologist Frimer and his colleagues showed in experiments how conservatives and liberals appeared to be almost equally averse towards learning about the knowledge beliefs of the others, even though in that case it meant giving up the chance of free participation in a lottery. The researchers in this set of studies stressed that the mutual lack of interest was not based on information fatigue. Instead, people were worried about becoming irritated and having to make an effort to find better arguments to support the knowledge beliefs of their own ideology and culture.[1]

We usually assume that we assess knowledge claims based on their Apollonian, 'epistemic' qualities – their plausibility, logical consistency, and even on the systematics of the evidence collection. Without being aware of it, we navigate our knowledge beliefs more based on our often nonconscious, Dionysian goal of not deviating too much from our culture. We instinctively resist or reject knowledge claims stemming from communities that are not our own. Yet questions abound concerning how people stay loyal to the knowledge beliefs that dominate their own culture. Using numerous examples, this chapter and the next will help us understand this phenomenon. We'll learn some more about why philosophers and other thinkers specialising in logic find the phenomenon problematic in the first place. The chapter will go on to show what the social sciences have to say about how culture-based knowledge resistance is developed, maintained, and challenged in various areas of social life.

Knowledge loyalty

The Colorado dad's knowledge belief that proper child-rearing should be kept separate from findings in scientific psychology ran deeper than a habit that he was unwilling to change. Comprehensive research on political conservatism in the US shows that trust in science in general among conservative communities has seen a declining trend since the 1970s.[2] However, political ideology turns out *not* to be a reliable background variable in predicting whether people trust science in general. Furthermore, if we look at people's trust in scientific claims on specific issues, (dis)trust in climate science is one of the few topics where political ideology makes a big difference. More on this later in this chapter.

Was there more to that father's firm belief in rearing children through tough love, beyond the imperative not to trust science? How about his own experiences of whether spanking is effective or not? Did the spanking make his boy and other children stop doing the bad things that had provoked the corrective action? In Josh's case, it seemed his corporal punishment had little effect: an hour or so after the spanking, he took his father's car keys and used them as a basketball, throwing them over and over into a rubbish basket in the laundry room. This second, closely related mischief should not have come as a surprise. In fact, several replicated studies indicate that, on average, around 75 per cent of children who have been spanked repeat the undesired behaviour after only ten minutes.[3]

Then there were my own knowledge beliefs when I was a 17-year-old exchange student in Colorado. I'd had no experience of child-rearing except my own childhood. I held an intuitive distaste for spanking, to be sure, particularly when it was happening in the same room. However, similar to the belief of that father, my own knowledge belief ran deeper than this. I'd carried decades of Scandinavian truth claims across the Atlantic and into this little boy's room in the Rocky Mountains. To say that my view on spanking at that time was 'science-based' would have been an exaggeration. Indeed, to call Scandinavian knowledge beliefs science-based would probably be an after-construction.

Instead, what took place was that both the man and I were engaged in furiously defending our respective cultures. Such cultural defence isn't necessarily founded on a complete trust that your culture holds the most valid knowledge belief. In the case of child-rearing, the belief concerns what methods are most effective in balancing behaviour correction, nurturing, and minimal harm. The culture that father identified with, referring to it frequently when he spoke, wasn't one followed by Christians in general, but specifically 'born-again, spirit-filled Christians', as he formulated it. When we try to understand what factors lie behind whether a community holds a high or low trust in science, it is common to make the mistake of lumping both conservatives and orthodox (fundamentalist) religious people together into one, science-distrusting category. What the latest surveys have shown, however, is that orthodox (fundamentalist) religiosity, and being an active part of such a community, is a much more reliable predictor for a low trust in science in general than political orientation. Of course, many conservatives are also affiliated with moderate or reformist religious communities or consider themselves non-religious. They show a higher trust in science.[4]

The defence of the knowledge claims that dominate in a given community can often be a display of cultural loyalty. What's the difference between trust and loyalty? The concepts partially overlap. For instance, you can trust that a person will be loyal to you. However, whereas you develop trust once someone has displayed qualities of trustworthiness, loyalty means that you stand behind someone or something *despite* their possible errors or flaws. To highlight how people may still stay loyal to the knowledge beliefs of their culture even when they privately think the beliefs are false, the social scientist Timur Kuran coined the term 'preference falsification'.[5] People's forceful interest in remaining accepted and appreciated in their community can make them falsify their preferences by resisting, corrupting, distorting, or impoverishing the knowledge that would indicate that their culture's knowledge belief is false. Most of us are prepared to be loyal to our social group, organisation, or culture in this sense to some extent, even when we sense that its knowledge belief might not be the most valid. Imagine the ambivalence I felt about the superiority of the Swedish child-rearing model (the way I oversimplified it) after the following dialogue between that Colorado father and myself:

'OK, so what do you do in Switzerland when your kid doesn't do what you tell them?' the man asked.

'Eh, Sweden; well, we tell him again!'

'And if that doesn't help?'

'We … we yell at him. Yeah, yell.'

'Fine, so what if he takes your car keys again, and loses them?'

'We yell some more, and tell him that he won't get dessert.'

'Alright, and what if that doesn't teach him a lesson?'

'Well, we … we … SHOUT!'

I knew there were far more effective ways than yelling and shouting in Swedish and other countries' post-spanking modes of child-rearing. But my memory failed me. Still, I remained loyal to what I perceived as the Scandinavian belief: that yelling and shouting are far more effective and far less harmful than even moderate spanking.

In this light, it's time to make a stronger proposition about cultural knowledge beliefs: people, groups, and organisations often assume that they seek to continuously improve their knowledge – moving their beliefs closer and closer to 'the truth'. However, such open knowledge-seeking is usually subordinate to people's wish for new information not to deviate from the conventional knowledge beliefs of the communities important to them. This means that the person or group who represents the knowledge claim becomes at least as important as the quality of the claim. The example of spanking, along with beliefs about climate change, suggest the following: we usually assume that we assess various knowledge claims based on their formal qualities, plausibility, logical consistency, and on how the evidence has been collected. Sometimes without being aware of it, we navigate our knowledge beliefs in ways that don't deviate too much from the culture with which we identify.

One of my interviewees, a philosopher and a strong proponent of climate change mitigation who preferred to remain anonymous, told me how he had experienced what can happen if people within the scientific community make mildly critical points about climate modelling. Climate modelling is carried out by creating a mathematical representation of the processes in the physical world that determine the climate. The goal is to predict how much the climate will change in various regions and to plan for the future. This interviewee has debated in the community of climate scientists and policy-makers that a certain type of modelling, called high-resolution climate projection, is often unrealistic since it's overly precise:

> So, what I often get is a very hostile reaction when I say anything critical about certain modelling endeavours that try to make climate predictions almost at the postcode level, [because] I'm sort of seen as being on the wrong side or giving arguments to the enemy. I betray the good cause. Are you with us or are you against us? It's a tribal affiliation. But I think nuance matters. I think it's really important for science to recognise what we don't know.

To resist a nuanced understanding of the limits to climate modelling has huge, practical consequences in real life, my respondent maintains:

> Every company with more than fifteen employees [in the UK] is supposed to have a climate adaptation plan that is premised on these projections. And they may misadapt completely. It would have been much better to have a reasonable spectrum of option and of robustness planning.

45

This 'tribal' tendency that my interviewee finds problematic also means that we instinctively resist or reject the knowledge claims stemming from communities that are not our own. Let's take a look at what the masters of reasoning, logicians, and other thinkers specialising in logic and decision-making say about that human propensity.

Irrelevant, but obsessively interesting

If we ask any expert of logic and argumentation to comment on the fact that most of us remain loyal to the conventional knowledge beliefs of our community, that logician would most likely look concerned. Then he or she would make clear that believing that something is valid just because it's a common belief in one's own culture is a logical fallacy. From the view of logic, such errors of our reasoning are like germs or viruses, disturbing and obstructing human progress and problem-solving. They don't make sense.

When that Colorado man and I stuck to our own cultural knowledge beliefs, defending them loyally and uncritically, we committed such a fallacy, the logician would tell us. At the individual level, the father committed the 'argument from authority' (*ad verecundiam*) fallacy. This error takes place when people or groups with power-based authority – for example, a parent, priest, or merely the most charismatic person around – expect others that don't have such authority to accept their knowledge belief as true. 'Might is right' is an expression that illustrates this. The Colorado boy who was spanked couldn't start an open deliberation with his father about the likely short- and long-term consequences of physical punishment. Their power relationship was too uneven for that.

At a broader societal level, the strategy of rejecting conflicting knowledge only because it comes from another culture is sometimes called the *ad hominem* fallacy. An example of this is when I judged that father's belief that moderate spanking is beneficial to be erroneous because it didn't come from a culture that was mine. Instead, it came from a culture based on orthodox religiosity and conservatism. I made the mistake of primarily focusing on the cultural identity – Midwesterner, conservative, evangelical Christian – of the person and his group making the knowledge claim. To avoid this fallacy and actually seek to acquire the best available knowledge instead, the logician would emphasise that we should recognise that it's irrelevant what culture the person who makes a knowledge claim comes from.

The logicians' criticism is in line with the principal – Apollonian – opinion of most people, to be sure. In my numerous interviews as well as informal discussions with all kinds of people – religious, non-religious, right wing, left wing, with high or low levels of formal education – all indicated a strong wish to be objective, absorbed by the issue in focus. This is true whether it concerns how to teach children to behave without harming them or to minimise damage to the natural environment while making sure that individuals and companies don't suffer financially more than necessary. Still, when we lead our lives in practice, particularly when we are under stress, it makes an enormous difference to us what group(s) a person belongs to when deciding whether we will let their knowledge belief challenge our own assumptions. Despite the critical assertions of logicians and other philosophers over millennia, few of us – not even the logicians themselves in their own private lives – are free from this sin against logic. Humans are irrational and primitive, logicians would say. People seem to display the opposite of what is so often treated as an ideal: critical, sceptical, Apollonian thinking, where we are always ready to revise our knowledge beliefs when seemingly solid alternative facts or arguments emerge.

The easiest thing would be to stop right here when discussing knowledge resistance: we could conclude by saying that all groups have traits of irrationality and primitivity. This would be a step towards sophistication compared to the public debate about knowledge resistance that usually concludes by saying 'they' (mainly people in other groups or cultures) are irrational and primitive. However, scientific discussions or analyses ending with the conclusion that various groups of individuals are irrational are rarely useful. I'd like to argue that it's most often not that people or groups are irrational; rather, it's typically the *assumption* of what makes up a rational person or group that is incorrect. Sure, it's a logical fallacy to care more about what culture the claim-maker comes from than about the quality of the knowledge claim itself. Nonetheless, the fact that this error takes place within and across all cultures is an excellent trigger for curiosity far more profound than I felt when sitting next to the Colorado man who had just spanked his child. Beneath the fallacy that people commit when finding the culture or person more relevant than the knowledge claim, we should ask: is there even something useful taking place when people commit that fallacy – useful at least to those who resist the knowledge claims of others?

Scientific v. religious communities

To better understand how resistance to the insights of other cultures can have a place even in seemingly open societies, it's useful to look at two very different ways of learning about the world: religion and science. Please note that this distinction is separate from the Colorado case about spanking.

Many people don't find it necessary to take sides between religion and science. Millions consider themselves religiously and scientifically inclined at the same time. This is more common among people who identify themselves as part of moderate or reformist religious communities. Many of them feel that this dual view enriches their lives. At the same time, the principles of religion and science are opposites in a few critical ways.

Science – and critical thinking in general – has its foundation in the scepticism that we saw in the introductory chapter. If you identify as being more towards the science pole, you demand evidence or logical argument before you accept a knowledge belief as valid. It is common to hear people who place themselves at the science-minded pole expressing a preference for seeing for themselves before believing something to be true. It is more interesting to note what happens when it is impossible to see for oneself. Among the group identifying themselves as science-minded, the second-best thing to seeing for themselves is checking what experts in the problem area believe and copying their knowledge beliefs. The reason that many people in liberal, democratic parts of the world usually subscribe to claims about climate change that are grounded in science and Neo-Darwinism is hardly that they have a first-hand mastery of this scientific knowledge. Instead, the reason is that they trust the principles and processes of scientists and science. Once you have built up enough evidence and logical reasoning that converges with what experts say, you remove your resistance, at least temporarily, and reach a knowledge belief comprising a naturalistic (unmystical) explanation. This is at least how many of us believe that we shape our assumptions. However, the next chapter will show that it isn't necessarily so.

In many domains, people can't engage in direct evaluation of truth claims. How many of us have the tools and skills to make first-hand assessments of climate data, the principles of string theory, or hazardous chemical substances in food products? A sign of people's indirect method of assessing truth claims is that a large share of Americans who believe in evolution through natural selection can't describe its principles.[6] Instead of evaluating the claims directly, most people evaluate the actors or groups that make the claims.[7] When assessing science, political ideology doesn't matter as much as one might think. The belief that vaccinations do more harm than good, for instance, is not significantly more common among political conservatives than among liberals or leftists. Nor is this the case when people are asked about whether genetically modified food is hazardous to their health or not.[8]

Religion presumably works in the opposite fashion. By opening our hearts to a divinity, we develop faith in that divinity. The knowledge or wisdom that is discussed in several religions, aside from the knowledge stemming from religious doctrines, doesn't require evidence or logical argument. By accepting and believing in spiritual truth without such mundane support, we show others that we have reached knowledge and wisdom. In some countries, this principle has been turned into governmental policy. For example, look at Turkey's institutionalised knowledge resistance, its official decision to prohibit teachers from teaching Darwinian evolution, even in science classes.[9] A 2006 article in the journal *Science* indicates that fewer than 25 per cent of people in Turkey believe that humans have evolved through natural selection.[10]

When there is a religious leader, people in the congregation see him (it's most often a man) as a mediator of divine wisdom. What he says, therefore, should be believed if we have faith. During my year as an exchange student in Colorado, I joined my host family several times per week at the evangelical church where they were members. This was expected of me as part of my cultural exchange programme. Ted Haggard – Pastor Ted – who led the services, made many knowledge statements during that year. If you are poor or sick, the fundamental reason is that there is something that isn't right in your relationship with God, he would claim. When Darwin developed his theory of evolution by natural selection, he had been inspired by dark, Satanic forces, they told us in the youth group of the church. Through religious healing, where church members lay their hands on the person's body while praying, they maintained that people can be healed from many diseases. The pastor gave many examples of this, including how homosexuality could be reversed through such healing.

As with the example of the risks and benefits of physical punishment of children, my point here isn't to assess whether Pastor Ted's knowledge claims were correct or incorrect. It is more worthwhile to examine how the church services worked as a process between pastor and congregation. Soon the formula became clear, a formula that was argued in very favourable terms in the various discussion groups of the church. The more challenging it was to believe the claims of the pastor or others with high status in the church, the higher wisdom and more profound knowledge people had if they could absorb the claims as correct.[11] In my interview with the artificial intelligence (AI) researcher Allan Dafoe, he explained the phenomenon of how believing in particularly challenging, or even obviously false, claims helps people create particularly strong bonds. He did this by referring to another scholar who distinguishes between epistemic beliefs and loyalty statements. It would probably be fair to categorise many of Pastor Ted's claims as loyalty statements. After all, he told us not to judge the statements with our minds but with our 'hearts', and that we should listen more through our spirit. This is how Dafoe explained the two types of beliefs:

> A lot of beliefs are not epistemic beliefs – a lot of beliefs are loyalty statements. To most humans, it doesn't matter to their daily lives what the truth value is of many big claims about the world. What does matter is that their group welcomes them, and feels like they are a loyal member.[12]

The scientific and religious principles of knowledge are – in principle – very different from each other. The former are ideally based on scepticism and constant revision. The latter are based on faith and loyalty to what the scriptures and leaders say. Thus, it's unsurprising that people who place themselves at the poles of science and religion end up in controversies. In the US, science denialism is a fairly common phenomenon. The idea is that each scientific claim, even if – or sometimes because – there is a scientific consensus that seems to contradict any writing in the Bible, should be rejected.[13]

The social function of knowledge

Discussions about fact resistance often end by recognising these differences between science and religion. However, if we find not only differences but also similarities between these two seemingly extreme opposites, we'll have moved towards a more thorough understanding of culture-based knowledge resistance.

Sociology and cultural anthropology identify at least two functions that science and religion share.

The first social function is to provide 'certified knowledge' in a community, with shared knowledge beliefs. It has become something of a cliche to say that science has become the priesthood of today. While there may be some merit in this assertion, it's also important to recognise in what ways it is severely misleading. 'Real' scientists (excluding some self-proclaimed experts) rarely aspire to obtain the truth, at least not the whole truth and nothing but the truth. Instead, they try to identify and reject what is false. In this way they aim to reduce uncertainty and reach high probability. Throughout history in all cultures, people have had an interest in obtaining access to 'certified knowledge' – knowledge considered of the highest quality above our daily experiences.[14] This interest shows no sign of fading. Together with Magnus Boström and others, I've done research on society's eagerness to label products and services as being less harmful to the environment, health, animal welfare, labour conditions, and gender equality. Such certifications or emblems – often produced with the help of scientific input – are comforting to people in advanced societies where it's impossible for each person to check everything for themselves. Moreover, some product labels have even been shown to have an impact on the knowledge beliefs of consumers who previously hadn't considered the potential risks to nature and society of those products. Goods that are labelled as being less harmful to the environment than comparable products have even been shown to make at least some people who were previously dismissive of climate-change concerns begin believing that climate change is actually happening.[15]

It's intriguing to compare religious predictions with today's certified knowledge produced by our secular 'priests' – scientists, experts in nongovernmental organisations, stock-market experts, meteorologists, and other intellectuals who seek to predict the future. To be sure, most sciences are immensely more accurate than predictions made by religion alone. Where scientists are inaccurate, they often make scientific points about this, frequently framing it as progress. They are correct in doing this. After all, they have been able to falsify what they or others previously assumed to be correct (see Chapter 6).

Still, the appetite for listening to who we perceive as knowledge authorities entails a high tolerance for errors. The most obvious example is weather forecasts. Even when meteorological claims that we will get a weekend of sunshine are challenged by the weather gods who give us hail the size of golf balls, most of us continue to follow the forecast, albeit with some level of cynicism and scepticism. Meteorologists admit that forecasts are far from certain predictions. However, many of us non-meteorologists don't account for the uncertainty calculations of this science.

The same is true for the stock market. Most people interested in following the stock market know how it's influenced by political instability, natural disasters, and other sudden and unpredictable worries among stock owners that within hours can make the whole market go south. Most research economists were surprised by the economic crisis in 2008. This has led to wide discussions about the value of financial prognoses. British newspaper the *Guardian* reported that during a November 2008 visit to the London School of Economics, Queen Elizabeth described the financial situation as 'awful'. She called it awful in light of what economists had told her about the devastating effect it would have for workers, businesses, and beyond. The Queen approached Professor Luis Garicano, a leading economist and director of research, and asked him succinctly: 'Why did nobody notice?' According to the *Guardian*, the distinguished professor stammered, unprepared for serious questions during the royal visit: 'Someone was relying on someone else [in the homogeneous community of traditional economists] and everyone thought they were doing the right thing.'[16] Despite society's trust in financial forecasting, no one took responsibility for the failure of forecasting the 2008 crisis that resulted in such massive problems. Still, stock-market experts continue happily to make bold predictions about the markets' future performance. Even more puzzling, many people – myself included – have a bizarre tendency to treat such uncertain predictions as some kind of certified knowledge that is worth trusting, at least partly. To have some provisional knowledge claim when we navigate our lives, an understanding that is partially shared in our community serves a central social function of social binding.

The second social function that science and religion may have in common also has to do with social cohesion: by developing practices and preferences in our community that clearly differ from those of others, we distinguish our community from other ones and strengthen our internal bonds. The social anthropologist Mary Douglas has studied historical religious beliefs in the Middle East in their cultural contexts. She was particularly interested in the time periods when the monotheistic religions (Judaism, Christianity, Islam) were founded. Religious beliefs in those days were substantial parts of the available knowledge, integrated into the entire lives of these cultures. This is why understanding religious beliefs from that time is very relevant to our goal of understanding knowledge resistance. A standard way of explaining today why certain types of food, animals, or practices are regarded as pure or impure in a specific religion is that such norms are substantive knowledge shared in religious form. For instance, pigs are considered unclean in Judaism and Islam (as well as among some Christians, such as Seventh-Day Adventists), some suggest because this meat, unless conserved and prepared correctly, can be dangerous to human health.[17]

But this doesn't explain why different religions, and congregations within religions, show such vast differences in what they consider pure, impure, sinful, and not. Mary Douglas identified an underlying pattern that could explain such differences. When comparing the practical religious claims of the 'new' monotheistic religions, she saw that these claims were the opposite of those of the previous religions. Animals previously considered holy were defined as unclean. Sacred rituals for contacting the old gods were rejected as ungodly, and so forth. The underlying pattern through which changes in religious practices took place in the transition to the monotheistic religions was one of social and cultural distinction more than anything else. By making new and opposite knowledge claims about the purity and danger of various foods and practices, the new religious formations could stick together and reinforce their sense of community. For instance, it was – and still is – prohibited for Jewish people to cook meat in milk, plant trees of different kinds together, and to wear clothes made of both wool and linen. All of these practices were seen as part of the rites of their heathen neighbours.[18]

Each religion and branch within each religion has some beliefs that everyone in the community takes for granted. These fundamental beliefs are not to be questioned. In the Catholic Church, people are expected to believe that the bread and wine used in the communion don't just symbolise the body and blood of Jesus, they *are* the body and blood of Jesus. Such unquestionable beliefs might feel like a straitjacket for some individuals in the community. At the same time, they provide people with a comfort zone consisting of shared basic beliefs, sometimes called faith. These unquestionable beliefs help to clarify to the people what makes them, say, Catholics rather than Calvinists.

In the early 1960s, physicist and philosopher of science Thomas Kuhn made a ground-breaking discovery. He showed how it's far from evident that scientific knowledge is accumulated and improved in a linear way over time. Similar to religious faiths, scientific disciplines and subdisciplines have comfort zones. One type of intellectual comfort zone is called a paradigm.[19] A paradigm is a shared view, belief, or set of claims about a certain part of reality that a big community of scholars try to learn more about. In all areas of academia, from the natural sciences to the humanities, paradigms serve similar functions, such as cultural distinction. For instance, in my own research area – about factors that could make society and individuals reduce environmental harm – paradigms are everywhere. If you follow the 'materialist turn', you claim that there is a massive paradigm shift – which you promote – in your entire research community away from studying, say, human motivation behind environmental harm and into studying how objects, goods, instruments, and their use are significant in the environmental harm caused by society. If you follow the 'argumentative turn', you belong to a research community which is likely to resist knowledge generated under the paradigm of the materialist turn. You instead focus entirely on which arguments and metaphors – not material things – various interest groups in the public debate and politics use to support their own view, and how some arguments and metaphors gain public acceptance while others don't. The rhetoric about 'turns' in academic disciplines is not unlike claims in fashion magazines about what's hot and what's not. Such claims are not mere descriptions; they typically imply a ridicule of and even a level of embarrassment at the previous belief in the old paradigm, or fashion.

Subscribing to one paradigm usually means downplaying, resisting, or ignoring the possible value that the other paradigms might have for generating valid and useful knowledge.[20] Outside academia, paradigms are apparent in diets, health tips, and food recommendations that all change over time. Paradigms are different from both religious faiths and cultural fads in one crucial respect: paradigms are based on the continuous and often rigorous collecting of data and evidence aimed at improving knowledge. A food diet can sometimes be created by a charismatic person with no expertise in health, to be sure. More often, however, people promoting a new diet use scientific arguments to explain the mechanisms that make the new diet superior to previous ones.

Despite this scientific basis of paradigms, Kuhn's discovery implies that we can only be sure about one thing concerning knowledge claims, including scientific ones: there's a tendency within cultural communities, such as academic disciplines, to stick to one way of understanding the issue in focus. People will accept this understanding as the truth and nothing but the truth, while resisting knowledge claims that challenge their paradigm. Over time, however, a few mavericks will develop evidence to demonstrate the weakness of the paradigm. This leads to a 'scientific crisis', and ultimately to a so-called paradigm shift. Then the community returns to consensus once again as it recognises the truth and superior relevance of the new paradigm – and so on.[21]

In an interview, the evolutionary psychologist Robin Dunbar pointed out to me that the built-in scepticism and slowness to accept novel ideas that break with existing paradigms have some benefits as well. He compares this with the system of law in Anglo-Saxon countries:

> The rule of thumb is that it takes a decade for people within your discipline to agree with you, and a generation for the rest of the world. The old people have either retired to their country cottages or gone. But this is not such a bad idea that it should be like that. It's like barristers in a court. Certainly, here under Anglo-Saxon law it's very conflictual. The barristers are trying to test the evidence for the truth of what you are claiming on both sides – challenge, challenge, challenge. In some sense I see the process of knowledge working in the same way. The older generation is going: 'come on, prove it to me.'[22]

Although scientific paradigms are concerned with improving knowledge, they are also cultural phenomena. As such, they are similar to other cultural phenomena in terms of the function of strengthening the social cohesion of a community and marking distinction from others.

Examples aside from religious beliefs include tastes, customs, morals, and etiquette. In distinctions from other beliefs, it's crucial to be able to resist, ignore, or forget previous, rival views. There is a social drive not to learn, or at least not to recognise that there could, in principle, be something plausible about the competing belief. Douglas here used the term 'structural amnesia'.[23] To resist as much as possible of the beliefs and practices of 'the others' serves a social function. This resistance helps new groups and communities be formed and strengthened. In order not to make us think this social dynamic belongs to the distant past, Douglas was quick to point out the relevance of structural amnesia in modern times: 'Certain things always need to be forgotten for any cognitive system to work.'[24] This is the case in modern groups, communities, and organisations of any kind.

The drive to resist some knowledge that doesn't match our culture is often related to social taboos and disciplinary limits.[25] We usually belong to more than one community, and it isn't always the one that provides us with the most well-grounded knowledge that is the one with which we identify most strongly. For instance, I personally know physicists and medical doctors who, as active and loyal members of religious communities, argue in favour of a creationist religious belief. However, it isn't that they do this *despite* their scientific expertise. Their scientific expertise makes them even more likely to argue eloquently in favour of the knowledge belief that makes the community perceive them as loyal.[26] Their clever arguments – signalling both intelligence and loyalty to their religious community – help to secure their inclusion and high position within their community. Using our Greek terminology, their well-reasoned, inner Apollo supports their Dionysian need for social inclusion. This reflects the core motivation of argument and exchange of knowledge beliefs: not to find truth but to strengthen our social bonds. Applied to social media networks, we tend to link with those of the same ethnic, religious (or non-religious), ideological, and educational profile as ourselves.[27] The knowledge beliefs that we share in such networks serve the function of strengthening social bonds, often at the expense of not having our knowledge beliefs challenged.

The right to our own values, but not to our own facts?

Sociologists and anthropologists see differences in values, norms, and morality as the main distinctive traits of communities. While every culture has values, norms, and morality, the *content* of these differs a lot between cultures. Remember Mary Douglas's recognition of how such differences are rarely coincidental. Instead, these differences are created to mark a distinction from other cultures – which day of the week is designated the holy day of rest, for example. Whether professionals within a scholarly discipline call people who seek help 'clients' or 'patients' is another example. Whether they call what people do 'behaviour', 'activities', 'agency', or 'practices' similarly reflects how scientific disciplines mark distinction from each other. Such alternatives have normative and moral overtones of how people *should* be understood and labelled.

There are ever-ongoing discussions about the differences in morality and values between various cultures. The moral psychologist Joshua Greene uses the term 'moral tribes' to show how groups separate themselves from others. Tribes perceive their own 'in-group' as morally superior to others – the 'out-groups'. The question Greene raises is how we could develop a common meta-morality or super-morality that all communities could embrace despite their differences.[28] This research area belongs to the same 'value work' as endeavours made for decades with human rights, sustainable development, and other international agreements intended to override tribal differences in norms and morality. But how about the subject of this chapter? It isn't just values that differ between groups. Cultural differences also include which knowledge claims are accepted as correct and which claims are not. We have also seen how a denial of knowledge claims made by other communities can serve the same function as a denial of the values that other groups cherish.

I'd like to make a proposition here: cultural groups, as well as human scientists who study the groups, are too quick to translate disagreements and controversies into 'value differences'. Of course, values, ideology, paradigms, and religious differences must be taken into account when we are trying to understand and resolve conflicts between groups. In this process, we should, however, pay more attention to the knowledge claims and knowledge resistance than is often done. Take the dispute between the Colorado father and myself about spanking. The easiest thing would be to conclude that we belong to different cultures with different values and ideologies. While this is correct, the issue is about more than values. It concerns two underlying knowledge claims: first, which methods of child-rearing are most effective in making a child stop repeating specific, bad behaviour (and by extension become a responsible adult). Secondly, which methods of child-rearing are the least harmful and most emotionally nurturing for the child in the short and long term. While some families may combine elements of both concerns, some parents will prioritise ensuring that their child becomes a responsible and well-behaved adult, even if that means the child may have a few emotional scars from their upbringing. Other parents, meanwhile, care more that their child's emotional health is good when the child grows up, even if this means he or she may display eccentric behavioural patterns that sometimes bother others. However, in Josh's room in Colorado Springs in the mid-1980s, both his father and I made knowledge claims about what type of child-rearing would serve both purposes. Our disagreement concerned data and empirical evidence, a disagreement that was strongly related to our different cultural belonging. To say it was *only* a disagreement over 'values' wouldn't just be insufficient, it would also be fallacious, 'circular' reasoning. Such reasoning doesn't lead us forward. Take the follow statement: 'The Colorado father and I differed in our views about child-rearing because we had different values.' It doesn't take much to change that statement into: 'The Colorado father and I differed in our values because we differed in our values.' Notice how that reasoning goes around in a closed, useless circle.

I believe many other disputes in areas of health, wellbeing, environment, scientific paradigms, and – yes – religion often include knowledge claims and resistance that must be addressed if the disputes are to be managed. Everywhere there are examples of tradition and habitual knowledge beliefs standing in the way of critical examination. Take, for instance, the fact that it wasn't until 2012 that the French health authority stated that it didn't recommend using psychoanalysis as the only treatment for autistic children. France is a country in which Freudian psychoanalysis has a deep-rooted tradition, not least in cultural and political analysis. This might be harmless and even generate stimulating discussions in reviews of books, theatre, and art. But during decades of increasingly sophisticated psychology and neuroscience that include advanced methods for studying the brain, it has become apparent that several foundational knowledge beliefs of psychoanalysis have been falsified. They were wrong.[29]

We have seen *how* resistance to the insights of other groups and cultures can serve social functions. Such resistance may mark cultural distinction and strengthen bonds. This raises a question that the next chapter will examine: *why* would it ever be worth compromising our quality of knowledge in a conformist way?

3

Why invalid claims can be valuable

Your refusal to say the emperor has no clothes is a signal that you belong to the group.

Allan Dafoe, AI researcher, in an interview for this book,
26 April 2018

The social warmth of the emperor's new clothes

So far, we have seen examples of knowledge resistance concerning grave matters: vaccination, the physical punishment of children, climate change, and so forth. But there are less serious, more light-hearted issues to consider. A candidate that comes to my mind is the global community of sound lovers who call themselves 'audiophiles'. Some audiophiles claim to have 'golden ears', and all of them carry a dream: to find the perfect sound. For most people, finding the 'perfect' sound isn't very hard: just visit a good concert hall and listen to your favourite music, or maybe visit a forest far from city life. But it isn't in the forests or concert halls that audiophiles' hearts begin to beat most rapidly. Their favourite hunting grounds are the large audiophile trade events and – even better, if they can afford it – their own living rooms. At costs that sometimes reach a high share of their incomes, they buy preamplifiers, end stages, turntables, speakers, cables, and a variety of other components. Audiophile culture also encourages continuous replacement, 'updating' or 'upgrading' equipment. This tendency to sell regularly their old components to buy new ones is a norm and is jokingly called 'audiophilia neurosa'. It would be reasonable to assume that these audiophiles are music lovers. Of course, some of them are, but in the audiophile culture the sound is primary; the quality of the music is secondary.

What does audiophilia have to do with knowledge resistance? The products, knowledge, and communication in the audiophile community include a lot of technical and scientific jargon. Still, audio scientists are very sceptical about whether all of the expensive components deliver better, or even different, results compared with products that cost ten times less. A number of rigorous, scientific, blind tests have been done, comparing preamplifiers, power amplifiers, and not least cables in different price ranges. Such tests often fail to identify any difference when scientists use measuring instruments.[1] It is also common that no differences are perceivable by the human ear when scientists perform double-blind tests.[2]

This seems to be a contemporary case of the emperor's new clothes. In Hans Christian Andersen's original story, the child's revelation when he points out the emperor's nakedness triggers laughter among the public. It also leads to embarrassment among the members of the emperor's inner circle, who had previously expressed superlatives about the clothes. In the audiophile case, many would say the acoustic scientists serve the same role as this child by revealing negligible differences between extremely pricey and much cheaper equipment. What might seem puzzling is that people in the audiophile world are familiar with the results of such rigorous, scientific studies.[3] The studies are regularly reported in audiophile magazines. Yet, unlike the emperor and his court, the audiophile community appears more strengthened than embarrassed by the comments from audio scientists. Despite the results of double-blind studies showing little or no difference in sound between inexpensive versus expensive cables, the audiophile journalist Malcolm Steward still reviewed one of the more expensive cables in these words:

> The most marked and worthwhile difference, I felt, was in the increased naturalness in both the sound of instruments and voices, which seemed more organic, human and less 'electronic', and in the music's rhythmical

progression, which was also more natural and had the realistic ebb and flow that musicians exhibit when playing live. In short, recordings sounded more like musical performances than recordings.[4]

I personally know nothing about this particular cable and don't wish to pass any judgement on it. But the quote serves as a great example of the elaborate audiophile descriptions about differences in sound performances that few – or sometimes no – people can trace.

Two points should be addressed here. The first is whether it is even a problem that some men (and audiophiles are predominantly men) join a community that lives by a myth. What actually is the problem of embracing outrageously costly sound equipment that, according to scientific studies, doesn't deliver any better sound than far more affordable components? Let the audiophiles resist the best available knowledge and waste their money on these items if they want to. It's their problem. This was my reaction when I first learned about this case. However, when I conducted interviews for this book, a leading scholar in a different problem area – megaprojects (bridges, opera houses, etc.) – gave me an economic argument that goes against this perspective on wasted money (more on this in Chapter 5). Secondly, even if at least parts of the audiophiles' appraisals would appear to be a case of the emperor's new clothes, it's nonetheless clear that these clothes seem to provide some real warmth to the audiophiles. People join a community based on knowledge beliefs that non-members not only cannot share but cannot even understand. Still, this example shares traits with knowledge resistance concerning vaccination, climate change, natural selection, and several other issues. They all trigger more questions than the one occupying us thus far, about the role that community attachment plays in how people resist knowledge. Also, all these cases now wait for us to address the deeper question: why does community-based knowledge resistance in general exist? Why do we so often let our knowledge beliefs be navigated by the community, even when its knowledge belief is wrong?

Evolution and knowledge resistance

To answer the question of why individuals and groups resist the knowledge claims of other groups, we first need to address an even more fundamental issue – that of why humanity has survived and, as a species, reproduced so successfully since its dawn, with few signs of stopping. This is a question asked by the evolutionary sciences, including, for instance, evolutionary psychology and evolutionary anthropology. Evolutionary scientists find a narrower issue particularly interesting: why did humans evolve, survive, and – as a species – reproduce so successfully during the 99.5 per cent of our history as the genus *Homo* when we lived as nomadic hunter-gatherers?[5] The reason evolutionary scientists are so interested in that period is that it accounts for so much of our history. This means that it's the hunter-gatherer way of life to which we are genetically adapted to the most substantial extent. Evolutionary scientists contend that many of those who did not survive that long and in some respects harsh period lacked some adaptive trait that was needed to procreate and raise children in those natural and social environments. Those who live today do so because their ancestors, with whom they share genetic tendency towards certain individual motivations and behaviours, adapted to the living conditions in ancestral environments, and it's the degree of adaptation to the environment that matters here.

It's in our genetic evolution that we should seek the fundamental reasons for community-based knowledge resistance. Key here is to explore the 'adaptive value' of various human traits, particularly those that exist in several, or all, cultures throughout history. An exciting opportunity offered by evolutionary explanations is that we can start our attempts at reaching an understanding using different starting points. The most straightforward way is to examine how people and groups resist knowledge, and then we can try to explain it in evolutionary terms (about adaptive traits, etc.). However, this runs the risk of telling just-so stories, for example claiming that the nose bone has evolved since we needed somewhere to put our spectacles.

An alternative way would be to do what evolutionary anthropologist Oliver Curry recommended to me when I interviewed him for this book: start from the evolutionary principles and use them to argue what adaptive traits must have evolved. Take, for instance, the five taste receptors on the human tongue. Instead of having people taste a range of different things, one could start by analysing which sources of nutrition were most important in hunter-gatherer society, which were very rare, or which types of plants were most dangerous to human health in those environments. In theory, this challenge to survival should have led to the evolution of one or several taste receptors that trigger a strong but unpleasant sensation. In this way of doing things, according to Curry, we should arrive at the conclusion that the taste receptors are not restricted to saltiness, sweetness, sourness, and bitterness, but also feature additional ones such as umami (associated with glutamates). Our essential need for fat suggests that there ought to be taste receptors for identifying that as well. We have a hardwired craving for fats, salt, and sugar – nutritional groups that were sometimes scarce but essential for survival in hunter-gatherer environments, albeit far too accessible to us today.

How about the inclination to take part in the knowledge resistance of one's culture? We first need to ask what major threats and opportunities the hunter-gatherers faced, conditions in which individual differences in handling knowledge claims could make a difference to their chances of surviving and reproducing. Could it be 'genetically adaptive' to the strongly social environment of hunter-gatherer societies to unite with others in the group in their knowledge resistance?[6]

There is one resource that was – and is – of paramount importance to us humans who, compared to other animals, are slow, weak, fragile, and energy-demanding, and have offspring that take a long time to grow up. The resource – if we insist on using this crude term – is other humans. Sure, it's good for us to have friends, family, networks, and so forth. This may sound as if the social factor is an 'extra' that brightens our lives and something we could survive without. However, evolutionary psychology takes the social factor one step further. Humans that live today are still genetically adapted to hunter-gatherer societies. In the physical and social environments of these societies, social exclusion and loneliness meant an increased chance of dying early without having reproduced. The entire existence of hunter-gatherers was based on the group sticking together. This was crucial in order to hunt and share large animals, take care of the young, and protect each other from rival groups.

The evolutionary anthropologist Robin Dunbar, who I also interviewed for this book, has combined neuroscientific and anthropological methods. By doing so, he has identified that our brains can develop stable relationships with a maximum of 150 people. It is no coincidence that the average number of 'friends' on social media, where distant acquaintances are often added to signal how popular we are, is also roughly 150.[7] This was the approximate number of individuals in hunter-gatherer groups – and still is in the few remaining indigenous societies in various parts of the world.

What was the most significant threat to human prosperity, reproduction, and safe raising of offspring in hunter-gatherer societies? While not subject to the stress factors of modern life, anthropological and archaeological studies still indicate that people lived under more immediate threat from other humans than most of us do today. To be sure, hunter-gather society is often portrayed as a harmonious Eden, with food to which humans are genetically adapted, fewer infections, and – on average – only four-hour workdays needed for hunting, gathering, and building shelters.[8] The further away from the inner circle hunter-gatherers found themselves, the higher the risk was of them being harmed or losing their partner or children. Each man in hunter-gatherer societies had between a 1/3 and 1/4 chance of dying an unnatural death, compared with 1/100,000 in the US and Europe in the early 2000s.[9]

However, as we all know, social bonding was – and is – necessary not just in order to avoid being murdered. The whole safety net of care has traditionally been dependent on people being accepted as members of an in-group. Even if hunter-gatherers managed to reproduce, the chances of their offspring surviving to adulthood were highly reduced because of limited opportunities for caretaking.[10] There is no longer any doubt that people get sick from social exclusion and isolation.[11] The pain we feel from social exclusion is the body's genetic, evolved alarm signal. The signal screams to us that – at least had we lived in a hunter-gatherer society – we are at tremendous physical risk and must do whatever it takes to reduce this risk. During such circumstances in a hunter-gatherer society, people who had a higher ability to distinguish their in-group ('us') from out-groups ('them') would have been better adapted to survive and reproduce. It was also highly adaptive to be seen by one's in-group as someone who really belonged.[12]

How should people be best equipped to convince others they belong to their group? By having evolved nonconscious mental processes, including self-deception and compromised critical thinking. Such bases for knowledge resistance would reduce tensions with the main knowledge beliefs and values of the group. When we wish to be a member of a group – such as a religious, political, or even a scientific community – it isn't just for conscious, tactical reasons that we often don't challenge their fundamental knowledge beliefs. We are equipped with the capacity to believe the dominant knowledge claims of the group in question. Why? Because our body language and nonconscious signals communicate far more to others than our clever and well-measured words do.[13] Therefore, a crucial part of human adaptation in hunter-gatherer society must have included the ability to deceive ourselves and allow ourselves to be fooled by others in some matters.

Of course, our knowledge and beliefs are not the only cues that people use to distinguish group members and friends from 'the others'. In my interview with Robin Dunbar for this book, he mentioned that he and his colleagues had identified what he called six pillars of friendship. The six pillars, things crucial to have in common with others in order to feel united, are local proximity, a sense of humour, language or accent, educational background, music taste, and worldview. If we consider who these pillars, particularly in ancestral societies, were most likely to lead people to favour, to feel safe with, and to protect, the answer is their closest friends, who were in turn highly likely to be their closest kin – individuals that had more genes in common with each other than with other individuals. Dunbar's six pillars are also tied to the evolutionary process known as kin selection.[14] This refers to the preference for helping and supporting people that are closely related to us genetically, which increases the chances that our shared genes will survive and spread further. This shows that the six pillars, including a shared worldview, haven't only helped us identify trustworthy individuals with whom we are inclined to develop a relationship of 'reciprocal altruism' (in which someone may be happy to offer a certain amount of help, but will then expect something in return), a term coined by another anthropologist, Robert Trivers.[15] Among the six pillars, shared worldview is the one that is most directly related to what we're looking for in this chapter: explanations for why groups sometimes resist knowledge because it comes from other communities.

Sitting there in a medieval cloister room at Magdalen College in Oxford interviewing Robin Dunbar, I was at first really excited to hear about the six pillars, to the point that I felt increasingly impatient as he walked through each factor on the list. It was particularly fascinating to learn about studies in musicology that had shown that humanity started to sing – and laugh – before they had developed language. During a few seconds, I was transported back 250,000 years to a fireplace on the savanna. My group and I were singing and laughing free of all other – often tiresome – verbal exchange. What I was really hoping for, however, was that 'agreement over facts' would present itself as a factor at the end of his list. But it never came. We discussed earlier that religion and science have some traits in common, but that there are also immense differences between the two. Remember, as mentioned earlier, we have 'the right to our own values but not to our own facts'. Wasn't there any place for this wisdom in the pillars identified by Dunbar and his colleagues? The closest pillar was this vague 'shared worldview', which encompasses shared ideology, religion, knowledge about the physical world, knowledge about the social world around us, and whom to trust. I felt this was too much.

Now, I believe that Dunbar and his colleagues were probably pointing towards a critical insight by mixing ideology and knowledge into what they call 'worldview'. This mixing seems entirely consistent with what we have learned so far in this book about how people relate to knowledge. People instinctively recognise the worldviews of others along with the other pillars within a small amount of time – facts, values, ideology, morality; the more signs, the better. Maybe this is what we need to keep in mind when trying to understand why people and groups absorb and stick to some knowledge claims while rejecting others.

Knowledge tribes

From what social and evolutionary scientists would predict, individuals and groups don't often keep normative issues (values, ideology, and morality) separate from descriptive ones (facts and knowledge). The two types of issues at least seem to serve similar roles in keeping a community together, strengthening trust, and in identifying who doesn't belong to the group. The term 'tribal' comes to mind here. In all societies – from advanced industrialised societies to traditional ones – it's possible to find special loyalties, clear separations between in-group and out-group, boundary drawing, and so forth. This has been shown scientifically in several aspects of human life. The most obvious one is morality.

The moral psychologist Joshua Greene uses the term 'moral tribes' to show how our morality works.[16] The capacity for moral thinking, such as developing rules based on a sense of fairness and reciprocity, can be found in all societies. Nonetheless, all people have various moral biases in their thinking. We have seen above how people favour and prioritise the wellbeing of their in-group compared to out-groups. One such area is religion, as we saw in the previous chapter. In all societies, groups practice some form of religion. This capacity is universal. Still, religious faiths and non-faiths are in many areas the basis or a result of lines drawn between the in-groups and out-groups. These lines are usually drawn with the social function of strengthening tribal favouritism and loyalty within the group.

Some scholars even maintain that the capacity for religion has evolved not just with the function of strengthening in-group loyalty in general. Religion has also provided a stronger potential for succeeding in war.

Moreover, and inversely, success in war increases religious belief. This capacity, those scholars hold, includes the human inclination to twist and distort one's view of reality. Overconfidence is a crucial trait here. People exaggerate their own group's strength, talent, and unique relationship with the divine. There are numerous cases where war leaders and a significant number of their soldiers believe that they will be victorious in battle even if their enemies have far more men or stronger weaponry. 'Remember how David beat Goliath!'[17] Does that mean that we should widen our understanding of tribalism to include not just the normative issues such as moral values, but also the epistemic matters of facts, knowledge, and claims about how the world works? This is a radical step which opens up a very complicated world. In such a world, communities don't just differ in their convictions of what is right and wrong. They also differ in their beliefs of which knowledge claims are correct and incorrect. We should, I think, recognise that our tribalism – our hardwired inclination to divide people into 'us' and 'them', evaluating 'us' as superior – often includes how we estimate 'our' *knowledge claims* in comparison with 'theirs'. In academic terms, we all sometimes blur morality (how groups should behave) and epistemology (what is valid knowledge).

Still, there might be good news here for those who hope for greater unity between communities in how the world works and what society's main problems are. I've already mentioned that this discipline is anchored in evolutionary science. It tries to see how morality is adaptive to various social and physical environments. This includes our universal ability to distinguish right from wrong as well as each culture's specific moral stances on various topics. The moral psychologist Jonathan Haidt contends that in the same way as taste receptors evolved, enabling people to identify nutrition and avoid poisonous plants, evolution has provided us with half a dozen 'moral foundations'. All cultures navigate between these moral foundations when shaping the norms that guide actions, albeit with different moral content in different cultures. According to Haidt, these moral foundations, consisting of pairs of opposing factors, are:

- care/harm
- fairness/cheating
- loyalty/betrayal
- authority/subversion
- sanctity/degradation
- liberty/oppression.[18]

What do the moral foundations have to do with which knowledge claims people in various cultures perceive as true or false? The connection is almost impossible to see from the first glance at this list. There is an overlap between moral claims and knowledge claims. As it turns out, people within the two types of culture – value conservative and liberal-leftist – embrace different moral foundations to a different extent. Most apparently, conservatives – often nonconsciously – find authority and sanctity particularly important. Liberals and leftists find care and certain forms of fairness especially important. People from each group favour moral measures that are in line with their favourite moral foundation. Among conservatives, these measures would include a stronger police force (authority) and patriotic rituals (sanctity). Leftists and liberals, on the other hand, would favour ensuring equal numbers of women and ethnic minorities on boards of directors (fairness) and progressive taxes (care). Liberals and leftists are more likely to believe that a knowledge claim is true if it's framed as a fairness or care issue. Conservatives, on the other hand, are more likely to believe a knowledge claim is valid if it's framed as a question of authority or sanctity. The idea of framing (something we will come back to several times in this book) is that people or groups can never perceive or understand the world in a neutral way. Here, evolutionary science, sociology, and behavioural economics are in full agreement. To make sense of the world around us, we must place the parts of the world we are to understand in a culturally constructed package or frame.[19]

Chapter 2 discussed opposing views on the physical punishment of children. The practice is in fact banned in Sweden. Such a ban might seem – at least if you are a liberal-leftist – to be a textbook example of an enlightened, scientifically grounded piece of legislation. This assumption might be strengthened by the fact that those who were against the introduction of a ban came mainly from the conservative side of the political spectrum. Even conservative politicians were split on this issue, however. Consistent with religious orthodoxy being a stronger predictor for how much communities trust scientific expertise, the loudest voice against the proposed ban didn't just come from any conservative politician, it came from a conservative politician who was also a minister in an evangelical church. He used phrases that fit the general conservative emphasis on (parental) authority among Haidt's moral foundations. Yet the politician's main arguments actually fit best within the moral foundation of sanctity. He asserted that the Swedish state should respect its Christian heritage, which would include honouring the Bible verse: 'because the Lord disciplines those he loves, as a father the son he delights in'.[20]

The most probable explanation for the legal ban on spanking in Sweden can be found in the cultural context and style of the country in the 1970s when the ban was introduced (and afterwards). Reading the statements that underlie the decision, one finds psychologists and psychiatrists describing physical punishment in terms associated with morality and custom. Physical punishment of children is '*kränkande*' ('offensive') to children. Moreover, it is common with formulations where the value-neutral term '*barnaga*' ('physical punishment of children') is intertwined with the value-ridden term '*barnmisshandel*' ('child abuse').[21] The Swedish government, media, psychologists, and psychiatrists appear to have navigated the process based more on liberal-leftist moral foundations, and less on hard, scientific facts. Although claims were made about scientific support for a ban, specific data were rarely presented.

At the time Sweden introduced the ban, no comprehensive and systematic studies had to my knowledge been completed on the long-term consequences of moderate spanking. More extensive scientific studies of physical punishment on children have since been conducted. Their overwhelming and consistent message is that physical punishment of children increases several risks for psychological problems.[22] The studies also show that physical punishment of children is ineffective in correcting undesired behaviour.[23] However, this topic allows us to see the intense power of our culture-based knowledge resistance. Swedes in the 1970s held strong knowledge beliefs about the harm caused by spanking, but these beliefs were not based on extensive scientific studies. On the other hand, the culturally based knowledge beliefs of Americans still make them resist the by-now extensive scientific findings showing the harm and ineffectiveness of spanking.[24] In 2014, 76 per cent of men and 65 per cent of women in the US (both Democrats and Republicans, with different proportions of the two) claimed that 'a good, hard spanking' is 'needed' (effective and not harmful).[25]

Let's take another example notorious for dividing liberal-leftists and conservatives, one where political ideology actually is a robust and direct predictor. I have mentioned it several times already, but here we can place it in a new light. The example concerns whether to believe that scientific claims about human-made climate change are valid. A far higher share of liberals and leftists than conservatives hold the knowledge claim that climate change is happening and that it's the result of human activities, including greenhouse gas emissions from vehicles and the burning of fossil fuels. We have also seen that the more the two cultures have learned about climate change over the years, the larger the gap seems to have become. Paradoxically, conservatives appear to reduce their belief in climate change the more facts they are given about it, while liberals and leftists become increasingly convinced that climate change *is* happening the more facts they receive.

However, it's important to think about how climate change has been framed over the years. The framings have been constructed along these lines: climate change undermines the solidarity that we should show people in the Global South and future generations (fairness – predominantly liberal-leftist framing); addressing and reducing climate change is to care for those people and life forms that are most in jeopardy due to risk of flooding, excessive heat, and drought (care – predominantly liberal-leftist framing). Scholars, from moral psychologists to political scientists, hold that a significant reason why conservatives resist knowledge about climate change is that climate change has been framed with moral foundations that resonate among liberals and leftists.[26]

If we think about climate change or nature conservation in general, there is arguably very little – or nothing – that in itself ought to resonate and trigger concern so much more among liberals and leftists than among conservatives. We have the term 'conserve' for starters, the word stem of conservatism. Some scholars and politicians have been pondering on how climate change could otherwise be framed. Suggestions include the framing that humans are disobeying God out of hubris, destroying his creation of nature and climatic balance (moral foundation: authority). If conservatives do recognise climate change, they could frame this by pointing to a lack of respect for the homeland: if humans *do* cause flooding, droughts, and other extreme weather, then this is an offence to our home country. This framing ties to the moral foundation of loyalty to the nation, something that strongly resonates with conservatives.[27] Finally, we could even posit the framing of climate change as a risk that threatens 'purity'. Climate change leads to increased risk of infections within the country thanks to unusual changes in temperatures. This might resonate more among conservatives; purity is a trait that lies close to the moral foundation of sanctity, and purity – including fear of germs – is particularly strong among conservatives.[28]

If framing is as powerful as many human scientists think, it could help to raise the share of conservatives who believe in the reality and dangers of climate change. However, scholars involved in climate change debates argue that it's too late to reframe climate change so that its reality and urgency would resonate among conservatives and liberal-leftists alike. In fact, Pope Francis made a conservative reframing of climate change when the US president Donald Trump visited him in 2017 by giving Trump a signed copy of his encyclical letter 'Laudato Si' from 2015. In the letter, the Pope called for a political response to climate change. He echoed the sentiments of other religious leaders, saying:

> The climate is a common good belonging to all and meant for all. The Bible tells us to minister to the needs of God's creation as an act of worship. To ignore those needs is to dishonour the God who made us and that is just what we're doing by walking away from this [Paris climate] accord.[29]

Still, President Trump pulled out of the Paris agreement on climate change a few weeks later. This and similar experiences have made scholars and practitioners involved in renewable energy, electrification of transportation, and the like recognise that climate change has become too politicised.

Apollo and Dionysus

Value matters such as morality are often intertwined with what knowledge claims we think are true or false. When we think about community-based knowledge resistance, most of us are able to turn on a mindset where we perceive such resistance as absurd and irrational. This is also the mindset we have when we argue that people have the right to their own values but not to their facts. Values are fluffy, culturally rooted ideas along with religion, norms, and ideology. Whatever values we hold should be up to us, like personal taste. A liberal motto has been formulated about this in Latin: *de gustusibus non est disputandum* (in matters of taste there can be no disputes). The previous chapter and this one have hinted at causes for the human tendency towards resisting knowledge claims from other communities. Reflecting on how problematic knowledge resistance is can be easy from a distance. When we are out there, with real issues at stake – particularly social ones – knowledge resistance becomes a deep inclination, not just in 'them' but also in 'us'.

To illustrate this dual tendency in which people relate to knowledge I have already introduced you to the Greek gods Apollo and his half-brother (or half-sister, as he is sometimes portrayed) Dionysus. Apollonian treatment of knowledge can have a highly adaptive value. If you are inventive, logical, sceptical, science-minded, and always ready to tell the truth, this can lead you to receive much respect from your group. You are likely to come up with technical inventions and ideas about how the group should be organised, how work should be divided, and so on. There is something, for instance, in the role of the medicine woman or man that seems to be in line with some of these characteristics. The trust that people develop for you is consequently an Apollonian trust. It's a trust that your knowledge claims are sound, measured, well-reasoned, and that your judgement has been reached without influence under pressure from others.

However, what happens if you openly challenge others in your group? What if you say you don't believe in their knowledge claims, which are the dominant ones in the group? For instance, you might suggest among your liberal and secular peers that human-made climate change isn't real. Or you could hold that humans are the result of a world created by an individual, male God slightly more than six thousand years ago. Perhaps you have come to the conclusion that the (knowledge) beliefs of some of your rival groups seem more reasonable and plausible than your own. Moreover, your individual integrity and independent thinking makes you reassess and question most of the taboos and social norms of your group.

There could be good factual reasons for all your scepticism. However, there are high risks here. In today's modern social settings, the risks may at first not seem dramatic. Most of us are part of several groups with somewhat different profiles and values. Still, there is an interesting thought experiment you could do. If your social circles are mainly liberal and most of your friends and family have a high level of formal education, what would happen if you start to select and recite detailed statistics indicating that a much higher number of refugees could be helped if your country didn't accept any further refugees but instead diverted all resources designated for refugees to organisations in the countries where people are at risk of war? Or what if you started to endorse the notion that we should stop trying to mitigate climate change, and instead redirect all climate funds to preventing malaria and Aids? On the other hand, if you belong to traditional and conservative circles, consider showing statistics about the risks of extensive gun ownership or about the impossibility that the world is just six thousand years old. With such an uncompromised, Apollonian approach to facts and knowledge – even if formally correct – you would risk being excluded from your group.

Most of us don't consciously calculate the benefits of treating knowledge and facts neutrally versus the risks of being socially excluded.

Instead, it's done automatically in our minds. Sometimes this automaticity of conforming beliefs can stretch to hideous claims. Among many Germans in the 1930s, there was the widespread belief that Jews were the leading cause of the economic troubles everywhere in the country. This belief became mainstream, even though fewer than 1 per cent of the population was Jewish.[30]

In cases where people are not indoctrinated but doubt that a specific claim is correct, their emotions may still tell them to be polite, treat others with respect, not cause a stir, and so forth. During my high school year in Colorado Springs, after Pastor Ted's services in the evangelical church, I didn't once ask the others if they really believed everything Ted had said. I never asked if they genuinely thought that poverty and ill health were rooted in an insincere or otherwise dysfunctional relationship with God. I didn't ask if they would put all their money on the possibility of 'curing' homosexuality with healing or psychotherapy. Nor did anyone else that I heard of in that community ever challenge Pastor Ted's knowledge claims.[31] Today, in my more liberal circles, I haven't discussed any radical alternatives – conservative or progressive – to my own country's mainstream refugee or climate policies. Nor have others that I've heard of in these liberal circles. This silence is partly derived from the genetically rooted, Dionysian priority of showing loyalty to our own group, unless the issue concerns direct and imminent risks to the health or wellbeing of our community. To our inner Dionysus, it's the group that matters above all. Evolutionary science shows why this approach can have benefits for the individuals within the group since loyalty increases the chances of collaboration. This includes knowledge loyalty. The whole meaning of loyalty is that you stick with a person or group *even if* they are incorrect or – from an Apollonian perspective – full of other flaws. Loyalty, therefore, implies some sacrifice.

Our human ability to show loyalty makes group stability and a degree of social predictability possible. This often benefits the individuals in the group more than if there were a constant threat of knowledge controversies that would split up the group. Still, in our social lives, we oscillate between treating knowledge in the Apollonian and Dionysian ways.

Most often we find ourselves in between. We act on rumours, previous assumptions, habits. Only cautiously and gradually do we revise our knowledge beliefs from time to time in ways that remain well calibrated with our peers.

The dramas within and between people's brains

What does it mean when we say people oscillate between treating knowledge in the Apollonian and the Dionysian ways? Is it possible to say something more daring – and at the same time scientifically valid – about how the Apollonian and the Dionysian sides are related? How do they interact when groups form, hold, and challenge their own knowledge beliefs? Let's use some less metaphorical language. Supported by evidence from evolutionary science (about self-deception),[32] behavioural economics (about fast and slow thinking and cultural biases),[33] and also my own work on human interests and social motivation,[34] it's fair to say this: knowledge refinement and truth-seeking (our Apollonian side) are usually subordinate to our deeply social interests (our Dionysian side) in maintaining or strengthening our position in the in-group. This doesn't mean that groups or individuals are not interested in acquiring valid knowledge. Yet many times when we are eager to get the knowledge right (the Apollonian side) we do this in a context where it's also socially rewarding (the Dionysian side) to get it right.

Think about various school situations. When it's socially rewarding among their peers to raise their hands and answer correctly, and to get as high marks as possible, children are likely to strive towards this. The Apollonian and Dionysian sides are in concert (if we here, for the sake of simplicity, assume that the knowledge children acquire in school is correct and valid). This is also how much of the world outside of school works as well. Although it isn't always the case, as we shall see later, employees in most bureaucratic institutions are probably rewarded socially by producing accurate figures, facts, and so forth, most of the time. Knowledge resistance is more likely to come into the picture in social contexts where people's Apollonian interest in gaining correct knowledge goes against their Dionysian interest, the desire to maintain or strengthen their position in the community. There, one should expect individuals and groups to prioritise – often nonconsciously and instinctively – their Dionysian interests. This is the most critical lesson in this entire book and the most reliable explanation for knowledge resistance. Knowledge resistance makes it more likely that people will strengthen their social bonds and maintain or increase their social status. This means that people should be expected to be firmly pressured – from within themselves as well as from their social surroundings – to resist information that would entail more accurate knowledge. In such cases, people and groups are often most motivated to take the route that helps them strengthen or maintain their social position.

Again, much of group-conformist knowledge resistance takes place nonconsciously. A classic set of experiments on this was conducted by Solomon Asch in the 1950s. In this study, each setting had groups consisting of eight male students from Swarthmore College in the US. Each group was placed in a classroom. Only one person in each group was a real participant, unaware that the other seven were actors who had been told how to answer in the experiment. The task was to assess which of three lines of different lengths on a series of pictures shown to each group had the same length as a fourth, separate line. The actors maintained that two lines that fairly obviously didn't have the same length actually did. In a significant number of cases, the group pressure from the actors made the real participant believe that the false claim was true, which seems absurd from a rational point of view. Without group influence, on the other hand, participants could easily see and report which of the three lines was of equal length as the target line.[35] It isn't far-fetched to assume that several social settings in the real world are characterised by a group pressure similar to that enacted in these conform experiments. For instance, in a religious group that subscribes to a certain creationist doctrine, it can be highly rewarding socially to believe every detail of that doctrine is literally true. There, it can be equally rewarding to resist centuries of scientific evidence indicating that life has evolved through Darwin's principles of natural selection.

Intriguing differences have been found between adults and children. Many large groups of adults resist having scientific claims about evolution by natural selection challenge parts of their religious beliefs. Scientific assertions and abundant data are often insufficient for stimulating people to incorporate an evolutionary understanding of life on earth into their belief system. This goes both for placing the scientific knowledge side by side with a religious belief and for replacing the religious belief with a strictly science-based one. In such cases, Dionysian, community-oriented processes often prevail over Apollonian ones. Apollonian thinking is mainly used to select arguments for why mainstream biological science is wrong. Among children aged between 14 and 16, on the other hand, how much they know about evolution by natural selection has a strong correlation with how likely they are to hold a knowledge belief in the theory. Among adults, however, the polarisation in this issue is far more complicated.[36] There can be several reasons for this, as we will discuss later in this book. For now, we can hypothesise that adults might be particularly concerned – nonconsciously – not to jeopardise their sense of social belonging within their religious community. Young adults don't perceive the same social risk from accepting scientifically established knowledge.

A sociological lesson across a wide range of communities, from religious to academic ones, becomes apparent. It contends that the more the knowledge beliefs of one group deviate from those of another group, the stronger the social cohesion will be within each group. In other words, the more outrageous and unsubstantiated a knowledge claim is that members in a particular community hold, the more profound loyalty the members show the others in that community.[37] We can see this in some circles within the social sciences. For example, some scholars maintain that genetic differences between women and men either don't exist or have no role in why men are on average more violent than women. It helps to strengthen the sense of community to hold such a scientifically flawed view. The view serves to isolate these groups from academic communities. The latter explain the difference in levels of violence between males and females using an intricate interplay between genes, biology, and culture.[38]

Next time we are puzzled by seemingly extreme knowledge beliefs among specific groups, we should stop repeating the question of why groups can't just unite in a collective recognition of the best available facts. There are several reasons not to get stuck with this question. What makes up the best available facts is often far from obvious or clear-cut. We should also remember the earlier-discussed social bonding effect within the group that 'knows differently' from other groups. There is a sense of warmth in the exhibition rooms at the audiophile trade shows. Men nod to each other in shared amazement at the night-and-day differences in sound quality they perceive that different cables help produce. The audiophiles do this even if, or maybe because, science has found no such differences. The warmth doesn't come only from the hot tubes in the amplifiers or from body heat. It also comes from sensing that one truly believes something different to what most people do. And one shares this with others united in an exclusive community.

There are many exceptions to the pattern that people give our inner Dionysus priority while Apollo gets the reduced role as Dionysus's servant. In that description, Apollo gets to search selectively for signs that the erroneous, culturally established knowledge claims are correct. The exceptions are often admirable and touching. They are perfect plots for storytelling: think about the children's tale I've already mentioned – incidentally my favourite children's tale – 'The Emperor's New Clothes' by Hans Christian Andersen. Sometimes the exceptions come from real life. There are the whistle-blowers that are we hear about on the news. These are heroic people who go against the knowledge resistance of the rest of their community. By laying the facts bare – despite the risk of being excluded, ostracised, imprisoned, or even executed – they fight for transparency and justice. Research shows that the motivations of whistle-blowers to put the facts straight and unveil knowledge resistance are often mixed and diverse. The motivation might even change over time. It can range from frustration about their own situation or that of others to a broader concern about justice and fairness. Sometimes there may be hope that justice and fairness will win in the end. There is often a wish that the social position of the whistle-blower and other truth-seekers may be re-established or even raised.[39] Still, the strong social motivation that most of us are usually governed by makes whistle-blowing a marginal phenomenon. It demands support from policies and laws to become more common. Several countries have in fact introduced bills that protect whistle-blowers. Wise policy-makers and authorities realise that unveiling hidden or ignored truths is usually good for society, at least in the long run. They also realise that most of us will avoid whistle-blowing unless we get formalised social protection for doing so. The dramas within and between people tend to favour the Dionysian need for social bonding over truth-seeking when truth-seeking makes people run the risk of social exclusion.[40]

Adaptive, but not necessarily good

So far, we have seen how culture-based knowledge resistance can be 'functional' and 'adaptive'. It may sometimes help members of a group stick together and feel like a 'we', increasing their motivation to collaborate and support each other. This raises a question: if we include facts and knowledge into what distinguishes 'tribes' – including modern ones – does this mean that we have to accept that every tribe has its own truth? This topic will be elaborated upon in several chapters in the rest of the book. It would be a horrible mistake, I will argue, to claim that just because we live in knowledge tribes – as I believe we do – this isn't something we could, or should, do anything about.

The fourteenth Dalai Lama – a leader of one group of tribes – said the following about his own Buddhist knowledge beliefs:

> If science proves some belief of Buddhism wrong, then Buddhism will have to change. In my view, science and Buddhism share a search for the truth and for understanding reality.[41]

Although I'm not a Buddhist myself, I find this perspective admirable. It reflects great courage and comfort that the tribe(s) of Buddhism cannot only survive but can also prosper by being open to new knowledge claims. This includes knowledge from the outside that challenges the prevailing one of the community. Let's keep that perspective in mind when we examine how the whole range of tribes relate to knowledge that challenges them – from scientific to religious communities.

The Dalai Lama's sentiment is admirable, as is what Pope Francis emphasised about the importance of taking scientific warnings about climate change seriously. At the same time, not all instances of knowledge claims are this clear-cut. In several cases there isn't overwhelming scientific evidence that points in the same direction. Sometimes scientists within or across disciplines position themselves in paradigms that contradict the paradigms of other scientists. The following chapters will discuss some cases where there is a scientific consensus as well as others where scientists disagree with each other. This will help us see the subtler mechanisms of knowledge resistance. These are rarely given sufficient space in the polarised, public debate about 'fact resistance', 'denial', and 'post-truth'.

Knowledge belief first, confirming evidence second

Rationality upside down

The culture you belong to provides you not just with norms for how to behave and what values to hold. It also tells you which claims about the world you should believe and which you shouldn't. This goes far beyond religious beliefs. It includes factual claims about how best to preserve your health, the environment, how to correct the undesirable behaviour of children, and how to reduce crime. Sociology and anthropology were among the first disciplines to clarify how deeply embedded our beliefs and knowledge claims are in the culture we live in. People are neither freely choosing nor rational individuals, at least not rational in the traditional economics sense. Instead, we 'live through institutions'.[1] All our thoughts, reasoning, and decision-making are in a social and cultural context. This has coloured our thought process before we have made up our minds about what is real, false, certain, uncertain, and so forth. It's no coincidence, for instance, that certain leftist or green communities are likely to reject research findings that challenge organic agriculture (where no pesticides are used). The scientific claim – correct or not – that a global transition to organic agriculture would be incompatible with food security and reduced greenhouse gas emissions is categorically rejected.[2]

Let's leave the focus on debates between groups from different cultures for a while, and instead give the individual a bit more attention. What can we learn about how individuals shape their knowledge beliefs when not in a debate? How do people make use of facts and arguments when they decide what is true or not? This is an issue where there has been, and remains, a lot of dispute – between the human sciences and between many groups outside of academia.

In my interview with Bent Flyvbjerg, an economic geographer, we discussed how knowledge and power are related. He maintained that particularly people in power handle knowledge and decisions in the reverse way of what is conventionally seen as rational. And they are fully aware of what they are doing:

> There is this [conventional] rational model that if you make decisions, then you need to have to have knowledge of the basis on which you make the decision. Power doesn't think like that. Power thinks: 'We're going to make a decision. We want as many degrees of freedom as possible. We actually want no knowledge, we want to do what we want to do without being restricted by knowledge.' That's how people in power think.[3]

To be sure, Flyvbjerg's experiences of how influential people are fully aware of how they resist knowledge when they make decisions should not make us generalise that all people are fully aware and tactical. However, his claim that people often begin by identifying their desired conclusion and after that ignore or shape knowledge to fit that conclusion is indeed correct among society more widely.

An abundance of research has emerged on this topic. Some of this research ruthlessly contradicts the previous standard view of how individuals reason with each other. In one example, 2 groups comprising a total of 662 people were selected to participate in a survey as part of a study examining the role of facts and arguments for a person's knowledge beliefs.[4] The researchers placed the participants in groups based on whether they believed that violent video games increase aggression. The groups differed in knowledge beliefs about the possible cause (video games) and effect (aggressive behaviour). The researchers acknowledged that while values vary extensively around video games – not least among parents – there are still many facts out there that might be misunderstood. Those facts might make a difference at least so that people on either side of the debate may complicate their view of video games and move closer to the other side. Researchers gave both groups fictitious articles making 'factual' claims about the effects of violent video games. One article argued that violent video games may cause aggressive behaviour. The other claimed – through equally sophisticated arguments – that violent video games don't provoke aggression. What would be the 'reasonable' way of being influenced by the two articles? It's fair to speculate that most of us would answer in similar ways. By accessing facts and arguments – as in those two articles – that speak for as well as against a knowledge belief, people have a higher chance of becoming more nuanced. Acquiring two-sided information ought to make us less insular, less predictable, and more interesting people. When responding to a survey question about the effects of violent video games, obtaining information and arguments from both sides ought to make people avoid the extremes of 'Strongly agree' and 'Strongly disagree', an instead feel more comfortable with the more moderate answer options.

Before revealing the results of this study, let's take a closer look at the origins of this idea that facts, regardless of what side they come from, most often make us challenge, modify, or give more nuance to our knowledge beliefs. This is a question that might be as old as humanity, and one I can't answer with certainty. After all, what Daniel Kahneman calls 'thinking slow' is a universally human capacity that includes allowing new inputs to challenge our previous knowledge beliefs.[5] The assumption that this Apollonian dimension is what governs most or all of our decision-making processes can be found in traditional economics. Not that economists would say that people have an endless appetite for more facts and knowledge as a goal in itself. However, the basic idea in traditional economics is that people need to be 'fully informed'. How else would they be able to make all the consciously rational decisions that economists believe people are making?

Traditional economics assumes people are 'rational' by nature – with the motivation and capacity to seek out the best information to reach their well-defined goals. Systematic processing of facts and arguments before people decide is how economists assume humans operate. Similar views of human decision-making are found in the broader notion of rational choice. The assumption is that being as informed as possible is the primary interest of most people – scientists, in particular. Stated differently, getting the facts and arguments straight, and by extension solving the issue at stake in an optimal way, is how people operate. The notion – not unlike the ideal among logicians – is that people shape, or ought to shape, their decision-making process according to the following order. First, people study and contemplate the available facts and arguments systematically and without any predefined favourites. Then, they develop a verdict of what – on balance – ought to be the most valid knowledge claim. From this verdict should follow that people incorporate this belief or make a decision. Alternatively, people may hold a knowledge belief, only to have it revised in light of strong counter-arguments and evidence. It's according to this logic that many of us construct narratives describing how we have made our decisions or shaped our beliefs.

I've spent many of my years as a social scientist trying to understand why people do what they do in specific contexts. Why do some people under some circumstances make strong efforts to alter or maintain their daily practices in ways that cause less harm to the environment? As mentioned in Chapter 1, for instance, I visited cities and the countryside in Massachusetts in the US as well as in southern Sweden conducting interviews with householders about why they chose to change (or maintain) their heating systems. Questions also covered how they chose between alternatives. For example, how had they reached the decision to switch to a biomass boiler or to ground heating? How had some of them made the choice to connect to district heating (in Sweden, where heat is generated in a municipality or region at a central location and then distributed to households through insulated pipes) or to use direct electricity (from nuclear power, hydropower, wind power, etc.)? And how had some households decided to stick to their old oil-powered boiler?

When preparing for these studies in the early 2000s, I assumed that people would mix environmental arguments (except those who kept their oil boilers) and political views with situational claims. These would include, or so I thought, how they had been influenced by neighbours and friends, as well as practical considerations. At the same time, their decision-making would presumably follow somewhat different patterns in various residential areas. I also expected to find cultural differences between the decision-making processes in Massachusetts versus southern Sweden. My initial worry was that the people of every household – across urban and rural areas – would create politically correct rationales after their decisions had been made. I hoped that people wouldn't mainly offer cliched phrases about the – undoubtedly enormous – importance of passing on a green, clean earth to the next generations. In the end, I got some mixed arguments, but they gave me almost none of the expected environmental rhetoric. Initially, I congratulated myself for having created such a disarming atmosphere where people didn't feel obliged to portray themselves as ecological saints. Yet, the balance – or lack of balance – between the rationales they expressed behind their choices have intrigued me to this day. Regardless of which heating systems they had chosen – between ten and fifteen remarkably different options – most of the householders emphasised one advantage as the overriding one for their own decision: their choice entailed 'by far' the lowest cost, at least in the long run. This rationale was stated even by households who had decided to keep their old oil boiler. One of the 'oil boiler' families in particular has stayed in my vivid memory – a woman and a man, 41 and 43 years old, living outside Växjö in southern Sweden in a quaint little wooden house. Both of them were in good health and led active lives. This didn't prevent them from arguing along the following lines: 'If we'd have invested in a different heating system some years ago, that would have made sense. But now when we're approaching old age, we have way too few years left for making such an investment a reasonable one.'

Taken as a collective, the complete cohort of households considered most or all of the financially relevant factors. These included the current price of fuel, cost of the new equipment, uncertainties related to energy supply, interest rates, maintenance and repair costs, and time used for running the equipment. No household, however, had taken *all* economic factors into account. They had picked a few and ignored the others. It was particularly interesting to compare households that had focused on the same three or so factors. These factors were, for example, the price of the equipment, the interest rate for the loan required to buy it, and price of the fuel. Even when emphasising the same factors, different households in several cases ended up with different types of equipment and energy sources. The conclusions they all claim were the main basis for their respective decisions.[6] The point isn't so much that they emphasised financial reasons for the specific choice they made. Rather, I was fascinated by how most householders – unsurprisingly, it was mainly the men who did the explaining to me – constructed a story to themselves and me. The story concerned how they had started out as a blank slate. They had been entirely open to all relevant facts and plausible uncertainty calculation before they had made the optimal decision. However, none of us is truly a blank slate.[7] We enter situations with different degrees of risk aversion, ways of envisioning the future, specific knowledge, experiences, influence by peers, and so forth.

What do the findings of how these householders perceived their own decision-making say about people beyond Western societies? This is a crucial question that has two parts. The first concerns whether it is a universal human trait to assume – often erroneously – that one's decisions are *economically* rational? From my examination of cross-cultural studies in economic and evolutionary anthropology, I think it's fair to answer no to that question.[8] The acronym WEIRD has been developed by scholars comparing how people in different cultures make decisions, and concluding that decision-making in Western, Educated, Industrialised, Rich, and Democratic societies doesn't represent cultures in general.[9] There is something with Western cultures, albeit spread globally, that should make us not expect people in all cultures to believe so strongly in their own economic rationality. This Western (or North-Western) way of thinking was analysed by the sociologist Max Weber in his classic book *Protestant Ethic and the Spirit of Capitalism* in 1905.[10] Seventy years earlier, the French political scientist and diplomat Alexis de Tocqueville had written the book *Democracy in America*. He stressed that American culture does not consist of greedy people. Still, de Tocqueville was struck by the materialist focus among the Americans he met:

In the United States, a man carefully builds a home to live in when he is old and sells it before the roof is laid. ... The taste for material gratifications must be regarded as the primary source of that secret restlessness revealed by the actions of Americans and the inconsistency they exhibit every day.[11]

In sum, the view among individuals that they make complex decisions in financially optimal ways seems to be far from universal.

The other part of the question is whether it is a universal trait for humans to assume – often erroneously – that they make their important decisions based on a conscious and rational calculation in the broader sense. If we agree that it is, we recognise that people's goals could be rational beyond just saving money and time. The goals might be increased comfort, concern for others, the pleasing of God, reduced harm to the environment, and so on. The 'conscious and rational' part would be that individuals start with one or a couple of these goals. Then they collect information neutrally and openly about how to maximise or optimise the satisfaction of the goal in question. On this basis they make the optimal decision. The universal and evolution-based potential for self-deception identified by several evolutionary and social psychologists makes it highly likely that this type of narrative about one's decision-making prevails in all cultures at least some of the time.[12] This potential enables people from all cultures to convince themselves and others that they make systematic, well-grounded decisions, most often founded on a systematic process that optimally satisfies their explicit goals.

More realistic descriptions than the above-mentioned robot-like systematics of decision-making processes that most of us fool ourselves into believing can be found in quotes from fiction writers, artists, and politicians. Such quotes are based on their everyday experience rather than lofty philosophical ideals. Here's one such quote, said to be from Mark Twain: 'To a man with a hammer, everything looks like a nail.' Stated prosaically, we first make up our minds, often without being aware of it, then we make feverish efforts to find evidence and arguments that confirm our position or decision. Take the video game study mentioned above, in which two groups with polarised views on whether violent video games cause aggression were given two articles containing factual claims in both directions. Perhaps surprisingly, neither group became more nuanced or moderate in their beliefs about the potential risks. On the contrary, members of both groups moved closer to the extremes of their former position. The results suggest if you had initially believed that playing violent video games doesn't provoke aggressive behaviour, reading both articles would most likely have made you conclude decisively that those games are not risky at all. So much for our hopes of becoming multi-layered and nuanced by getting both sides of the story.

The same phenomenon has been identified in a broad range of issues. These include whether the death penalty deters violent crime,[13] whether nuclear accidents make subsequent nuclear power safer,[14] and knowledge beliefs about the efficacy of the HPV vaccine.[15] It has even received a name: 'biased assimilation'. The phenomenon is related to a wider human tendency to which the social psychologist Leon Festinger gave a term in the mid-1950s that has become far better known: 'cognitive dissonance'.[16] Let's use Festinger's theory to understand the puzzling video game case. How could people's beliefs become more extreme despite being given arguments in both directions? People seek consistency between their emotions, knowledge beliefs, and decisions. Being confronted with an argument that goes against their prior beliefs creates an unpleasant, psychological dissonance that needs to be removed. One way to remove it is to alter the knowledge belief. This could be done, for instance, by moving away from thinking that video games cause aggression and into thinking they don't. However, based on inertia, habitual thinking, and pressure from the beliefs of their peers, it's more likely that people develop an absolute trust in articles that support their prior conviction. This also goes for the pieces that criticise articles that hold the opposite argument. The result: a more extreme version of the belief they held earlier.

Cognitive dissonance theory can also help to explain parts of the reasons most or all householders in my energy studies described an elegant and systematic decision-making process. Regardless of which heating system they had selected, most householders believed that their individual household had identified and chosen the most financially sound option. Think about the situation: you have taken out a big bank loan and made an irreversible investment that will affect you for a decade or more. Imagine the frustration – or dissonance – you would live with on a daily basis if you admitted to yourself and others that there were probably much more cost-effective, durable, practical, and environmentally friendly alternatives available that you ignored. Research indicates that when people have made irreversible and costly decisions, they are mainly inclined to construct narratives about a well-balanced, and fully informed process by which they arrived at that decision. Such a story typically concludes that the narrator chose at least one of the best options available.[17]

Further research has broadened this perspective by incorporating biology and neuroscience. In this way, science has been able to investigate and partially explain the neurological basis for the seemingly reverse logic that people use. They first shape their beliefs and then select, as well as exploit, specific facts to support them. Behavioural economics is a relatively new discipline that has found a niche here. It has taken as its duty the discovery and cataloguing of what is perceived as distortions in how people process information and form knowledge beliefs. Behavioural economists recognise that these distortions, which they call 'biases', have evolved biologically. A concept relevant to knowledge resistance is confirmation bias – in short, how people have a tendency to confirm and select support for previous beliefs. I will describe and explain this and related biases later in the book. For now, it suffices to draw upon a couple of foundational claims of behavioural economics. The human biases are rooted in biological evolution, and are therefore universal, existing in all cultures. Some biases exist and are expressed separately from the social and cultural context. This view may inspire the following question: is there some knowledge about the world that we are inclined to believe? Among the examples mentioned above about why people and groups resist knowledge, is there something special about certain topics? Is there something in some issues – regardless of culture and social context – that makes us more likely to resist knowledge about them than about other matters?

Too strange to be imagined?

It may seem strange to us, in the early part of the twenty-first century, that it seems to have taken until a few decades into the nineteenth century before people were able to develop in writing the possibility that humans might have evolved gradually from other animals. We know that some ancient Greek thinkers, notably Anaximander of Miletus (*c*.610– *c*.546 BC) suggested that the first human came from a fish.[18] However, to call him – or any of the other early thinkers – the first Darwinist, as he was referred to for a while in the twentieth century, is a silly exaggeration.

All it would take to develop at least a simple version of the idea of gradual evolution would have been to sit down and look at one's toes. In hindsight, our toes, with their seemingly useless claws that we call nails, appear similar to those of so many animals. This should lead us to wonder why, throughout history, more great thinkers didn't question whether, aside from the shared trait of all being divine creations (something that most cultures seem to have believed in some way), humans had evolved gradually and slowly from other animals, making us closely related physically and biologically. Here I leave aside more spiritual ideas such as those that can be found in many non-Western religions, ideas about reincarnation or pantheism. There has, of course, always been tremendous religious pressure preventing thoughts of evolutionary theory in many parts of the world. On the other hand, people have throughout history managed to write other things in secrecy – consider, for example, all the religious dissidents who have been bold enough to challenge the religious privileges of state churches. If they had happened upon the idea of evolution, they would probably have tried to spread it. As would influential people in the many text-oriented cultures that didn't place as much religious pressure on their citizens as in the long, monotheistic periods of the West. It really is fascinating to think that no person influential and courageous enough to spread a similar idea before Darwin and his colleagues had ever reflected on their own body in the Darwinian way. How could this be?

An evolved resistance to the idea of evolution?

There is a psychological and evolutionary argument which contends that there must be an immense resistance – not just from cultures and religions but also from our biologically evolved mental modules – to sowing the seeds of an idea similar to Darwin's. Even after Darwin had published his revolutionary ideas, decades into the twentieth century these were still misunderstood and juxtaposed with an equally 'ungodly', but for the most part faulty, notion. This was Lamarck's theory, developed in the early nineteenth century, that offspring inherit the characteristics that their parents acquired in the environment. For instance, the theory would contend that giraffes have long necks because their ancestors stretched their necks in reaching for food in higher tree branches and this useful characteristic was passed on to their offspring.[19]

Let's expand the notion that some knowledge claims are particularly likely to be subject to resistance since our evolved mental modules find them counter-intuitive. Could it be that such knowledge resistance is a more general phenomenon? Maybe several of the other areas where this book has so far identified knowledge resistance are similarly counter-intuitive. Note that 'counter-intuitive' doesn't necessarily mean that the claims are too intricate or complicated. Try for yourself to study and learn the details of various creationist stories and religious doctrines. You'll find immense intricacy and advanced thinking. Rather, 'counter-intuitive' here means that the claims are more difficult to believe *spontaneously*. The reason that some scientific claims might be counter-intuitive would be that they differ from the types of problems our brains have evolved biologically to solve. Those among our ancestors who could solve the latter problems had higher chances of surviving and reproducing, predominantly in hunter-gatherer settings. Let's continue the example of why it was challenging for people to come up with similar versions of, or spontaneously believe, the Darwinian idea. The claim that humans have evolved through random mutations over thousands of generations seems to be very difficult to internalise. Added to this difficulty is the fact that no individual has ever witnessed the evolutionary process in real time. The process is too slow to be incorporated into our intuitions and common sense; we have to *learn* it. Even then, it's difficult to grasp. Those who discovered it – Darwin and, in parallel, Alfred Russel Wallace – did so through thousands of studies and observations, and tremendous creativity.

In my interviews with human scientists, I brought up the possibility that there might be something counter-intuitive about evolution by natural selection. Javier Lezaun, a social scientist at Oxford University who studies public understandings of science, reacted in this way:

> No, I'm not sure. To use the example of evolution: if the argument is that evolution is very counter-intuitive, people are naturally going to be inclined to resist it. But if you look at the alternative arguments about intelligent design or anything you can read in the Bible, that's as counter-intuitive as anything you can find. And those people seem to be fine with that level of counter-intuitiveness. I don't think we are wired to accept some realities as more counter-intuitive than others. But that's my disciplinary bias.[20]

The view that it's religion – not evolutionary science – that is counter-intuitive is found among many social thinkers that identify themselves as agnostic or atheist. J. L. Mackie, a leading philosopher who criticises religion from the perspective of logic, gave one of his books the telling title *The Miracle of Theism*. Daniel Dennett, another philosopher who has been called one of new atheism's 'four horsemen', has also indicated how absurdly counter-intuitive he thinks that religious belief is. In an interview, Dennett told the journalist about religious friends and acquaintances who have said that they pray for him: 'I excused those who said they prayed for me and I resisted the temptation to say, "Thanks, I appreciate it, but did you also sacrifice a goat?"'[21]

Many of the religious and mythological narratives may both impress and puzzle a modern, secular person by their fantastical and limitless imaginary. Secular people have heard about evolution by natural selection since their early school years. The raising of this awareness has been followed by natural science teachers in school confirming that there is a scientific consensus about the validity of evolutionary theory. As a

95

consequence, these secular people are tempted to conclude that evolution is at least as intuitive as religious narratives.

What, then, is the plausible answer to the question of whether evolution by natural selection is as easy to imagine and believe in as the religious doctrines? I don't think it is. And I'm not alone. Scholars, among them literary studies scholars, psychologists of religion, and anthropologists, have identified several similarities between religious stories and children's tales. These scholars have also been able to show the social and evolutionary relevance of both religious stories and children's tales. The common character of such stories and tales belongs in what the psychologist Jerome Bruner calls our narrative mode of thought. Its opposite is our systemic mode of thought. When referring to Bruner, the risk perception analyst George Gaskell described the two modes in this way in our interview:

> The narrative mode has a story, a person. It has a person that has motives, and it has a conclusion. In science [at least in principle] we use the systemic mode. It's impersonal, it's logical, it uses statistics, et cetera.[22]

Recent studies show that believing in a personal God (reminding us of fathers or mothers around us) who has created a final version of woman and man comes easily to us. As in the narrative mode, religious texts reveal God's motives and a purpose where each of us is important. They also provide a conclusion about how we can fulfil God's wishes and what happens if we don't. It's much easier to believe in such descriptions – typically provided in the narrative, Dionysian mode – than in impersonal, statistical, Apollonian descriptions of how *Homo sapiens* has evolved through gradual changes generation after generation.

To consider that *Homo sapiens* is still evolving through mutations and adaptation to the natural and social environment is particularly challenging to think spontaneously. Ask 4-year-old children how they see the world around them, regardless of the faith of their parents. You are likely to witness their propensity towards what developmental psychologists call 'promiscuous teleology'. Everything is there for a purpose. Berries grow on the bushes so we can eat them. Clouds are there 'for raining', and so forth. This recognition of how preschool children reason has been studied by the cognitive scientist Kelemen, among others.[23] The reasoning is very similar to the outlook of a tall and skinny priest, the Abbe Marignan, who Guy de Maupassant described in the 1880s in the short story 'In the Moonlight':

> Everything in nature seemed to him created with an absolute and admirable logic. … The dawns were made to rejoice you on waking, the days to ripen the harvests, the rains to water them, the evenings to prepare for sleeping and the nights dark for sleep.
>
> The four seasons corresponded perfectly to all the needs of agriculture; and to him the suspicion could never have come that nature has no intention, and that all which lives has accustomed itself, on the contrary, to the hard conditions of different periods, of climates, and of matter.[24]

My point isn't to depict this teleological thinking as infantile just because the priest shared it with preschool children. Instead, it's the profoundly human propensity of this thinking I'm getting at. If we turn to supernatural thinking, Darwin himself realised that a belief in a spiritual force is a universal, human phenomenon. This is how he formulated it:

> a belief in all-pervading spiritual entities seems to be universal; and apparently follows from a considerable advance in man's reason, and from a still greater advance in his faculties of imagination, curiosity and wonder.[25]

'Universal' doesn't have to mean that *everyone* is religious or spiritual. It rather means that religion and spirituality can be found in cultures around the world today and throughout history.

Contemporary evolutionary scientists have searched for specific adaptive value with a religious belief in our ancestral past. These scholars claim that different types of societies are supported by different spiritual and religious beliefs.[26] For instance, in hunter-gatherer societies, it was particularly common to find pantheistic or animistic beliefs. The spiritual entities in focus had a mixture of human and nonhuman traits. These traits represented part of the ecology, including the food supply of hunter-gatherer societies. Those individuals with a substantial capacity for holding a spiritual belief had it canalised into polytheism and animism. Such a capacity helped them to collaborate with other people not only in their hunting and gathering but also in raiding and ambush, the primary form of violent activity in those earliest forms of human society. Small groups of men (rarely women) that were kin, with little or no planning and without permanent hierarchy within the group, entered the territory of another group. The goal was to obtain by force resources such as women and food.

Nomadic hunter-gatherer societies gradually gave way to so-called village agriculture (between three thousand and ten thousand years ago) with permanent settlement. Spiritual beliefs became more often polytheistic. Gods had more human traits and were less of a mixture of animals and humans. The warfare of this era was increasingly militia-based, and almost all able males participated. They were not always kin and had to develop a quasi-kin relationship where they were willing to die for each other. There was more planning in the warfare of village agriculturalists than in the raiding of hunter-gatherers. Moreover, there was a stricture hierarchy and allocation of specialised tasks. When the aggressive acts had ended, the men who had survived went back to their agriculture.

In the third broad phase of societal development, which has been called city-state agriculture and industry, monotheistic religions became more prevalent. In monotheistic religions, God isn't fully human in character; he or she is a supernatural force organising and governing society. Monotheism has mainly been found in technical-agricultural, city-state-like societies. These include large cities and nation-states. This is our current subsistence system. Very crudely put, we have lived in such a system for around three thousand years. Most of us are not directly involved in agriculture. We specialise in different activities but live within a global super-organism. Warfare in this society is to a greater extent professional, highly hierarchical, and without the kin group connections of earlier types of warfare.

Each specific kind of religion is accordingly tailored to strengthen the internal cohesion of a particular kind of society, as well as the ability of that society to be successful in warfare. The great variation in the chances of people's survival and reproduction throughout history, this view contends, has depended in part on how well warfare and religion have served each other. In groups or societies where warfare and religion have served each other successfully – in the sense above – this has on average been beneficial to individuals within those groups or societies.

At first sight, it may seem unclear how the type of spiritual belief, social order, and aggressive activities go together. For our purposes it suffices to keep in mind three things. The first is that the degree of hierarchy that is useful in a specific type of warfare goes hand in hand with the degree of hierarchy between the deities and the humans in a particular era. In a hunter-gatherer society, there doesn't seem to have been a tremendous bottom-up reverence to the supernatural entities. Reverence to higher deities is greater in polytheistic religions. The greatest level of submission is found in the extremely submissive role that humans have vis-à-vis God in monotheistic spirituality. The same difference can be found in the level of hierarchy in hunter-gatherer raiding groups (low degree of hierarchy), militia warfare (medium degree of hierarchy), and professional warfare (extreme hierarchy based on rank). If people who, helped by their religious beliefs, in each type of warfare stick to the level of hierarchy that is most suited for prevailing in the violent activities, the religious beliefs have had adaptive value. Those individuals with the capacity to unite with others in a group based on a religious faith have in that case increased the chances of winning the conflicts. This entails increased chances of getting access to resources, such as food, status, and mates. We should remember that to these people, beliefs in supernatural entities were in line with their intuition, no matter how fantastical the beliefs may seem today when drawn out of context. We should also remember who these particularly religious people were: our direct ancestors with whom we share our genes, and our fellow humans living today.

The second issue concerns how beliefs in supernatural entities may increase collaboration within a group. In Chapter 2 we saw how religious belief could make people compromise a bit with their immediate, individual self-interest. There is, of course, the kindness – for kindness' sake – that religion sometimes fosters within the group. Besides, religion may provide believers with the instrumental reasons for helping each other. The political scientist and evolutionary biologist Dominic

Johnson shows this in the title of his book: *God Is Watching You*.[27] If you help your fellow group member, God will reward you; if you don't, God will punish you. However, what does this strengthened collaboration within a group of the same beliefs mean for the relationship *between* groups? As we could see above, the human capacity for believing in supernatural entities also seems to strengthen the in-group for warfare between groups. What does this have to do with knowledge resistance? Warfare facilitated by a common religious belief within a group seems to go together with certain aspects of knowledge resistance. Self-deception and in other ways skewed thinking are common aspects. They have, throughout history, made people (mostly men) more inclined than not to take part in warfare. Those participating in combat have rated the benefits of participating in war – including an honourable death – as higher than the risks, compared with those of hiding and deserting. The beliefs concern, for instance, the probability of gaining something desirable if one engages in warfare (access to mates, social status, material resources). They also concern the likelihood of being injured or killed compared with if one doesn't take part. To this can be added the misleading sense in a war that the other men are your brothers (pseudo-kin), and that your nation is your mother, father, or uncle. In Sweden, we sometimes call our country Mother Svea. Plenty of other such examples exist. In sum, such beliefs – boosted by misleading metaphors – have historically turned people into useful warriors. Their particular spiritual beliefs have been adapted to the specific type of warfare likely to take place in each respective era.

The final point is that these eras – hunter-gather, village agriculture, and city-state agriculture – are united in a fundamental sense. They all show a universal, human capacity and inclination to believe in supernatural entities. Darwin seemed to be right that this is inherent in many if not most of us. This supports the claim that spiritual beliefs – with different forms depending on social and cultural context – are more intuitive to us than some scientific knowledge beliefs. It's tempting for groups that perceive themselves as scientifically informed and enlightened to assume that they are 'liberated' from supernatural beliefs. These secular people may in some cases see themselves as free from the types of 'automatic' moral conclusions that religious people often draw from their worldview. However, intuitions close to supernatural beliefs are alive and well there too. This human tendency to draw supernatural conclusions in life may, for instance, have influenced the long period of what has been called social evolution in the nineteenth and twentieth centuries, which we will return to in Chapter 7. Many people translated the scientific recognition that humans have evolved through natural selection into a quasi-religious imperative. The superhuman entity wasn't (necessarily) God. Nevertheless, there was the 'the natural order', which social evolutionists claimed somehow dictated that the inequalities between individuals and between cultures ought to be there. Why? Simply because inequality was there as a fact. To reduce inequality would be to tamper with the natural order. Also, that certain countries had more advanced technology and conquered countries inhabiting predominantly people with darker skin was erroneously interpreted as a sign of the 'natural' superiority of the former. The substantive research behind the excellent book *Guns, Germs and Steel* shows how the more fortunate geographic locations of the con-quering countries explains most of that success.[28] Social Darwinists drew the quasi-religious conclusion that it was not just their right to conquer and bring order to the uncivilised countries of the Global South, it was a moral duty of the 'white' countries to do so. A belief in God played a key part here. But there was also the quasi-religious belief that society should imitate the natural, evolutionary order. Far from incidental, it was groups at the top within the technologically advanced countries who used these arguments. Thus, the arguments follow the simple 'us v. them' rhetoric and the biases towards 'us' that I introduced in the Introduction and Chapter 2.

From what we have learned about knowledge resistance, we shouldn't assume that people have advanced these arguments as a conscious tactic. The claims have necessarily been made as a strategic means to improve their own groups' chances of getting access to resources from what they portrayed as 'inferior' cultures. Through various types of self-deception and overconfidence, many people believed in this image of cultures and that some were morally obliged to conquer others.[29] To draw conclusions from a belief of what one's own group is morally bound to do regardless of the consequences lies very close to a religious or quasi-religious way of thinking. Remember, for instance, the example in Chapter 2 about the Colorado father spanking his 6-year-old boy. Although I could see the father's tears when he caused his son pain, the main argument the father gave me for proceeding with the punishment was biblical: it says in the Bible that the father should punish his child physically after a wrongdoing – supposedly regardless of the consequences.

An additional sign of how easily religious-like beliefs come to us can be seen when you open any biology book that tries to make evolution more intuitively understandable. That's a challenge that authors writing about evolution have, not just when they write for the general, busy public but also to other evolutionary scientists. In all such writings there is (erroneous but pedagogical) formulation portraying evolution as a personal and intelligent actor. Accordingly, evolution by natural selection 'experiments' through mutations to 'solve problems'. Evolution is described as having intentions, goals, of trying to meet the organism's needs, and so forth. The core of Darwin's theory is the exact opposite. Evolution has no intentions and no intelligence. It only *is*, and often ruthlessly so. Still, that we as humans – or any other living organism – just exist without an intention behind that existence seems to go against our intuition. Therefore, the Darwinian story needs to be translated into a more intuitive, quasi-religious one. This is necessary even so that evolutionary scientists can understand it, not just intellectually but also with their hearts (= intuition). In everyday life today, there are many examples of how intuitive supernatural beliefs seem to be to us. For instance, quite a few secular football fans have in studies reported that the fate of their favourite team is to some extent dependent on whether they watch the game on TV and support the team from their couch.[30] Deep down I know that I contributed – if only a little – to the Swedish tennis player Björn Borg's defeat of John McEnroe in the final at Wimbledon in 1980. We cheered, yelled, and cursed that beautiful June day. We did this to support him. Our support radiated into the twelve-inch black-and-white

TV that we had brought to the little summer cottage my father had rented in southern Sweden. Björn Borg himself was known to take the supernatural very seriously. His temporary beard, hairband, and many other details gave him some supernatural advantage. And he won.

Processes as objects

Another case discussed in this book, climate change, turns out to have a primary characteristic in common with the notion of evolution by natural selection. Moreover, both cases have something in common with another scientific claim that has been subject to much knowledge resistance: the astronomer Kepler's discovery that planets move in ellipses at a constantly changing speed. These three cases share the fact that they are based on knowledge claims of ever-changing processes. As cognitive scientists show, however, we humans have a strong tendency to think about processes as objects.[31] According to evolutionary theory, evolution never stops as long as there is life. Not even *Homo sapiens* is a finished object or entity. Albeit slowly, humans continue to change from generation to generation. Still, it's far easier for us to conceive of humans as a finished, fixed 'object'. Something similar appears to happen in the case of climate change. Our intuition seems to tell us that the weather is changing while we think about climates as regional but constant. In fact, those who are sceptical of the idea that human-made climate change is taking place become more certain in their dismissal when the weather is unusually hot. The same weather causes those who believe climate change exists to become more certain in their belief.[32] From a scientific perspective, neither reaction is accurate, since single weather events say little or nothing about climate change. Some researchers claim that people, including those with high, formal education, share a specific intuition. It contends that societies can avoid causing climate change by continuing to emit greenhouse gases at the current levels, as long as these rates are not increased.[33]

Further support for this 'object bias', our inclination to interpret processes as fixed objects (some moving by themselves and others not), is found in child psychology. When children are just a year old, they have already developed knowledge about the characteristics of several objects. They are aware that toys, for instance, are persistent over time, even when they can't be seen. They also know that most things don't move by themselves. People, on the other hand, can move by themselves, have goals, and respond emotionally to various situations. One-year-old children know this as well.[34] These are universal findings. As to processes, however, it takes until the age of 7 until children are even in principle able to distinguish objects from processes. In cognitive tests, 5-year-olds have been shown to believe a story (a process) can be skinny (like an object can) and that a fight (a process) can be fat (like an object can).[35] The age gap between when children can understand the characteristics of objects (aged 1) and when they can distinguish processes from objects (aged 7) supports the claim that children are not blank slates, equally likely to learn and believe one thing as they are to learn and believe another.

The persistence of this core system is responsible for the object bias among mature adults. This is the tendency to apply knowledge of physical objects to temporal processes.[36] Most of us see fixed 'objects' that a less-biased observer might more accurately understand as a process. Think about the entity of a person. We see others – and ourselves – as more or less fixed, stable entities that we expect to remain consistent over time. The few exceptions to this common expectation about other people are when we know that particular circumstances apply – when they are under the influence of chemical substances, under extreme stress, sexually aroused, and the like. This goes against findings by neuroscientists showing how fundamentally an individual's various brain regions increase in activity in different situations. The variation is so extensive that it might be more accurate to think of an individual as more than one person. Immense, individual changes take place in us as people throughout our lives. Changes are seen in our bodies, of course, but also psychologically and in our way of socialising. If we took a personality test early in our lives and repeated it three or four decades later, many of us would probably come across as entirely different personalities. Still, we tend to assume that we know what 'the real me' is: something stable, almost like an object. We assume that there is always a stable 'object', a fixed person, waiting to be identified. Still, the individual – like the natural, global climate, and many other entities that we perceive as fixed objects – is in fact subject to constant change. This would make it more accurate to describe these objects as more like processes. Climate change is particularly interesting in this respect. From what we have learned here, dismissing climate change can't only be explained as stubbornness or conformism within a community. It is also a result of what could be called object bias. Such a bias seems to be genetically present in people, and could be added to the plethora of cognitive biases making people inclined to resist certain well-established knowledge.

Another bias can be tied to a resistance to acknowledging research findings indicating that the benefits of vaccination outweigh the risks. In the case of the measles vaccine, all systematic research indicates there is no risk that the vaccine could cause autism. The whole idea of vaccination goes against intuitive 'common sense', which includes a strong tendency to be highly averse to risks of contamination. This is an aversion which has served us well throughout human history. However, that aversion can become highly risky in itself if it makes some people avoid crucial vaccination.[37]

Cognitive biases are manifested in distorted views that are common concerning other risks as well. Fear of flying seems to stem from an exaggerated fear of the control one lacks when being a passenger on an aeroplane.[38] A tendency among heavy smokers to be subject to 'optimistic bias', downplaying the risks of smoking, is another example where people resist or twist the data available.[39] Combine these two biases and you get the outlook of my paternal grandmother: a heavy smoker with a strong fear of flying. And she isn't alone. Or rather she wasn't – I'm sad to say that she died prematurely, perhaps due to her smoking.

I think there is something important in the theme running through all these cases. The idea is that people have an inherently biased common sense that makes them more likely to learn and accept some knowledge claims than others. This notion gives a fresh perspective on ignorance.

Rather than 'emptiness', it's more apt to conceive of ignorance as based on what we are equipped with and genetically prepared for: biases, among other things. Psychology and behavioural economics have been very productive in 'discovering' hundreds of human biases.[40] Many of these biases are cognitive, and are concerned with how people on average seem to be inclined to resist insight into descriptions of reality that go against their genetically prepared intuition. To take the example of physical safety, many of us know intellectually that the risk of becoming a victim of violent crime is, in many places, the lowest ever. Still, many people don't feel that this is the case, and are in fact more worried than they used to be.[41]

Learning about human biases gives a certain insight into how we are made up. Yet it would be a mistake to assume that biases can act on us in a vacuum. Why? Because none of us lives in a vacuum where only our genetically prepared inclinations operate. We never perceive knowledge claims in a 'pure form'. They are always packaged – or framed – either by our previous experiences, by those who deliver the knowledge claim, or both. Take vaccination, for example. Scholars have attributed part of the reason some people decline vaccinations for themselves or their children to the way vaccination is usually framed. There are a lot of war metaphors surrounding vaccination: a 'shot' containing an 'enemy' substance entering our healthy body is like having an armed aggressor infiltrate our camp. But not presenting vaccination as a way of strengthening the body's army seems to be very constructive. Instead, it would be more accurate – and productive – to present vaccination as a way of strengthening our intelligence service. What vaccination does is to allow the body to identify an enemy. Moreover, the vaccine enhances our resources and hinders the chances of the enemy having an impact. The risk perception scholar George Gaskell gave me that suggestion in an interview for this book.[42] He, in turn, had heard it in a talk by William K. Hallman.[43] Similarly, reframings of climate change, evolution, genetically modified crops, and many other issues may increase our chances of accepting well-established knowledge claims supported by ample evidence. However, whether an issue is intuitive or not and how the questions are framed are two factors that together only explain parts of the knowledge resistance to the issue. It's easy to see the vast variation in how much these two factors impact people's knowledge beliefs. Many of us – despite wide differences in educational levels – don't believe in creationism. A significant share of the world population doesn't *really* believe in ghosts and fairies, even if such beliefs might be more intuitive than some naturalistic explanations.

Even if in this chapter I have tried to stick to 'the individual', this can only take us so far. There is obviously an enormous social and cultural influence here. How a person's community views science and critical, evidence-based thinking has a substantive influence on that person. Bloom and Weisberg have shown how sensitive children and adults are to what they perceive as the trustworthiness of the source of the knowledge claim. In some communities, science is held in low regard. These are usually communities dominated by non-scientific ideologies and 'common-sense thinking'. There, people are more likely to resist counter-intuitive scientific claims.[44] If the claims are framed in ideologically or physically threatening ways it's even less likely that the claims will be believed, even if they are valid. We should, in other words, continue to search for factors influencing knowledge resistance beyond the 'inherent nature' of knowledge claims. Where should we look? In cultural and social factors that, in turn, are rooted in evolutionary science. Previous chapters have examined how these factors can explain knowledge resistance between people of different cultures. The next section will turn to an additional aspect with a social and evolutionary foundation: knowledge resistance between individuals that belong to the same (or similar) group.

Trust me, I'm right on this!

Irrational intelligence experts?

In his book *Life 3.0*, the Swedish-American physicist Max Tegmark recalls a symposium on AI organised by the Swedish Nobel Foundation in which he and his wife took part. Very simply put, AI is the intelligence of computer systems that enables them, for instance, to recognise speech, translate between languages, and make unaided decisions. World-leading scholars on AI were gathered on a discussion panel at the Nobel Foundation event. The host asked them a question roughly along the lines of 'How should we define intelligence?' The panellists discussed, debated, and deliberated on this topic at length. Astonished and amused, Tegmark notes the outcome – or non-outcome – of the long panel discussion:

> there's no agreement on what intelligence is even among intelligent intelligence researchers! So there's clearly no undisputed 'correct' definition of intelligence. Instead, there are many competing ones.[45]

It isn't peculiar that different people need different definitions of intelligence depending on where they aim to apply the definition: to logic, planning, creativity, or even social skills. But the exercise of the panel was to agree on a broad way to understand intelligence, a definition – the smallest common denominator. But they couldn't come to an agreement.

I share Tegmark's amusement, but not his implicit astonishment. Instead of saying there's no agreement *even among* intelligent intelligence researchers, I will in the rest of this chapter try to convince you it would be more appropriate to say there's no agreement *because they are* intelligent intelligence researchers. Shouldn't it have been easy for these sharp minds to agree on a broad working definition of intelligence that could take us quite far? Tegmark gives such a description that remains useful throughout his entire book on AI:

> Intelligence = ability to accomplish complex goals.[46]

Even those of you who don't spend your days thinking about intelligence could probably have come up with a similar definition yourselves. On the face of it, the panellists had not accomplished the explicit, complex goal in question. They couldn't develop a broad and basic definition of intelligence on which they all agreed. This seems irrational, doesn't it? Unintelligent, even? Behavioural economists in particular are quick to point at the irrationality, distortions, biases, and errors of decision-making when people deviate from the explicit goal in question. Behavioural economics with its focus on biases and nudging may seem rebellious and paradigm-shifting vis-à-vis traditional economics. Still, the former remains loyal and subservient to the latter by sharing its ideal of what would be truly 'rational' for people to do: to consistently respond to incentives in ways that maximise the satisfaction of their explicit, often material interests.[47]

But is it necessarily irrational or even bad to follow our nonconscious motivations instead of our explicit goals? As the psychologist Barth notes, it's over-simplistic and unreasonable to conceive of the conscious and explicit parts of our minds as good, and the nonconscious, implicit parts as bad. To categorically hold that the conscious is good and the nonconscious is bad is to fall into the seventeenth-century philosopher Descartes's and (three centuries later) the physician Sigmund Freud's black–white divisions which don't hold up to current scientific standards. Contemporary research with a basis in evolutionary theory has found Descartes's and Freud's distinctions 'completely, inconveniently wrong'.[48] To be sure, and contrary to traditional economists, behavioural economists find it problematic to argue that this ideal equals reality. Still, behavioural economists mainly analyse the gap between this ideal and reality. They provide tips and tricks for how the individual can fool his or her 'irrational', 'biased' brain in order to become more like the model of an economically rational person. Thus, this subdiscipline rarely goes further than discussing the gap between people's decisions and the explicit and concrete goal in question (in the case of the panellists, the goal of delivering a useful definition of intelligence).

Let's say that the AI discussion panel didn't achieve its task as a temporary collective. Does this also mean that the individual panellists had acted irrationally in their stubborn resistance to the insights of the others? So far in the book, I've placed considerable emphasis on groups and cultures as the most essential entities behind knowledge resistance. I haven't done this because groups have interests separate from their members. That's a contentious area which lies beyond the scope of this book. Instead, this book has focused on group-based knowledge resistance because such resistance seems to favour individuals (and their genes) within the group. Still, in order to assess whether it was less than rational of the AI panellists not to agree on any proposed definition of intelligence, we should consider two things. First, there is the lesson from previous chapters that people haven't evolved to be primarily truth-seekers. Rather, humans have evolved successfully since they generally prioritise their social motivation if this deviates from the quest for the most logical arguments and valid knowledge. Second, we should give special attention to the situation in which each separate individual on the panel finds his or herself.

Whereas the economic sciences often take an interest in the individual, much of social science downplays the role of the individual, portraying him or her as an unessential invention of Western culture. What mainly matters are groups and cultures. Evolutionary science doesn't show a particular interest in the individual either. To be sure, 'individual selection' is a term in evolutionary science. However, more often discussions about the individual in an evolutionary context are a misinterpretation of the evolutionary biologist Richard Dawkins's idea of the selfish gene. It isn't individuals that are selfish, according to Dawkins, it's genes. Consequently, many evolutionary scientists have criticised what they perceive as an overemphasis of individual selection and individual self-interests. Instead, this science – or group of disciplines – is interested in genes and their potential for maximising the number of their copies that are passed on globally. These are processes where kin groups are often more interesting than the single individual.

At the same time, we shouldn't forget that individual success (regarding survival and reproduction) throughout humanity's long history has implied an increased likelihood of success among one's own children and relatives as well. Individual success manifested in social status in a group is always connected to successful collaboration and reciprocity with others (reciprocal altruism). As we all know, no man (or woman) is an island. All this adds up to the following assumption: individuals and their particular interests are probably a relevant 'unit' to examine when trying to understand social as well as evolutionary processes. For this book, how individuals engage in debates, problem-solving, and knowledge exchange is likely to be integral to parts of social and evolutionary dynamics.

Why do we reason anyway?

There is a stream of thought that examines the situation of the individual before concluding what would be the rational or irrational reasoning of this person. This stream of thought analyses how people reason, and recognises that humans haven't evolved primarily as truth-seekers. It's called the argumentative theory. This thought stream is not on a mission to advise how each person should process information in a less biased way. Instead, one of its founders, Hugo Mercier, has gone back to the more fundamental question of how – and why – people debate and reason with each other. Mercier and his colleagues have observed many debates and problem-solving processes. They analyse in detail how participants make use of various types of information and arguments. By reasoning, Mercier and his co-researchers refer to 'inferential mechanisms that pay attention to and produce, reasons'.[49] Argumentative theorists have ended up with the following conclusion: people don't reason with others primarily to reach 'the truth' or 'the optimal result' in an objective sense. Instead, people reason with the underlying – often nonconscious – aim of producing the best justification for their own knowledge claim. In turn, people are mainly motivated to provide the best reasons for resisting and rejecting knowledge claims of the other party. People reason to convince others of what is true. In short, they argue to win.

This finding resonates well with the social scientific and evolutionary perspectives introduced in Chapter 1. It's plausible that, throughout history, individuals with an unusually high ability to find reasons that support their own knowledge beliefs had higher chances of enjoying a high-status position in the group. This, in turn, has increased the likelihood of the individual being able to produce offspring (individual selection). Moreover, it has on average helped to raise the status of the close relatives. This may have led to successful reproduction for them as well (kin selection). Consequently, Mercier and his colleagues maintain that 'reasoning remains the last and most important bastion of individualism in epistemology and science studies'.[50]

To convince others that one is 'right' is a good basis for being influential in cooperation with others. This has mutual benefits for all parties involved, but particularly to someone in a higher status position. In sum, the underlying goal of winning the argument is something of which the individual is often not conscious. To be conscious of the goal of winning would make them appear as less than a truth-seeker and open-minded knowledge absorber.[51] In daily life, most of us may have noticed how important it is to have a colleague, friend, or spouse give constructive criticism on our ideas and written formulations so that we can make revisions and strongly improve what we are trying to say. Others are usually far better at identifying the flaws and shortcomings of one's work than oneself.

Not even our conscious and seemingly dispassionate reasoning is truly dispassionate. That contention is an important critique of how Kahneman, who I mentioned earlier, conceives of his two modes of thinking: the 'fast' versus 'slow' modes. Kahneman, who is one of the founders of behavioural economics, has claimed that 'one of the functions of [reasoning] is to monitor the quality of both operations and overt behaviour'.[52] This isn't what has been found in a wide array of studies on how people actually reason with each other, however. Kahneman exaggerates the integrity of reasoning as something separate from the social aspects of how – and why – an individual absorbs or resists another individual's knowledge claims. His image of fast and slow mental systems has solid merits. Still, it's crucial to note – as Kahneman sometimes fails to describe – that the two systems are in constant interaction. Not even the slow, measured, systematic, conscious processes through which Kahneman characterises reasoning and knowledge formation have truth-seeking as their dominant function. Instead, this Apollonian dimension is based on social rationality. It has the role of collaborating with the Dionysian dimension in making us adapted to the social environment we live in.

I share Mercier's view of reasoning and knowledge (resistance) as fundamentally social, relational phenomena.[53] Knowledge and reasoning can rarely be explained separately from their social context. Kahneman's slow mode of thinking, which I illustrate in Chapter 1 with Apollo, hasn't evolved primarily to make the individual remove or minimise the impact of *their own* fast, Dionysian thinking. Instead, the slow mode of thinking serves to remove or unveil the biases of *other people*. The slow mode of thinking helps the individual find support for their already established, biased beliefs. I also have to modify somewhat my claim that people oscillate between treating knowledge in the Dionysian (socially focused) and Apollonian (knowledge focused) ways. Rather, the two gods constantly interact, not least when we are engaged in so-called serious reasoning, although the proportions of the influence of the two differ in different situations. Apollo is particularly alert when scrutinising the other person's reasoning. When searching for a convincing argument that the impulsive and fast conclusions drawn by his brother Dionysus are plausible and valid. We shouldn't forget that communication types other than reasoning – for instance, small talk and gossip – don't have to be connected to the specific social motivation of winning and influencing others. There are other social motivations, such as striving towards shared beliefs in order to bond with others, displaying one's knowledge, skills, and so forth. Knowledge resistance can also be a common phenomenon in conversations where we keep confirming each other's knowledge claims as valid even when evidence speaks against these claims.

High intelligence makes people more effective knowledge resistors

In discussions where all parties are interested in developing standpoints and finding reasons for that standpoint, it would be logical to think people with high intelligence are particularly likely to excel. When you are a sociologist, as I am, you are usually very sceptical of the idea that traits such as intelligence can be objective. I find it hard to agree that IQ tests measure traits that can't be impacted by our cultures, the biases of those who developed the tests, and so forth. Moreover, IQ tests have changed over time, which further points to the 'impurity' and cultural embeddedness of IQ measurements. A prevailing contemporary view among experts on IQ testing is that one of the few things we can be entirely sure of is that people with high IQ are very good at IQ tests.[54] Still, even if we buy into this scepticism, it is intriguing that scholars have seen differences in patterns of reasoning between people who score highly on IQ tests and people who do not. The differences run counter to what at least I believed before I studied the results.

We might think that people with high IQ are better at identifying the various aspects and angles of things. However, this isn't where these people excel. Instead, a higher intelligence primarily makes people more sophisticated at sticking to their current knowledge beliefs and resisting challenging information. For instance, how do people within communities sceptical of climate change, such as evangelical Christian communities, and who show a higher level of intelligence and scientific knowledge relevant to climate change, conceive of climate change? They are even more confident that human-made climate change does not exist than their fellow community members with lower scientific knowledge levels. Intelligence, and sometimes even scientific competence, have the potential to make people more knowledge resistant. This paradox is tied to the evolutionary function of argumentation and much of our knowledge (in cases that don't concern short-term life or death): to convince others we are right and to prove loyalty to our community. In prehistoric environments, these abilities and inclinations probably had highly adaptive value.

Back to the – presumably intelligent – panel of AI scholars. For the panellists to develop a definition collectively that everyone would agree on would, of course, be the way to reach the explicit goal in this exercise. This would meet perfectly the social motivation of the single panellist who was most influential – the panellist who gets to make the definition and manages to bring the others onboard and share it with her or him. However, in this case, no one managed to convince the others of such a definition. The reason was that no one was allowed to take the lead. The second-best outcome – for all of them – was instead to agree on disagreeing. In this way, everyone maintained her or his prestige and esteem. Maybe several on the panel even raised their esteem by advancing sophisticated and impressive arguments on the way. If you agree with me on this reasoning, you will also agree that the panellists used their intelligence and that they acted in a 'socially rational' way. They did this by resisting the compulsion to develop a shared and accepted definition of intelligence.

Kirkebøen and his colleagues, also scholars of decision-making, ought to agree.[55] They have investigated what is at the heart of it all: what makes people let go of their knowledge resistance. Put differently, what makes people allow themselves to change their minds, their knowledge beliefs. These scholars echo the argumentative scholars' claim. The quality of the result, the knowledge outcome in an objective sense, is usually not what people prioritise. Instead, these researchers point to the decision process (or the knowledge process) as key to whether people change their minds and are satisfied with this. Such processes are highly social. They involve assessments of how dominant other parties have been. This includes the issue of whether others have tried to make the person feel inferior, or whether that person's own arguments have been taken seriously. Who has tried to influence the individual, and how, also matters greatly.

What we should learn from this

What should be brought home from the findings of this chapter? We have seen that even serious and systematic reasoning – highly Apollonian – between particularly intelligent individuals serves the deeply social (Dionysian) function. Reasoning first makes individuals more interested (often at a nonconscious level) in shaping their knowledge claims quickly. Then the reasoning process involves an interest in finding the most powerful arguments and evidence that support this view. It no longer seems plausible to conceive of that as irrational. Nor does it seem reasonable to give the monopoly of the term 'rationality' to socially immune, fully conscious, and systematic knowledge processes only aimed at the truth. When social motivation and truth-seeking conflict, winning the argument is the social motivation that often overrides the interest in getting the facts and arguments right.

Equally important as what should be brought home from this chapter is what shouldn't be brought home from it. The answer is that we in this book should not end up in hardcore relativism. In hardcore relativism, all groups and all institutions – religious institutions, scientific institutions, political institutions, and civil society organisations – are seen as equally arbitrary in their knowledge claims. Scientific institutions more often operate based on the ideal of critical debate and deliberation than religious institutions. That's the reason that most of us – even among those who are religious – would be more likely to take our sick child to a science-based medical doctor than to a spiritual healer. It isn't that scientists are different kinds of people from religious leaders. Both should be expected to prioritise their social interests in acceptance and prestige in their own community rather than by truth-finding, should these goals be in conflict. Both are, at their core, socially rational. However, the social norms and rules differ so much concerning how knowledge claims are handled in the two cultures. In scientific communities, unsubstantiated knowledge claims are punished, as a rule. In religious ones, such claims can be accepted as higher truth or elevated to the status of 'faith'. Scientific communities usually conduct far more effective scrutiny of unsubstantiated knowledge claims.

In the norms, rules, and routines of various institutions – science groups, companies, religious congregations, or any social group – lie limitations in how substantial our resources are, of money, time, skills, and competencies. These limitations raise questions often posed by traditional economics. To what extent is knowledge resistance a result of limited resources? It's crucial to learn in a nuanced way about the rational-choice approach to understanding knowledge resistance. This is the topic of the next chapter.

5

Knowledge: what's in it for me?

Fully or optimally informed?

Many of us might occasionally reflect on how much we know and would like to know about various things – politics, fine art, history, and so on. When we do this, do we also associate our knowledge with costs, economisation, and optimisation? Such terms may sound awkward, aspects that ruin the spontaneous joy of learning things. Formal education is another matter. Most people need to make a calculation before choosing what career to pursue. In addition to listening to our hearts, most of us first weigh the costs of gaining the particular job skills against the opportunities and salaries if we choose to become carpenters, civil engineers, plumbers, or art historians. In this chapter on the cost of knowledge, however, I'm thinking about knowledge aside from our specific choices of formal education. I won't discuss more formal issues of educational costs, research policies, or costs related to intellectual property rights.

A reason that costs, economisation, and optimisation sound awkward is that people usually perceive knowledge as one of the intrinsically good things that should be considered separate from strategic calculations of cost. Cost appears as irrelevant when discussing knowledge as it does when talking about friendships between children playing in a sandpit. There seem to be some areas of life that simply shouldn't be translated into costs, or where cost calculations don't seem relevant. Perhaps knowledge and curiosity could be candidates for such areas.[1] At the same time, the phrase made world-famous by Milton Friedman, traditional economist par excellence, is that 'there is no such thing as a free lunch'.[2] No activity is strictly speaking free – someone has to pay with time or money. The moment you find Jules Verne's classic book *Around the World in Eighty Days* on the street, pick it up, walk to a park bench, and start learning about countries and cities, your meter starts ticking. How could this be? According to any economist, spending time and effort – if not money – on reading and learning entails an 'opportunity cost' (the cost of the missed opportunity of doing something else). Instead of reading that classic, you could have stayed a bit longer in your office doing some extra paid work.

Although the idea of the ubiquitous opportunity costs of knowledge may appear valid – albeit stressful to some of us – a few things need to be clarified. What – if anything – do strategic calculations of costs have to do with knowledge resistance in our daily lives? The first challenge I ran into when investigating the idea of knowledge costs was the idea in classical economics of *Homo economicus* – the perfectly economically rational person. The idea contends that such a person makes sure that they are fully informed before making any decision. Knowledge resistance, in contrast, means that the person avoids becoming fully informed. Is there any way that the economics idea of fully informed individuals can be compatible with the focus of this book – people's inclination to resist some knowledge? How could it ever be 'rational' to resist knowledge when economics preaches that being fully informed is a prerequisite for making rational decisions? The answers from economists come in various versions of 'rational ignorance'. The contention is that our ignorance is more often than not based on our active and strategic calculations of the costs and opportunities that additional knowledge would entail, given our fixed goals.

The second issue I had to struggle with was whether it is possible to be 'fully informed' and at the same time 'knowledge resistant'. Some economists argue that it is. To what extent, and in what ways, do people actually resist knowledge based on such calculations and economising with their resources? Traditional economists routinely conceive of cost as anything that goes against an individual's preferences. Cost doesn't have to take the form of money and time, but can also be effort, emotional consequences, and more. However, to make the cost perspective of knowledge resistance clearer, I will focus specifically on monetary and time-related costs. We will see how individuals, groups, and cultures resist knowledge as a way of economising with their time and money. Finally, we will discuss whether the economists' notion of rational ignorance can go hand in hand with the conclusions of previous chapters: that people and groups resist knowledge mainly based on their motivations to act in socially rational ways.

'You always know what you're missing'

As noted in Chapter 4, the rational-choice understanding found in traditional economics assumes that people follow a particular order when they develop their knowledge beliefs. First, information and data enter their minds. Second, they process this input – mainly consciously – assessing its validity, systematically using various arguments. Finally, they develop knowledge beliefs as a consequence of this processing. What does rationality then mean according to the rational-choice approach? It leaves the definition of what the goal would be relatively open, as long as it's reasonably stable, explicit, and substantive. Such a goal could be increased comfort, material standards, health, or an improved environment. To be rational is to optimise how our means – such as time, learning ability, and money – are planned, arranged, and used to best reach the goal in question. As you can see, it is very similar to Tegmark's definition of intelligence, discussed in the previous chapter, which contended it is the 'ability to accomplish complex goals'.[3] Very often the rational-choice approach of traditional economics assumes that people's preference is to increase or save the means – money and time – in order to use these resources in reaching their other goals. How about 'rational ignorance'? How could it be rational to be ignorant when economics treats the state of being fully informed as a prerequisite for making rational decisions?

To learn more about this, we need to go back to the economist who was among the first to work on the notion of rational ignorance: George

Stigler. In the early 1960s, he proposed a strong version of economic ignorance. According to Stigler, people who are rationally ignorant have made accurate calculations about the knowledge they resist. Before they resist knowledge, they have systematically assessed the costs and benefits of searching for the information in question.[4] Rational searchers are aware that the time and money costs of searching for the information they decide to remain ignorant about would outweigh the benefit to their striving towards the goal in question. Key to Stigler's version of rational ignorance is that people may very well be conscious of their own ignorance. They accept that the opinions and beliefs they will hold based on this ignorance could be wrong.[5]

Take the example of climate scientists or science commentators who try to reach out to the public via the media. Even if the individual is a climate scientist, some economists argue that it might in some cases be rational for that climate scientist to ignore certain knowledge. What might be seen as knowledge resistance of the public, due to some economic rationality, may actually be a case of knowledge and presentations about uncertainty being costly for the media, since news stories that analyse the full uncertainty and complexity of a phenomenon might be more difficult to sell to the public. Say you are a climate scientist and feel it is essential to reach out with a message that we should work harder to mitigate climate change. Uncertainties are always involved when assessing the risk levels of an issue as complex as climate change in different geographic regions. However, if your aim is outreach via the media, it might be rational to downplay scientific uncertainties even if you are aware that such uncertainties exist. In order to conform with the logic of the media, many communicators about climate change downplay such uncertainties even to themselves. They may fear that complicating the picture could foster further climate-change dismissal. Therefore, to portray climate change as a clear and entirely certain phenomenon, regardless of the region, may well be a case of rational ignorance.[6] This reasoning is consistent with how many economists try to reconcile rational ignorance with the idea of the 'fully informed' *Homo economicus*. To be rationally ignorant, the person has to know precisely what type of knowledge he or she doesn't have. Moreover, the person must have made a correct calculation that acquiring this kind of knowledge would be costlier than it would benefit the efforts towards reaching the particular, stable goal, whatever it may be.

How would traditional economists explain why people differ in terms of how loss-averse they are? Stated differently, would these economists explain the variation in how much different individuals dislike losing nonmaterial things, such as their current knowledge beliefs? Intriguingly, the notion of an entirely rational and purposeful ignorance has been expanded by economists who study loss aversion. It's well known that people differ in how averse they are to losing something substantive: time, money, comfort, safety, and so forth. Perhaps this difference in loss aversion also illustrates the different levels of knowledge resistance that can be identified between people. The economist Elbittar and colleagues claim that they have found such a difference. According to them, highly loss-averse people are more likely than others to resist alternative knowledge, for instance about politics, which challenges their current knowledge beliefs. Loss-averse people find a loss of their current knowledge belief costlier than do people who are less loss-averse.[7]

Stigler's strong version of rational ignorance was soon applied to the area where it's still mainly used: political participation. Why is it that so many voters in several countries remain ignorant about political issues, not least environmental and health policy issues? In his book *Democracy and Political Ignorance*, Ilya Somin advances the argument that 'most political ignorance is actually rational behavior for most citizens'.[8] As a single individual, argues Somin, it costs more to learn about the political programme of each political candidate before going to the voting booth than the beneficial difference that it makes in that individual's life:

> even a voter who cares greatly about the outcome has almost no incentive to invest heavily in acquiring sufficient information to make an informed choice.[9]

Accordingly, it would be more rational – at least financially – for the person to spend that learning time on work. This would not only earn the individual more money but it would also provide more money for the common good via taxes. Yet Somin makes it very clear that his view of rational ignorance doesn't mean that he thinks that such a rationality is good. In fact, he is very troubled by it, claiming that political 'ignorance is a kind of "pollution" of the democratic process [that can result in] potentially dangerous outcomes'.[10] Somin's belief about people might be cynical; people only act on the principle of 'what's in it for me' or 'what's in it for my household'. However, claiming that Somin is cynical doesn't represent sufficient grounds for rejecting his explanation.

The term 'pollution' has its literal parallel in another global challenge: how to deal with the fact that it might be rational to the single individual to pollute the environment. As we all know, everyone is far worse off if people act out of direct, selfish rationality. Likewise, we would all be far worse off if everyone ignored politics and didn't participate in the democratic system. This is true even if such knowledge resistance might benefit the individual from a short-term, selfish perspective. Something to take home from the strong version of rational ignorance is that we – and especially policy-makers – shouldn't expect people to act in ways that deviate sharply from their short-term, individual rationality. Policy-makers ought to develop structures and systems of incentives that make people's short-term, individual rationality converge with the common good. It should be made worthwhile not just for the collective but also for the individual to learn about politics and to reduce their environmental harm.

Still, there seem to be fundamental flaws in the assumption that we, when we resist knowledge, never can make mistakes. For one thing, there is something odd and circular about the reasoning that people who ignore knowledge can never make mistakes. As it turns out, we don't have to leave economics to find such criticism.

'You pursue rational ignorance but sometimes fail'

It's easy to agree with Somin about how people's ignorance of politics and society poses a danger to democracy. But is it correct to say that this public ignorance is sufficient evidence for Stigler's claim that a person's rational ignorance is a strategically selected knowledge resistance based on her or his full awareness of what knowledge that person chooses to ignore?

Let's take the example of the fact that a significant percentage of people with low incomes still vote for a government that favours a reduction of accessible healthcare for such people. To be sure, some of these voters may not be ignorant of such plans for changes in the welfare system. However, in the instances where voters are unaware of the political intentions of the party they vote for, is this rational ignorance? Here, it's difficult to say that Somin and Stigler are wrong and that such ignorance would be irrational. From an individual's perspective, one vote makes a very marginal difference. To become politically knowledgeable takes a lot of time and effort with high opportunity costs. In some cases, the person would be able to use the time and effort saved by remaining ignorant about politics and instead spend more hours working, earning money, saving, or purchasing private health insurance. This knowledge resistance resembles what is called 'the tragedy of the commons'.[11] This is a condition where what is rational for the individual leads to problematic public outcomes where everyone suffers, or at least low-income people in this case.

However, there are examples from other economists that are challenging to Stigler. Evans and Friedman make a critical reflection about Stigler's notion of the infallible, rationally ignorant person. They ask about what they call 'one of the greatest bouts of mass economic error in history': the financial crisis of 2007–8.[12] I mentioned in Chapter 2 how Queen Elizabeth made an eminent economics professor nervous by her very reasonable, straightforward question of why nobody had noticed that the crisis was on its way. The financial crisis involved massive ignorance among financial experts as well as among the wider population. It would have been beneficial for all of us if the financial experts had at least acquired the knowledge needed to predict and – better still – prevent the crisis. Contrary to the example above about costly political knowledge, ignorance about the impending financial crisis was not a case of the tragedy of the commons. It seems paradoxical that even the economic experts who became victims of the financial crisis (since their stock lost much value) acted on rational ignorance, and that they didn't make mistakes here.

How can that ignorance be explained? Is it, as Stigler suggests, possible for people to be entirely aware of what they ignore so that all instances of knowledge resistance can be fully informed? Evans and Friedman don't think so. Their alternative is that people can be 'inadvertently ignorant' of facts. Without intending it, a person makes genuine errors when they (a) are ignorant of relevant information; (b) are misled by information that is false; (c) are misled by information that is accurate but irrelevant; or (d) misinterpret information that is accurate and relevant.[13]

Consider, for instance, the point that the political economist Karl Marx made about ignorance among workers who were heavily exploited by factory owners. How were workers in the nineteenth century able to accept their treatment for so long before an inevitable revolution took place? Marx held that the whole of society was rife with mystifying, false, and distorting knowledge claims elevated to ideology. This ideology was created and maintained by the ruling classes. For instance, workers were led to believe that their living conditions were fair. They were told that market exchanges were also fair and that the immense inequality was sanctioned by God or by Mother Nature.[14] Social thinkers inspired by Marx also point to the false belief in some contemporary societies. The mantra is that if you only work hard, you have a realistic chance of moving from the lowest to the highest strata of society. Many children in poor families put all their efforts and hopes into the dream of becoming a professional sportsperson or rock star. This happens even in families where the special talent isn't even there.

Some Marxist thinkers may agree with Evans and Friedman, asserting that the main obstacle to people's welfare is that knowledge is often not only uncertain but also distorted. This causes people to miss essential insights needed for them to strive more efficiently towards better lives for themselves, and to mobilise with others in similar situations.[15] Such inadvertent, accidental ignorance, these authors argue, is neither irrational nor rational, because rationality, as well as irrationality, involve a decision. Inadvertent ignorance, on the other hand, exists regardless of whether one makes a decision. Such ignorance persists even if people act rationally. Inadvertent ignorance is an inherent part of the human condition, according to these economists. Nobody is omniscient. Every person faces uncertainty and false knowledge claims. Many times, we lack an overview of all knowledge from which we can select what to ignore cost-efficiently.

If ignorance is to be better understood, this human condition is a necessary insight, and Evans and Friedman's inadvertent ignorance might be a plausible candidate. People can resist knowledge based on rational calculations of costs. However, the human condition that includes uncertainty, false knowledge, and lack of a full overview makes perfectly cost-rational ignorance difficult, and sometimes impossible. This perspective is common sense. People do their best to gather the most important information, but from time to time they fail. You might walk around with a headache and wonder whether this is connected with your use of a mobile phone. The Internet offers almost unlimited amounts of information on health risks. However, it's very challenging for a layperson to identify the most relevant sites that are also reasonably trustworthy. It is not always the case that combining the sources and believing in their average takes the person to the fact of the matter. Some sources might say that radiation from mobile phones causes headaches. Others say that holding up a mobile phone makes your neck tense, which may cause a headache. Meanwhile, other sources might indicate no correlations at all between mobile phone use and headaches. The challenges of drawing an accurate conclusion from such diverse factual claims may lead you into adopting an incorrect knowledge belief. Alternatively, you might simply give up the hope of finding the knowledge you're seeking.[16]

I ran into an entirely different example when doing the interviews for this book. Bent Flyvbjerg and I discussed the fact that many megaprojects around the world end up costing far more than initially predicted by the actors involved. Such megaprojects include bridges, urban renewal projects, sports arenas, dams, and extensive cultural facilities. Each time a megaproject exceeds the estimated costs – often by hundreds of per cent – the revelation is met by surprised voices. It isn't far-fetched to assume that resistance to taking uncertainties into account are at play here, along with ignorance of lessons from previous megaprojects. One particular example is the fantastic opera house in Sydney, which ended up costing at least fourteen times more than had been estimated in the initial calculations.[17] Surely ignorance and knowledge resistance must have played a part. But is it apt to talk about a *rational* ignorance, in Stigler's sense, here?

In my interview with Flyvbjerg, I began by taking the perspective of Stigler, noting that knowledge resistance must have taken place. 'But look at the outcome,' I said, 'one of the most beautiful and loved architectural creations in history. In the long term, who cares that the planners ignored knowledge that would have revealed that Sydney Opera House would become far more expensive than their initial calculation?' I went on to offer another example: Michelangelo's paintings on the ceiling of the Sistine Chapel – without any doubt a work of true genius that thousands of people appreciate every day. 'Who cares today if it cost more than initially assumed?' I asked. However, Flyvbjerg provided a broader perspective, albeit one less romantic than mine. He held that the planners may well have tried to be rational in what information and knowledge they recognised and ignored, but they failed to raise uncertainties that would have been possible to know in advance. If they hadn't ignored such information, the costs might have been reduced. This could have meant opportunities for additional buildings as beautiful as the Sydney Opera House or more paintings as breathtaking as those in the Sistine Chapel, Flyvbjerg argued. In other words, while the planners might have believed that they acted rationally, they still ignored great opportunity costs, an ignorance with suboptimal consequences. Flyvbjerg pointed out the main opportunity cost that the world had to pay:

> Even though Australia and Sydney got maybe the most spectacular building in the twentieth century, the rest of the world didn't because Australia screwed up systematically and thoroughly by mismanagement and avoiding knowledge and expertise. That architect never got to build another

major new building, basically. So that's the real cost of the Sydney Opera House. Australians look at it narrowly. If you look at it from a world point of view, it might be that we lost a Michelangelo, we lost a Leonardo, and so on.[18]

Evans and Friedman, on the other hand, would perhaps be a bit more sympathetic towards planners who miscalculate megaprojects. They would maintain that there will always be things that planners don't know in advance that would be valuable to know.[19] This resembles what US Secretary of Defence Donald Rumsfeld in 2002 called 'unknown unknowns'.[20]

It's a common-sense assertion to say that we sometimes make mistakes and face uncertainties when we navigate our private and professional lives. Still, it would be overly simplistic to believe that Stigler's rational ignorance and Evans and Freidman's inadvertent, accidental ignorance are the only existing types of ignorance. Nor is it convincing to draw the conclusion, which Evans and Friedman do, that people either succeed in making a rational choice of how much information to resist or fail completely in this task. A person's decisions are not binary in this way because a person's preferences are not stable throughout his or her life.

'You are several, rational incarnations over time'

As a critique of the two previously mentioned perspectives, other economists have come up with a quite fascinating alternative. It's not that a person can never make a mistake when ignoring knowledge in order to optimise the way towards reaching one stable goal, as Stigler believed. Nor is it that a person either succeeds in ignoring knowledge or fails to optimise the way towards reaching one stable goal, as Evans and Friedman imply. If the notion of rational ignorance is to survive, we mustn't understand the individual as *one self*, who is rationally ignorant concerning stable goals throughout her or his life. Instead, each individual should be perceived as *several selves* living in different periods of time throughout life. Each individual is in conflict with his or her future selves. What a person's rational ignorance is during one period may come into conflict with that same person's rational ignorance in another period. The individual's knowledge absorption or resistance must be in phase with these revised preferences if the person is to be rational.

The economists Carrillo and Mariotti refer to extensive data from cases of knowledge resistance about how high the risks are that various practices pose to human health.[21] Take smoking, for instance. These scholars note that both smokers and non-smokers believe that the probability of developing lung cancer due to smoking is five times higher than the US Surgeon General's findings (based on extensive data).[22] The general public's overestimation can't only be due to the perceived costs of knowledge (as Stigler's view would contend). Nor can it only be caused by the human condition of error and uncertainty (as Evans and Friedman would claim). Obtaining accurate statistical information about many health risks is quite easy today. It is accessible and it costs very little in time, money, and effort for most people to acquire it. So why are people still so ignorant about what appear to be the best available figures concerning health risks? To answer this question, we have to move away from economic theory and towards psychology, Carillo and Mariotti argue. Non-smokers might resist information and knowledge which correctly indicates that smoking is five times less risky (for lung cancer) than people commonly believe, knowledge that would increase the risk of them becoming smokers. The scholars call this knowledge resistance 'voluntary ignorance'. They describe it as an individual tool for self-control. People resist knowledge in this way to protect themselves from hazardous behaviour that they would regret later. What Carillo and Mariotti are saying is that people can be irrationally ignorant from their present self's perspective, by resisting inexpensive and accurate information. At the same time, this can be rational to their future selves, by helping them avoid hazard and regret later on. The economists draw the conclusion that people are 'time-inconsistent' decision-makers. A person is 'a collection of incarnations with conflicting goals'.[23]

One example of this would be when scientists cheat, claiming to have obtained new and path-breaking results. In the case of measles vaccine, the physician Andrew Wakefield at the time maintained that he had high-quality evidence showing that the vaccine significantly increases the risk of autism. He ignored the indisputable claims about how his study had been flawed in many ways. From the perspective of the interests of his incarnation at the time his article was published, his ignorance of these facts might have been rational. Wakefield received, for instance, financial benefits from convincing others about his 'findings'. For his subsequent incarnations, however, this ignorance was probably less rational. Consider all the criticism and shaming that came his way, culminating in the official withdrawal of his article from the prestigious journal *Lancet*. Still, this hasn't stopped him from continuing to spread unsubstantiated claims about the health risks of this vaccine.

Another example is how people act today as if they accord significantly more value to their short-term preferences than their future preferences. People smoke today and drive cars powered by fossil fuels, for instance. This might be a sign that they downplay their future preferences of staying healthy or of leaving an equally liveable planet for future generations.[24] Where the individual actively chooses not to acquire all available information, this is a case of rational ignorance. It must be strategic and rational to resist the information. Otherwise, the economically rational, multiple-self individual would use it. The information costs very little and hardly delays decision-making. From the perspective of traditional economics, this way of handling the critique of rational ignorance is brilliant. By claiming that the individual isn't one but several selves living in the same individual but during different times, these economists don't have to abandon the idea that each person has stable preferences. The person's stable preference is just limited in time and lasts only until he or she is a new self. The individual's incarnations acquire as well as resist knowledge as a means to best satisfy the incarnations' respective preferences.

Perhaps the analogy of the individual as many selves with conflicting goals saves the economists Carillo and Mariotti. They can still claim that each self that has a say on decision-making will act 'rationally', even though many decisions may seem irrational from an outside perspective. In the case of planners and decision-makers on megaprojects that routinely end up being far more expensive than originally estimated, Bent Flyvbjerg gave me several explanations. One stood out. Flyvbjerg, quoting the philosopher Friedrich Nietzsche, asserts that 'power makes stupid'. According to Flyvbjerg, Nietzsche was of the view that people in power don't understand even what's in their own long-term interests. This is why I introduced miscalculated megaprojects in the earlier section about how people pursue rational ignorance but sometimes fail. However, the notion of the individual as multiple selves provides us with an alternative explanation. The ignorance among planners and decision-makers about realistic costs might be better understood as entirely rational to the time-limited selves of these planners with one megaproject in focus. The problem for these planners is that they discount their future interests in completing subsequent megaprojects at far lower rates. According to Flyvbjerg, the same goes for rich people in contemporary society:

> The rich think that it's in their interests to become richer and richer, so that's their rationality. They think they're acting rationally in doing that. And they don't see that they're actually undermining their own basis of living, their own businesses so to speak, and that's an example. It's irrational. They are short-term. They are very ideological.[25]

Each incarnation, if the individual has a so-called myopic bias, over-emphasises his or her current self's preferences and underestimates the preferences of his or her future selves. Thus, that person will prefer to resist knowledge that could be used by future incarnations at the cost of not taking the optimal current decision.

What should we make of this understanding of what it means to be human? Are you a series of selves over time? Is each of your selves best defined by its stable preferences (within a specific time period)? Do such stable preferences entail a rational resistance of knowledge that goes against the explicit and substantive goal within a specified time period? It makes sense that there are conflicts between a person's different selves when he or she, for instance, ignores knowledge about the risks of living in material abundance using a lot of fossil fuels today. This knowledge would be of interest to the person's future selves. However, are all of an individual's preferences – current or future ones – about substantive, explicit things? Are all our preferences connected with material comfort, monetary optimisation, environmental quality, or even health? Is everything about Apollonian issues, or are there other interests that are missing here? Perhaps there are additional interests that are at least as motivating to us. Such interests might drive us more in how we choose what knowledge to believe and act upon and what to resist or ignore altogether.

'You're much more than the above'

All the perspectives described above on costs as the basis for knowledge resistance are intellectually stimulating. It's hard to deny that costs in time and material resources play an essential part in how we deal with the information and knowledge around us. They affect how people deal with, and filter, the massive flow of information and knowledge claims with which they are confronted. The consideration of 'what's in it for me' enters the minds of most people when they hear about yet another issue. There are so many issues that fight for our attention and knowledge acquisition. We are frequently confronted with information about how to reduce harm to our health and the environment, which companies to support or boycott, and how to become still better informed before making any decision.

Nonetheless, radical knowledge uncertainty is intrinsic to the human condition, as we recognised above. For instance, as sociological research shows, it's just impossible for people to make fully informed choices about how to identify the least environmentally harmful products and services. Consider tomatoes. They might be grown with the use of large quantities of pesticides. At the same time, the same tomatoes could be grown with low levels of energy use in greenhouses. To introduce a third factor, we could say that these tomatoes might be transported in a way such that medium amounts of greenhouse gases are emitted, for instance by boat. There is often no 'synthesised knowledge' about such diverse parameters. How to assess the environmental impact of these tomatoes with types that score differently on each factor is far more complicated than just summarising the three and comparing the sums. This is a key reason why consumers resist some information in the marketplace: information overload is common. To make things more complicated, certain information is false or exaggerated.[26]

However, the aspects of information costs mentioned earlier are far from the entire story of what is going on when people resist knowledge. People are neither perfect nor imperfect, economically motivated actors at their core. This isn't what human rationality has evolved to be. Thus, the economist Lemieux probably has the logic backwards when he maintains that 'individuals will buy information only up to the point where the information yields no more net benefits than just following signals emitted by others'.[27] Lemieux's claim implies that people begin with an individual, explicit utility, some goal. Then they 'buy' information – with their money, time, and effort – but only up to a specific, calculated point. This point is where they stop 'buying'. Here, they change conscious strategy into one of imitating others. This imitation does not amount to what in the biological world would be called parasitism. The resources of others don't seem to be reduced by the imitation. Rather, biologists would label the strategy 'commensalism', where this shrewd imitator exploits the information efforts made by others, although he doesn't seem to harm them in the process.

Yet, given what the evolutionary and social sciences know about human interests and motivations, this is not how people usually operate. Lemieux seems to turn our order of motivations upside down. The rationality that runs most deeply in people is social. Beneath their calculations about substantive costs in money, time, or even to their health or the environment, people are engaged in another and more fundamental type of calculation, often nonconsciously. It has to do with whether it would work against their deep-lying interest in maintaining or strengthening their social bonds and positions. This is not to say that we don't make use of the efforts others have made in acquiring knowledge, by imitating some of their choices. We do that all the time with people we trust, and it's oftentimes highly economical. Many of us find it most convenient to copy our savvy friends' choice of hard drive size, weight-loss diet, and home heating system. Still, the core function of such copying is social, which is more apparent in fashion, music taste, and travel destinations, but is true also for the more 'technical' choices above or even for political preferences. To imitate others or to share knowledge with others so they can imitate us serves most fundamentally the function of strengthening group bonds and enhancing trust.

As to the example of rational ignorance among citizens about politics, we shouldn't forget that it's common that a majority of the population votes. In many countries the majority follows at least some political news reports before voting. Why? One reason could be that complete ignorance before voting may well be socially irrational. Among several groups in society, there is an expectation that members should inform themselves at least to some degree. In many groups, people are probably expected to know at least a little about the political candidates, the main issues, positions, and stories surrounding an election. Without that basic knowledge, people are likely to deviate from the norm, which in turn creates a risk of reduced esteem. This doesn't mean that everything is well concerning the political participation of the public in any country. However, it means that there is some reason for hope regarding the chance of increasing civic engagement among the public. By designing political news and schemes for participation in ways that converge with people's deeply social interests in keeping up with the basic political awareness of their groups, the chances are that civic engagement will be increased.

As the perspectives of rational ignorance in this chapter focus on 'substantive' costs (time, money, effort, health, and environment), the Dionysian, deeply social interest and the social rationality associated with it are overlooked. This is the first factor that needs to be incorporated into any analysis of costs behind knowledge. The second factor that needs to be considered is what takes place beneath the strategic and consciously planned, Apollonian level of people's decision-making. Here, the difference is striking between the various human sciences:

evolutionary psychology (with its biological basis), the social sciences, and traditional economics. The evolutionary and social sciences treat processes of knowledge resistance as in many respects nonconscious. This is evident in biology when it examines the 'lower' organisms (since cells and most organisms are not assumed to have consciousness). Yet even when it comes to people, evolutionary psychology and parts of the social sciences conceive of resistance in the case of knowledge as often not taking place primarily at the conscious and strategic level.

In line with those disciplines, this chapter makes the claim that not even knowledge resistance is fully conscious unless it's evolutionarily adaptive for us to be fully aware of it. There are several reasons for this. Firstly, habits, routines, and sticking to the conventional knowledge beliefs of one's community saves much mental energy. There is an irony embedded in the discipline of economics. This discipline is supposed to be preoccupied with resource-saving and economisation. At the same time, economics usually resists common biological knowledge about one of the most critical areas of resource-saving in human life: how the enormously energy-demanding brain must continuously minimise its use of energy. Many brain processes concern nonconscious, instinctive, and developing semi-automatic habits. Such energy-saving processes of the brain include going with the flow of taking common knowledge beliefs for granted.

Secondly, in many cases, it's socially favourable for a person or group to remain nonconscious of the reasons for their knowledge resistance. Such lack of awareness – sometimes even self-deception – is an efficient signal to others that the person is honest in her or his beliefs.[28] Classic examples include when President George W. Bush convinced the US and its allies that Iraq possessed weapons of mass destruction. Bush resisted all signs that Iraq didn't possess such weapons. He didn't recognise the weaknesses and flaws of the claims that contradicted his unalterable belief. In this way, Bush could, through words and body language, convince large parts of the Western world that he was honest in his beliefs. Because he probably was honest. On the cover of *The Economist* on 15 July 2004, Bush and the British prime minister Tony Blair can be seen together through a detective's magnifying glass a couple of days into the Iraq War. Above them the headline reads: 'Sincere Deceivers'.[29] The chances are this was true. Again, my point is not to identify a limited number of people who cause particular harm through their knowledge resistance. On the contrary, my understanding of knowledge resistance is that it is universal. This means that it risks causing particularly great damage when people in power are not confronted strongly enough in their knowledge resistance. The example of Bush and Blair certainly falls into this category.

How about the knowledge resistance of the scholars in the eminent human sciences that I interviewed for this book? How, and on what basis, did they in their work draw borders between what was relevant and irrelevant for them to know? Some interviewees seemed to stick rigorously to their own discipline or even their narrower subdiscipline when doing research about human motivation and interests applied to health, the environment, and wellbeing. These are research areas where many disciplines and subdisciplines are involved. They often study identical or similar phenomena but use different methods, assumptions, theories, and concepts. I asked these narrowly focused scholars why they didn't try to learn from or collaborate with other disciplines or subdisciplines. After all, they all study partly the same things. Wasn't there a risk of reinventing the wheel unless they built bridges to neighbouring disciplines? When speaking about themselves, all these interviewees, regardless of their subjects, explained the borders they had drawn between relevant and irrelevant knowledge as a type of rational ignorance (although they didn't use that term). They explained the process the way that economists like Stigler or Somin conceive of rational ignorance. It was a fully conscious, determined, and infallible knowledge resistance. Terms similar to the rational ignorance perspectives were used by my interviewees. To broaden one's knowledge and perspectives 'takes a lot of extra time' and 'is costly', and 'one has to choose what's most relevant'. I find it intriguing to compare this with an entirely different case that we looked at in Chapter 4: householders who told me what had motivated them to choose a particular type of heating system. Everyone I interviewed in that study was convinced that they had optimised their decision-making process. This had made their choice entirely in line with their one explicit, overriding goal (in that case to minimise financial cost).

As to the scholars in the human sciences, they all stated that there was one overriding goal with their work. It was an Apollonian one: to produce novel findings of the highest quality. Optimising the way towards that goal was the only reason they gave for resisting knowledge from neighbouring disciplines. They described issues such as social status, opportunities for tenure, chances of obtaining funding, and so forth as mere means to the knowledge goal. Still, although this goal sounds obvious for scientists to have, there is something odd here. All of us – regardless of our occupation – know that we have to economise with time. Limiting the influences from neighbouring fields and areas that we allow ourselves to be subjected to is one way of economising with our time and effort. On the other hand, everyone with a basic awareness of previous, path-breaking discoveries and innovations knows that when a culture isolates itself and avoids learning from others, the result is usually repetition and recycling of old knowledge. I would venture that all renowned human scientists know about this risk very well. We should note that this risk jeopardises the reaching of the overriding goal that all these scholars emphasise: to produce novel findings of the highest quality.

Given their explicit, overriding goal of producing novel findings at the highest level, my human scientists' self-proclaimed rational ignorance seems partly less rational. However, could there be another reason why they appeared less than rational in this respect? Could it be that they weren't telling me the truth regarding what their overriding goal was? Or were they not even being honest to themselves? My understanding is that the interviewees were telling the truth, but only the part of the reality that they could see most clearly for themselves. An individual may have more than one goal at a time – for instance, one explicit goal about producing novel knowledge and another implicit one about maintaining esteem within one's scientific discipline. This duality is different from the economic view above that each person has several selves that each prioritises explicitly and strategically one specific point in time. Instead, a scientist's goals held at one point in time may be in conflict with each other. Economics often fails to recognise this. In fact, none of the three economic perspectives above takes this profoundly human trait into account. As a collective, economists who are interested in ignorance claim we always do one of the following three things. We know and accept the knowledge we are missing in the pursuit of one fixed and explicit goal, such as generating novel, high-quality research findings. Or we strive towards one set goal but make mistakes when assessing knowledge claims. Alternatively, each of us is made up of several selves each striving towards one fixed goal at a time. Each self absorbs only the knowledge instrumental to that specific goal.

To be sure, these human scientists – renowned within their own discipline – portray their own rational ignorance as a process they choose strategically for the Apollonian sake of maximising novel knowledge production in the world. However, this also needs to be interpreted at the Dionysian, deeply social level. Recognition and esteem within one's culture are key drivers for what people prioritise. Scientific disciplines are examples of cultures. Ask the moral psychologist Jonathan Haidt, who sees the isolation of particular subdisciplines and schools of thought as a very tribal tendency. He notes that knowledge isolationism is based on the human inclination to stick to one's own tribe. This includes instinctively evaluating one's own tribe – or subdiscipline – as better than the others.[30]

From an individual perspective, the scholars' narrow, disciplinary focus makes better sense if we understand it as following the logic of social rationality, given the incentive system that is in place at universities. The incentives that increase social status are most often confined to the number of published research papers scientists deliver within a narrow, disciplinary focus in prestigious journals. Absorbing knowledge and influences from neighbouring – often rival – disciplines involves risks. It may reduce a scientist's esteem, at least temporarily. As the evolutionary psychologist Robin Dunbar told me from his own experience: 'You'll always be accused of not being an expert.'[31]

No one becomes an instant expert in the rival discipline. Still, if you as a scientist manage to create something novel using influence from rival disciplines, this could be highly status-enhancing, but after years of scepticism from one's peers. During those years of scepticism, your peers are likely to perceive you as unfocused. You might also find you have more difficulties in getting funding for your research. Therefore, it might appear most socially rational to stay loyal to one's mother discipline. It is also increasingly common to stick to one's subdiscipline or sub-subdiscipline, resisting insights from outside. In our interview, Robin Dunbar explained why such loyalty is particularly common among older scientists:

> Having spent your career developing your idea, some 15-year-old comes along and says 'no, no, you're wrong'. Your reaction is: 'This can't be right, because if it's right everything I have done is wrong, and it means I have to start again. Here I am, aged 50.' The natural defence mechanism is to say 'no, no, that must be wrong'. What you end up with, unfortunately, is a complete opposition, which prevents you from figuring out which bits are right in the new things. You ought to be able to say: 'What do we do to articulate these two views together?'[32]

As mentioned in previous chapters, both our explicit, substantive, Apollonian goals and implicit, deeply social, Dionysian goals are real and authentic to us. Still, when the two are in conflict, we should expect the deeply social, Dionysian goals and interests to be the ones we prioritise in many cases. If taxpayers, research councils, and political authorities think it's important that scientists and other knowledge producers exchange ideas more across disciplines, the reward system for 'good science' will need to be broadened. This needs to be done in ways that also the Dionysian, deeply social goals can be reached by opening up and exchanging insights between disciplines and cultures.

The ignorance of thinking that ignorance is foolish

Recognising the phenomenon of rational ignorance can sometimes help us make sense of what on the surface might seem an egotistical aversion to knowledge. However, even those of us who are not economists must admit that not even knowledge acquisition can be spared from some restrictions. This includes the time and money we spend on it. We should also acknowledge that people absorb or resist some knowledge based on their explicit goals. When choosing what route their child should take to school, parents might try to collect information that is as specific as possible. The history of accidents on the various streets in relation to the number of people who use them every day seems like relevant knowledge. Once the parents have this information, they can decide what route they should tell the child to take. The parents are likely to rationally ignore data about accidents on these streets from the nineteenth century. They will probably also ignore data from streets in a different part of the planet. This is common sense – nothing strange here. Moreover, understanding the principles of rational ignorance can make us more humble, avoiding assumptions that all people who are suffering but who seem to have the ability to change their situation are irrational, resisting the reality of what would be best for them to do. For instance, a criminal might rationally ignore advice about the possible benefits of leaving their gang, in cases where that community actually provides that person with a minimal level of safety and sense of belonging.

While the rational ignorance perspective could be seen as a cynical phenomenon where people are seen as cold, selfish machines, it doesn't always have to be so. For instance, media coverage of apocalyptic climate devastation could lead to a sense of powerlessness. It is important to real-ise that a sense of powerlessness – often created by a lack of democratic openness to public influence – makes it more rational for people with little power to avoid learning more about the issue at hand. In such a situation it is more rational to narrow their scope to their own lives and those of their close relations. Why spend time, effort, and money trying to reduce risk or harm where you have almost no influence? To be sure, no one should find this reaction satisfying. However, there is not much point in calling the individual disengaged or selfish. Rather, it should be the job of politicians and civil society leaders to provide ways in which it becomes meaningful and 'rational' for people to move away from that rational ignorance and towards engagement.

If cost in terms of time and money is to be fully understood as a basis for knowledge resistance, it must be analysed not only at the overt, explicit, Apollonian level. People's explanations for how they draw their knowledge borders regarding time and other resources is only one part of the story. The underlying, often nonconscious, Dionysian level is also always operating in people's brains. Their deeply social interests guide what knowledge and facts to find relevant or irrelevant, valid or false. How they economise with knowledge should always be analysed as part of people's social rationality. Substantive and deeply social interests behind knowledge resistance often go hand in hand and reinforce each other. In cases where they don't, people and groups can be expected to prioritise social interests. While this chapter has mainly discussed substantive, direct costs for the individual or group at stake, the next chapters will examine other reasons for knowledge resistance in greater depth. As we'll see, these reasons exceed the narrow and explicit calculations of 'what's in it for me?'

6

When knowledge is responsibility and ignorance freedom

Knowledge resistance as strategy

As we learned in the previous chapter, knowledge is costly in substantive terms. Yet it is not only demanding concerning the resources of time, money, and effort it takes to increase our understanding. In this chapter, we'll look at two additional sides of knowledge. The first is how knowledge carries with it a moral and social responsibility. The second is the reverse of this: how ignorance may open up to opportunities that would have been difficult if you knew 'too much'. Convincing others – and yourself – that you are ignorant about specific occurrences can in some cases be of great value. This chapter will investigate these two sides of knowledge, and how they may give rise to knowledge resistance. The fact that knowledge resistance might have benefits for some people and groups doesn't mean that such resistance should remain unchallenged. I will show examples that range from knowledge resistance that most of us can sympathise wholeheartedly with, to resistance that is just cynical and appalling. This will lead to a brief discussion about the moral dimension of knowledge resistance. Where should the line be drawn between when it is acceptable to remain ignorant and when it is not?

Avoiding the burdens of knowledge

Ignorance can in some instances be not just cost-effective, but also beneficial. Thus, it makes sense that people and groups fend off knowledge from time to time. In the realm of entertainment or of significant real-life events, it is extremely common that people wish to remain ignorant, at least for a while. The benefit of not losing the 'drama' of movies, books, or sports games, or of finding out what gender a child will have, is reflected in people's common, explicit wishes that others not spoil the surprise in advance.[1] In studies from various countries where women have attended an amniocentesis, the women have been asked if they wish to know in advance their child's sex. In Germany, Spain, and the Netherlands 31–40 percent of the women preferred not to know. Most of them explained this with their preference for surprise and fun.[2]

Whereas the wilful ignorance in such not-very-burdensome issues is unproblematic and understandable to most people, the wish not to know about the graver side of life deserves far more attention here. Such knowledge resistance might at first seem irresponsible or disloyal. Still, as the psychologists Ralph Hertwig and Christoph Engel show in their overview of reasons for 'deliberate ignorance', resisting knowledge about future risks or problems doesn't always have to be a sign of irresponsibility or the like.[3] That such knowledge resistance doesn't have to be an escape from responsibility becomes apparent when one considers the increasingly sophisticated health information that is available nowadays in more advanced societies. In addition to the many benefits of this development, some types of health information put enormous – and possibly unwanted –pressure on people. This pressure is likely to increase in the near future, as advancements in artificial intelligence (AI) enhance the quantity and quality of health prognoses about social categories and individuals. An intensified public debate about how a 'right to ignorance' about one's own health prospects could continue to be honoured – a right already stated in the World Medical Association's 1995 'Declaration on the Rights of the Patient' – is likely, given the pace of the advancement of AI.[4]

As the famous psychologist Abraham Maslow – he who developed the pyramid of needs – put people's apparent need for some limits to knowledge decades ago:

> We can seek knowledge in order to reduce anxiety and we can also avoid knowing in order to reduce anxiety.[5]

The vast amount of health information that is available to individuals makes many people question the principle of the-more-the-better. Many of us draw the line at least somewhere concerning how much medical data we wish to access. The decision theorist and psychologist Gerd Gigerenzer suggests that this line-drawing is rooted in our anticipation of regret when we think about what would happen to us if we – like Cassandra in Greek mythology – learned about future events that we can't do anything about. Cassandra was given the gift of prophecy about events that she couldn't alter as a curse, set by the god Apollo, after she had declined his romantic advances. This, Gigerenzer assumes, might have led her to the same type of regret that many of us anticipate when we consider how we would feel if we learned about the conditions of ourselves or significant others.[6]

In specific instances, medical information about an individual can point with full certainty at her or his future diseases. Most cases, however, provide figures about the probability of illness. Findings in the psychology and sociology of risk show how the latter type of cases – the uncertain ones – are usually the most difficult ones to handle. Knowledge about uncertain risks is, firstly, emotionally stressful. Also, learning about uncertain risks is cognitively problematic. Humans are notoriously bad at incorporating statistical calculations and translating into measured and optimal decisions.[7] To absorb additional knowledge is often to accept being faced with new and challenging choices with several uncertain outcomes. Information about diseases raises other questions that force people to make further decisions between alternatives with either a certain or uncertain outcome. All this puts pressure on the individual to decide on issues where she or he used to remain blissfully ignorant.

Difficult personal choices

Amniocentesis, the medical procedure that can be used to diagnose foetal abnormalities, is an example of the kind of tests that different people may feel very differently about. Information generated through amniocentesis can raise the issue of whether having an abortion would be the most humanitarian thing to do. Some couples actively avoid this and other genetic screenings in order to avoid making what they feel are overwhelming choices. Better to have 'nature' or 'God' decide.[8]

When discussing various medical screenings, it's easy to empathise with some people's resistance to acquiring the maximum amount of information possible. With further progress in medical science, the right to knowledge resistance is becoming an increasingly relevant topic. At the same time, it's partially a personal issue as to whether we feel better once we have received more information about a diagnosis. Once people suspect they have a disease and they have the chance to obtain information about it, it's common for them to wish to have that information. In a study concerning cancer, 52 per cent of people in a survey said that their anxiety was reduced once they had received information about their disease; 10 per cent claimed the opposite.[9] To be sure, 10 per cent may seem like a small share, but it still shows that receiving the maximum amount of information about one's health isn't for everyone. In addition to personality differences, there are other factors relevant to this difference. They include how people perceive the efficiency of the cancer treatment. Whether they have the sense of control and self-efficacy to cope with the knowledge also makes a significant difference.

Responsibility to make things better

So-called strategic ignorance isn't only the avoidance of knowledge about bad things that might happen. Many of us also resist knowledge for the opposite reason. We sometimes prefer to remain ignorant about the good causes we could contribute to. There have been studies of how people with highly conscientious personalities sometimes handle information about support for humanitarian causes. They have shown that such people sometimes resist this type of knowledge. By doing so they reduce the pressure on themselves to contribute to charity, for example. According to the economist Nyborg, duty-oriented people are sometimes even willing to pay money in order not to get such information. They are particularly inclined to avoid information about the high social value of a particular contribution to a good cause.[10] Again, the psychologist Festinger's term 'cognitive dissonance' from the 1950s gives us one possible explanation for this phenomenon.[11] By resisting knowledge about the high social value of a contribution, conscientious people can avoid the uneasy dissonance between their knowledge and an omitted input – their passivity.

Although this example is connected with economic costs, it differs from the theme of the previous chapter on using knowledge resistance to reduce costs. There we covered how people may resist some knowledge to obtain only the optimal information – optimal in the sense of the type and amount of information being perfect to enable the person to reach their specific goal. In the example of charitable giving in this chapter, people don't need to have such a goal. Instead, they are fighting some of their social conscientiousness. This illustrates a type of knowledge resistance familiar to many of us: avoiding reading horrible stories about war victims, for example, that raise the issue of how we could help (even) more than we do.

Studies such as the one by Nyborg help us deepen our understanding of the nuances of knowledge resistance. I agree with Nyborg that ignorance with a purpose (as above) isn't the same as complete unawareness of a problem. Nor is it a full unawareness that the person, group, or organisation could make a contribution to reducing the problem. Everyone knows that there is much suffering in the world. We also know that there are serious organisations that through each individual contribution can do an even more ambitious job in helping those who suffer. Instead of treating ignorance as binary – knowing it all or not knowing at all – Nyborg perceives ignorance as unawareness of scale, proportions, and figures. Everyone is familiar with our potential for helping others. At the same time, we may resist the more specific knowledge that might increase our cognitive dissonance. This includes how many beneficiaries there are, the magnitude of the problem, and how efficient our own contributions would be. It's often the details and practicalities that people and groups remain unaware about, Nyborg argues.[12] This is very important to keep in mind as we try to identify the subtleties of knowledge resistance.

In a different case, climate change, many people and groups resist some knowledge without being complete climate-change deniers. Some people only ignore what they could do about it, what political party would be more progressive in trying to reduce environmental harm, and so forth.

Responsibility not to make things worse

We have seen how people can resist knowledge that would entail difficult personal choices. They may also avoid knowledge that would create moral pressure to contribute more to good causes. There is an additional reason for resisting knowledge: our wish to avoid responsibility for some of the adverse outcomes we play a part in. Many people convicted of crimes try to convince their lawyer and the judge they didn't know the act was unlawful or had a high risk of harming others. Such claims rarely impress judges. At the same time, acting 'in good faith' may sometimes be a factor that reduces the responsibility and culpability in and outside of court. One of several strategic ignorers par excellence in history was Hitler's chief architect, Albert Speer. In the 1930s and early 1940s, Speer was employed to create the architecture of the Third Reich. Formally, he was separate from the plans of the horrors of the Holocaust and the other heinous schemes. However, historians have been able to show how Speer exercised strategic ignorance time and again. He made numerous active choices not to 'learn' about the awful acts that took place within the Third Reich that he was drawing on his architect's table. Speer avoided participating in conversations where atrocities were planned. Later he admitted that he didn't want to know. At the same time, it's tough to imagine that he would have been entirely ignorant.[13]

Examples of knowledge resistance aimed at reducing one's responsibility for adverse outcomes are numerous, in all areas from the most appalling war crimes to trivial cases in our apparently peaceful offices. All of us have been party to at least some less dramatic cases. Again, convincing others that we are ignorant of a problematic issue where if we knew about it we would have to assume some responsibility is often very difficult. We are not in full control of our body language, which according to some psychologists is how the majority of our communication takes place. This is one of the reasons a full consciousness and awareness in all situations hasn't evolved in humans (or any other species). It's often far safer for people to maintain genuine ignorance. Alternatively, people could deceive themselves into believing they didn't know the circumstances. Such self-deception sometimes takes place where knowing about the circumstances would make people responsible for solving the problems involved. It's often difficult to assess whether people deceive only others or also themselves that they are ignorant. This means that so-called '*strategic* ignorance' is often a misleading term. Strategic ignorance makes it sound as if the ignorance was always entirely conscious and planned, which it rarely is. At the same time, my interview with economic geographer Bent Flyvbjerg convinced me that, at least when it comes to powerful actors in big decisions, strategic ignorance is often better understood as fully conscious.[14]

> If power is not interested in types of knowledge or certain specific knowledge coming out then there will be knowledge resistance. It's often a matter of not even producing knowledge where power is not interested in it. So that knowledge does not come into existence in the first place. That's completely common.[15]

This type of knowledge resistance hasn't been discussed so far in this book. This is because most studies on strategic ignorance focus on how actors avoid knowledge once it exists. However, it's very important to recognise the most basic type of strategic ignorance, namely avoiding looking for information and knowledge in the first place. What happens then in the cases where knowledge that is uncomfortable to powerful actors and organisations already exists? According to Flyvbjerg:

> Should knowledge be produced that power is not interested in then power will fight it. And they have escalating means of how to do that. I illustrate it in my paper about uncomfortable knowledge. Various strategies, starting by simply ignoring it. That's enough sometimes. Or excluding experts. When the decision is really important, power will not include experts. The experts are going, 'What? Why aren't we included? We could have provided the knowledge that should be the basis for that decision.'[16]

Such exclusion of knowledge providers is far from nonconscious coincidence, Flyvbjerg argues. Nonetheless, since we have seen examples of strategic ignorance that appears to be either conscious or nonconscious, the next section will remain agnostic on that matter.

Deny, dismiss, and divert

Three strategies to resist knowledge that is uncomfortable are particularly relevant for this book. The social scientist Steve Rayner is the original identifier of these strategies, which are denial, dismissal, and diversion.

Denial as strategic ignorance takes place when an individual or organisation refuses to recognise the availability of knowledge that would entail undesired responsibility. When an organisation is in denial, it may ignore or be unable to acknowledge information even when individuals within or outside the organisation try to bring it to attention. The situation that Steve Rayner uses in his article on uncomfortable knowledge is when the UK Parliamentary Office of Science and Technology published a House of Lords report identifying that public confidence in science was low. The report stated that this low confidence was problematic. The Minister for Science and Innovation made the premature assumption that the lack of confidence was rooted in a low level of scientific knowledge among the public. As a consequence of this assumption, a large, five-year research programme was launched to investigate the public perception of science more closely. It turned out, however, that the public had very high confidence in scientists and engineers. Around 85 per cent of the public agreed with the description that these professionals contribute to society in very valuable ways. Instead, it was people's confidence in government ministers and civil servants that was very low. The public confidence was particularly low in ministers and civil servants responsible for ensuring food and other types of public safety. The civil servants, as individuals, recognised this result and believed it to be valid. However, the Minister – and thus the ministry as an organisation – denied the results. The Minister took the position of denial by refusing to change his original view that the UK was permeated by an anti-science culture and a public knowledge deficit in science.[17] If he had admitted the validity of the new findings – to himself and others – he would have learned that he and his ministry were responsible for the low confidence in science. He would have been forced to recognise his responsibility not just to improve the public perception of science but also to change the ministry itself in order to regain public trust in science.

A softer sibling of denial is what Rayner labels dismissal. This strategy admits the existence of an uncomfortable knowledge claim. However, 'dismissivists' call the knowledge irrelevant, invalid, imprecise, or the like. The example that Rayner gives is how the US Congress has treated scientific evidence of climate change. I agree with him that what is portrayed as denial of climate change is more often dismissal of climate change. Nonetheless, groups who repeatedly dismiss knowledge claims, even when these claims are supported by increasing amounts of data, are very tough to debate with. To agree on dispute resolutions with them is even more difficult. The amount of data and evidence may sometimes make dismissivists admit that there might be something important in the knowledge claim in question. But in other cases, dismissivists keep demanding what would amount to an absolute certainty, something which is never possible in science, as discussed in Chapter 1. When dismissivists demand 'absolute certainty', it is based on our human tendency to first reach our knowledge belief through Dionysian impulse.

After we have reached this belief, our Apollonian side struggles to find sound and reasonable arguments that confirm our belief. As a type of strategic ignorance, this pattern of dismissal serves the function of alleviating the responsibility of dismissivists. In this case, the responsibility is that of political leaders in the US (along with other countries) for addressing the changing global climate.

Another example of dismissing knowledge in order to reduce one's responsibilities seems to be how the UK government has treated the EU law of animal sentience. In the process of leaving the EU, the UK government has had to make a wide range of decisions about whether to incorporate elements of European legislation into post-Brexit law. The law of animal sentience is recognised in the EU as an important factor to consider in various legal processes that concern animals. Still, the UK government appears to have voted against the relevance of all these data.[18] The massive amounts of scientific evidence and advances in neuroscience indicating that animals feel pain and have emotions is in effect resisted – by dismissal – by the UK government. Beneath the seemingly blunt ignorance of the matter, the reason for this resistance lies plausibly in the special interest in reducing the responsibilities of UK businesses and others where animals are involved.

The third and last of Rayner's terms that are relevant to us here is diversion. The literature on strategic ignorance has its typical focus on how organisations from international to local level obscure knowledge to avoid responsibility. Diversion is key here. It refers to distracting attention from a problem or topic, including the awareness of its existence.[19] One type of diversion that deserves particular mention is 'sequestered knowledge'. This is the practice of hiding uncomfortable knowledge or making it difficult to access. In this way it may not easily influence decision-making.[20] But the preferred way of hiding uncomfortable knowledge isn't necessarily to lock it away. It's far more common to conceal it in piles of papers together with more palatable information. This gives the impression of goodwill. The organisation thus presents the appearance of complying with rules and of taking all information into equal account. In effect, however, the group is avoiding the uncomfortable information and thus the possible demands for accountability that the information may give rise to.[21]

A second type, 'distributed ignorance', is subtler. It refers to people's exclusive focus on their own work, while they may avoid or simply lack the broader, systemic problem picture. By resisting knowledge, even knowledge located only outside the group's focus area, the group can claim that it isn't responsible for anything that takes place outside their most narrow focus.[22] If the different pieces of information of various groups are not used together in order to build a more comprehensive picture, the strategically ignorant actors can avoid responsibility for contributing to the visions of the organisation as a whole. In principle, distributed ignorance can be resolved by putting the bits and pieces together. Yet there may well prevail a resistance to comparing and integrating the parts.

Importantly, neither of these types of diversion are necessary parts of unambiguous attempts at deception. There may be intricate mixes between strategic ignorance and innocent efforts to convey correct and relevant information. These types of diversion help organisations prevent others from getting access to or even asking questions about the information.[23]

Making use of our ignorance

Strategic ignorance doesn't take place only to avoid burdens. It can also be a way of seeking opportunities.

Accepting and welcoming ignorance

We have already discussed the simplistic and idealistic view of how knowledge ought to be generated. Individuals and organisations – particularly in work life – should acquire knowledge systematically and in a particular order. People should have complete control over the previous steps before they move to the next ones. In an effort to manage various risks, all uncertainty should accordingly be removed regarding the risks in question before dealing with them. For example, in work to reduce contamination of water supplies, the norm prescribes that people shouldn't act to control a problem until they know the exact conditions. Such conditions could be whether, and to what extent, there are contaminants in the groundwater. Ignorance, or even a lack of complete and precise knowledge, should be the opposite of action, the norm prescribes.

However, the complexity and unpredictability of many environmental hazards make it impossible to follow such a linear, highly controlled process. Acting only based on observable and known facts is not always practical. The sociologists Gross and Bleicher have studied this clash between understandings of how to deal with limits to knowledge. They show how – and why – it's unconstructive to assume that all restrictions to knowledge are anomalies that must be overcome before acting. Gross and Bleicher claim that the simplistic ideal of linearity leads to an unfortunate knowledge resistance. People and organisations exert strategic ignorance to avoid blame for not following such a linear, predefined procedure. By extension, people avoid acting. They stay passive in order not to face the question of what they have been doing specifically and why their explorations 'fail' every time. However, 'failure' is the wrong term, the sociologists imply. Not finding anything interesting or relevant is many times part of the nature of such nonlinear explorations. Avoiding blame can be seen as a benefit of ignorance and thus a reason for knowledge resistance. The message from Gross and Bleicher is that recognising our ignorance – and allowing for ignorance – may have huge benefits when facing problems, such as contaminated water and land. Unknowns will always exist. Acknowledging and accepting them increases the potential to act and discover both new problems and solutions, these scholars maintain.[24] They add an additional twist: 'we also address the possibility to creatively use and manufacture specified forms of ignorance'.[25] The lesson is that we should not just admit and accept ignorance, but also the *state* of ignorance as such. This would open up new opportunities for searching unrestrictedly for problems and their causes, as well as solutions.

Stressing one's ignorance and legitimising further research

The contamination example mentioned above concerns practically applied work to handle environmental problems. Is ignorance treated as blameworthy in science as well? Science is ambivalent in this respect. On the one hand, the philosopher Sir Karl Popper's principle of falsification is still influential.[26] To some people who are not very familiar with scientific procedures, it might seem as if scientists' task is to discover what is 'true'. They do that, although in a very vague sense. Popper didn't think that it was possible to identify 'the truth', and that those who try to deal directly with the truth are in the business of pseudoscience, not real science. He had a much higher respect for the opposite activity: identifying what is false. With his principle of falsification, Popper claimed scientists should mainly deal with showing which hypotheses are false and, step by step, removing false assumptions. That is the only activity that can lead to improved knowledge, from Popper's scientific point of view. Finding that a hypothesis is false should make scientists excited. Each such scientific finding makes our remaining beliefs a little less wrong. Falsification is, therefore, a positive contribution to scientific progress. The Danish scientist and poet Piet Hein has written a telling verse about this process:

> The road to wisdom? – Well, it's plain and simple to express:
> Err
> and err
> and err again,
> but less
> and less
> and less.[27]

This means that recognising the limits of what we know is considered in the scientific community as a sign of competence and maturity. Importantly, this respect for recognising limits of what we know is high within the scientific community but unpopular when politicians or the media wish to make use of scientific findings. A philosopher (who requested to remain anonymous) among my interviewees describes the difficulty scientists have in communicating their results to politicians and policy-makers:

> There is no desire in politics for detail and subtle results. So, if the conscientious scientist comes to politics and says 'this is what we know, this is what we don't know, here's the uncertainty, and here is what we have no clue about', then politicians aren't happy. So scientists don't communicate uncertainties [to politics or the media]. They have to give exact results [even if such results are unrealistic].

Let's return to norms within science. Identifying intriguing knowledge gaps (the things that no one knows) but managing to convince research foundations that we know how to fill these gaps are among the primary skills for which scientists are rewarded with research funding. Ask any scientist how to write a research application that is successful (likely to be funded) and at least some of them will suggest that you should have almost completed the research in advance of your application. This is the only way, they contend, in which you can show that you are aware of exactly what you don't know. Being aware of exactly what you don't know is the only way to convince funding institutions of what would be worthwhile doing, and what you are able to do. You must convince the foundations that it's very likely that your project will generate results, these scientists would say. In the sociologist Merton's terminology, most institutions that fund research only accept the 'specified ignorance' of scientists.[28] To persuade research foundations that they (the scientists) have specified ignorance in an area that the foundation finds important is a good starting position for obtaining research funding.

It is, of course, essential to fill predefined knowledge gaps, not least in medical science. However, many of the paramount discoveries throughout history wouldn't have been reached if specified ignorance had been the only type of ignorance allowed among scientists and innovators. Here are two classic examples. In 1945, Percy Spencer, an American engineer, elaborated on a magnetron that could beam high radiation waves. Suddenly, a chocolate bar in his pocket began to melt. Out of sheer curiosity, he put popcorn in a bowl next to the tube. Within seconds it began to pop. This became the knowledge basis for the microwave oven. More lifechanging in a fundamental sense is the story of how the Scottish biologist Alexander Fleming, while doing research on staphylococci, returned to his lab after a few days away to find that a blue-green mould had developed on one of his Petri dishes that he had left open by mistake. The mould turned out to be able to kill harmful bacteria without harming the human body. Fleming's ignorance of what he didn't know entailed the discovery of penicillin, which is often considered the beginning of modern medicine.[29]

It is probably the value of such profound ignorance that Gross and Bleicher argue for, although these authors focus not on research but on practical work in handling environmental harm. Both paramount discoveries and practical ecological risk management need us to allow time and effort to be spent on what we are not aware that we don't know. When it comes to research in academia, some research institutions and foundations are well aware of the limits to funding only specified ignorance. This is why they occasionally have calls for 'high-risk projects'. The goal is to give at least some room for truly open explorations of 'unspecified ignorance' – what we aren't aware that we don't know. Naturally, a lot of such explorations are likely not to generate any interesting knowledge. If we are lucky, however, a few of these wild and crazy projects may stimulate what the physicist and philosopher of science Thomas Kuhn called a scientific crisis. In such a crisis, the conformist way of thinking – the current paradigm – is challenged in a scientific discipline or knowledge area. To reach a refreshing paradigm shift, Kuhn saw it as crucial not to be stuck in the preconceptions of the old paradigm. He didn't use the term 'specified ignorance', where one is aware of exactly what one doesn't know but could soon find out. Yet he would have seen the limitation of science to deal with specified knowledge as a way to maintain the old paradigm. Kuhn noted:

> Almost always the men who achieve fundamental inventions of a new [scientific] paradigm have been either very young, or very new to the field whose paradigm they change.[30]

The free thinking that can come out of the ignorance of what we don't know was probably what he had in mind when pointing to the benefits of being new to a field.

Knowledge resistance to avoid partiality

In many of the previous examples of knowledge resistance, it has been difficult to show the extent to which the knowledge resistance has been consciously strategic – Apollonian. A significant share of the examples where people resist knowledge seem to be nonconscious and impulsive – Dionysian. Some cases would probably fall somewhere in between.

One category of knowledge resistance that without a doubt is entirely strategic at the conscious level is the ignorance that is actively cultivated within certain organisations to avoid unfair partiality in society. One of the most important psychological and sociological insights is that we all have biases that we can rarely rid ourselves of just by being aware of them; these Dionysian traits are too deeply rooted in us. It's not enough to try to think 'reasonably' about how unfair these biases are to others. Pulling ourselves together and thinking outside of these biases is particularly tricky when the issue at stake concerns people of other ethnicities, cultures, gender, social classes, and so forth. It could be confirmation bias, my-view biases, or biases favouring our kin, peers, and others who are like ourselves. Something can still be done about our biases, however, if we agree with others. First, we need to recognise that we, as separate individuals, cannot outsmart our own biases. Then we can create principles and rules together with others in society and organisations with a view to preventing biases from influencing decision-making where they shouldn't. Such regulations and principles often involve making us ignorant. This can be seen in many spheres of society and social thinking.

One of the most famous thought experiments about how to create a just and fair society is based on the idea that constructing a setting of ignorance can make us fairer. It's called 'the original position' and was developed by the brilliant political philosopher John Rawls. The theory is that in order to agree on what a just society should look like, everyone must put on a 'veil of ignorance'. This means that you are ignorant of what position you'd have in an imagined society. You don't know whether you'd end up rich or poor, enslaved or free, woman or man, black or white, queer or straight, old or young, sick or healthy. According to Rawls, this ignorance is the only way to get valuable answers from people that everyone in society can agree on.[31] To be sure, no theory of justice is perfect. The ignorance that Rawls proposes as a way, at least in theory, to reach a collective agreement about a just society has been met with critique as well. For instance, Rawls claims that no reasonable people who are ignorant of their individual fate would accept slavery in their imagined, ideal society. They don't know if they would be a slave were this society to become real. However, critics have said that some people who are gamblers might accept extreme social inequality in their ideal society, including slavery, because they hope and believe that they'd be a middle- or upper-class person in that society. This critique is rather beside the point I'm trying to make here, but I wanted to show that strategic ignorance may have its clear benefits when we try to develop justice.

Active and strategic ignorance of a similar type has been shown to be promising in other areas as well. One concerns attempts at developing and exchanging creative ideas on the Internet. If anyone thought that social media would be a melting pot of ideas and arguments to be challenged across groups with different experiences, reality has so far mainly shown the opposite tendency. It seems as if we enter social media groups to have our knowledge claims confirmed by our cultural peers more than anything else. Early studies of social media also show how masking identity and preserving the anonymity of the participants may increase the chances of developing a more creative discussion and more honest exchange of opinions.[32]

In my work as a university professor, ignorance as a tool for creating fairness is regularly a relevant, practical issue for me. When we grade student papers and essays, my colleagues and I have discussions of whether the students should be made anonymous. It is telling that there is still the view among some teachers along the lines that they don't need the papers to be anonymous as they always give their students the grade they deserve. They might offer their years of involvement in anti-racism activism as proof of their lack of bias. After what we have learned above about biases, can we be sure that long work experience and the 'right' human values make us immune to having the name of the students influence our assessments? I don't think so. Even where there is cultural awareness, there is still the risk of overcompensation. Consider a situation where you are a teacher who is extremely conscious of at least informal racial injustice in society. You are equally conscious that you are WEIRD (Western, educated, and from an industrialised, rich, democratic country). Moreover, you are aware that you are a heterosexual, middle-aged, liberal man in a dominant position relative to your students. How can you be sure that your status will never influence your grading? Several studies have shown that you can't.

Research has compared the results that junior high school students in Sweden achieve in standardised national tests (where name or gender doesn't influence the grade) with grades in the classroom as well as final grades. Getting good final grades is crucial for being allowed to choose a subject profile in high school. In the subject of English, 50 per cent more girls than boys got a final grade that was higher than the grade they were given in the national test. In biology, three times as many girls than boys got the highest final grade without having received that grade in the national test. And so on. The phenomenon is mockingly called 'snällhetsbetyg' ('kindness grade'). One reason this happens is that all Swedish teachers are probably aware of the gender inequalities where boys are on average shown to be pushier and more talkative in the classroom at the expense of girls. A second, partly overlapping reason for this bias in favour of girls' grades is that, as a national study shows, teachers in Sweden, on average, assess girls more on non-cognitive factors such as interests and motivation, whereas boys are assessed more on cognitive ones like knowledge, comprehension, and so forth. This has also been shown in classroom research.[33] To be sure, interests and motivation could perhaps be included as significant parts of what is graded. However, the point here is that the Swedish grading system, like any other, should supposedly be gender-blind, which it isn't.

In police forces – as with university tutors – there is sometimes the view that experienced police officers are blind to race and colour. Among the police in the US, for instance, police officers on average believe that they are far more colour blind than non-police people are, and claim on average not to see any differences in behaviour between people of different colour. Although in this section we have praised ignorance (or 'blindness'), there are several problems with this stated colour blindness. Studies indicate that individuals who perceive themselves as blind to colour often have difficulties interacting with people from racial minorities. For example, therapists who claim to have colour-blind attitudes were found to be more inclined to think that their black clients more than their white clients were responsible for solving their own problems. Also, black students have been shown to do worse in various cognitive tests soon after having interacted with white people expressing colour-blind beliefs. They scored better when they had interacted with white people who showed multicultural values (values where they recognised that there might be differences between people of different ethnic groups, but that every group should have the same rights). Perhaps these black students were more inclined to trust the abundant research – from laboratories to real-life observations – as well as their own life experiences showing that people are rarely *truly* colour blind; they might therefore feel more comfortable with people of another colour who admit that they are not ignorant to racial or cultural differences. In this example, however, it is essential that these people clearly show the view that people of all races and cultures should have equal rights and obligations. This ought to be a lesson for all of us, as police officers, university professors, or any other profession.

The lesson could be translated into several other demographic categories as well. Assuming that we or others are blind to gender might not always be the best mindset in the workplace, for instance. This has been shown in a study about how women and men on average react to various job descriptions. Certain occupations and academic avenues necessitate 'brilliance' of the people working there. Still, it turns out to be beneficial to women if this 'truth' is toned down or not even mentioned. The reason is that terms such as 'brilliance' work as dissuaders to women since brilliance is stereotypically associated with men. Women – including 'brilliant' ones – sense on average that the environment in a field that uses that word won't be welcoming to women. How should employers formulate the need for brilliance then? Research indicates that stating a field of work demands a lot of effort and passion is more effective in attracting women to apply.[34] The take-home message is that employers should not ignore gender differences. They should not struggle towards gender blindness. It is not constructive to maintain that women *should* react in the same way as male applicants to any job description. Instead, it seems better to discuss with both women and men beforehand what formulations are most likely to create different, gender-based reactions.

In society there are areas where it's possible to make ourselves ignorant to ensure fairness and a creative exchange of ideas. This is the case when, for instance, we grade student papers or assess job applications. Also, when we wish to develop an Internet group with the goal of developing new ideas, most arguments point towards doing this. Then there are tasks where it is impossible to construct such an ignorance. It might not be viable when walking the streets and interacting with people in real life. In such situations, research implies that we should recognise and admit our social and cultural astigmatism. Only then is it possible to continuously reflect and cross-check with people in other positions how the problem could be handled.

When knowledge resistance harms or helps

Over the centuries, valuable insights have been accumulated into how knowledge can strengthen power.[35] This chapter has hopefully made it hard to deny that ignorance may also have its benefits in specific situations. Some circumstances are more morally tolerable than others. There are those among us who embrace and others who resist results from genetic screenings and other methods for predicting their medical future. A significant proportion of the public prefers to avoid some of that information. Data that is uncertain and probabilistic creates particularly stressful decisions that many of us would rather not have to address.

Another category of strategic ignorance is arguably far more blameworthy: the ignorance that makes it easier for us to continue harmful activities we may be engaged in. Yes, there are horrendous examples of such ignorance in the history books and daily news, ranging from ignorance of war crimes to spouses claiming not to have known their partner had repeatedly abused their child for years. 'How could they not have known?' we ask ourselves. Still, there is often a blurred line between knowledge resistance that is consciously strategic and other knowledge resistance that is self-deceptive. Add psychopathology and long-term psychological violence to the circumstances. This makes it additionally difficult to answer that rhetorical question in an accurate way.

Aside from extreme instances, all of us are likely to ignore strategically some of the harm we cause through our choices in daily life. These include our negative impact on the natural environment, animals, or over-exploited workers who produce the goods that we purchase. Are we really ignorant of this? No, most of us are not. During much of my research career to date, I've devoted myself to studying how people, or 'citizen-consumers' as I call all of us in contemporary society, are quite knowledgeable about such impacts. Citizen-consumers are aware that compromises to animal welfare take place in industrial meat production. They are familiar with the downsides of mass consumption and fossil-fuel-based transportation's effect on the environment, animal welfare, and labour conditions.[36] To be sure, different scholars vary in their views of what aspects of production and consumption are more harmful than beneficial regarding suffering or its reduction. Still, most agree that some elements of manufacturing and consumption are highly damaging.[37]

More often than complete ignorance of such negative consequences, our strategic ignorance concerns practical and specific measures that we could take to reduce that impact. For instance, citizen-consumers sometimes avoid learning about and trying out public transport for their daily commute rather than using their car. Or they find other ways of leaving out of their minds and routine practices the acquisition of practical and specific knowledge related to how they could change some of their potentially harmful practices or become more engaged in their communities. Or it refers to who to contact and where to go to participate in organisations engaged in reducing these harmful practices on a larger scale.

Since most of us practice strategic ignorance from time to time and therefore are able to avoid making the positive effort that would reduce harm in the world, it is easy to conclude that such ignorance is 'simply human'. However, the so-called consequentialist traditions in moral philosophy find such ignorance as problematic as when we avoid becoming aware of the harm we are causing. Philosophers in these traditions, most notably 'utilitarians', are concerned only with the consequences of our actions and inaction, and find our intentions irrelevant. They maintain that avoiding the chance to reduce pain and increase pleasure in the world is as bad as doing direct harm by increasing pain. This is a major area where humans are likely to exert strategic ignorance. The moral psychologist Joshua Greene shows that the decision to avoid causing harm makes a different brain region particularly active compared to the region most active in making decisions about doing good to others.[38] Avoiding supporting a charity through which a person could have saved five lives is seen as far less blameworthy that taking five lives. The Dionysian part of our mind finds this to be common sense, but the Apollonian part doesn't necessarily agree. After all, the level of harm is identical across both cases. However, I would hold that our intuition that killing five people is worse than not saving five people isn't irrational. Instead, it's socially rational. This intuition has been vital throughout human history, instrumental in enabling trusting relationships between people. A strong aversion to actively harming each other has benefitted community cohesion and collaboration throughout the ages.

However, despite it having been socially rational and adaptive for humans throughout early history to feel that way, this doesn't mean it's morally defensible to avoid doing good when we can do good. The utilitarian philosopher Peter Singer's mission is to spread the gospel that we have just as strong a moral obligation to do good as we have to avoid doing bad. In an article titled 'The Man Who Didn't Save the World', he shows the irony of how people so often strategically ignore this utilitarian wisdom. The man that Singer refers to is a Saudi prince. In the Autumn of 2017, the prince bought a painting by Leonardo da Vinci portraying Jesus, titled *Salvator Mundi* ('The man who saved the world'), for $450.3 million. Singer notes that the prince could instead have done what Jesus told another wealthy man to do: give the money to the poor. That sum would have, for instance, made it possible for thirteen million impoverished families to grow about 50 per cent more food, or – alluding to one of Jesus's miracles – restored eyesight to approximately nine million people.[39] The prince must have been very aware of how it would have been possible for him to do something that would have reduced suffering substantially in the world, but it's fair to assume he ignored that alternative strategically. The reason is plausibly the social prestige that he envisioned in owning one of the most famous da Vinci paintings. The rest of us who ignore our own opportunities to do more to reduce suffering in the world exercise the same strategic ignorance as the Saudi prince. Only the scale differs. But it only differs if we strategically ignore the enormous amounts of harm we as individuals could avoid creating if we mobilised with others to maximise this utilitarian goal.

Conclusion

In this chapter we have learned about three strategies of strategic ignorance. These are to deny, dismiss, and divert information about how to reduce harm and increase benefits to society. We have also seen how people can make 'positive' use of their ignorance, or at least of their claims thereof. Knowledge can seem like a burden. There are quite a few innovation experts, philosophers of science, and sociologists who argue that ignorance can give people wings in some situations. These scholars claim that individuals and organisations should allow themselves and others the freedom of searching without being aware of what they don't know, perhaps not even what they are looking for, specifically. Many inventions and discoveries would not have been possible without such unstructured and nonlinear processes. Consequently, many agree that in science and innovation there must be room for searching for solutions to problems that no one knew existed. Such solutions have the chance of being path-breaking, paradigm-shifting, or – to use a worn-out term – game-changing.

Finally, strategic ignorance can be useful where fairness or creativity presupposes social and cultural diversity. In such cases, it's often advisable to construct rules to make all people involved socially ignorant. In my view, the widespread use and acceptance of such rules for impartiality – some of them millennia old, others brand new – are among the finest signs of human self-awareness and enlightenment. Establishing such rules reflects the recognition and reasoning of our own, built-in, genetically hardwired traits, such as biases. We can agree with others to control such hardwired characteristics by introducing rules that make us all ignorant. In this way social life can become fairer and more creative. Grading of student performance and job applications are particularly suitable for such rules.

From this chapter's focus on ignorance as a way of alleviating the burdens of responsibility, avoiding unfair partiality, and creating new opportunities, we turn to a factor that is often overlooked: how people resist knowledge claims because of their concerns about consequences. So far, we have mainly talked about outcomes to *individuals* and *groups*. The next chapter will broaden the picture: what role do people's concerns for broader, cultural, and socio-economic consequences have for the way they handle, and sometimes resist, knowledge?

7

What if the earth *is* round? Concerns about cultural consequences

I think bombs

The evolutionary biologist Robert Trivers has been called the Einstein of evolutionary biology.[1] I don't think this is an exaggeration. His findings on human collaboration and the parent–child relationship, for example, can hardly be overestimated. At the same time, Trivers isn't afraid of making claims about disciplines far outside of his own. One thing he has said about nuclear physics I find particularly fascinating – and challenging:

> When I read of nine billion euros spent on a supercollider in which tiny particles are accelerated to incredible speeds and then run into one another, I think 'bombs'.[2]

Many people might make the same connection as Trivers between nuclear physics and weapons of mass destruction, with the following truism: without knowledge produced in nuclear physics there wouldn't be any risk of nuclear war. Does this mean that accepting nuclear physics as a field that creates knowledge must also imply that we must accept the risk of nuclear war? Or can we treat nuclear physics as a discipline that provides 'amoral', neutral knowledge? Think about another 'product': electricity. It can be used for everything from the electric chair used in executions to lamps used in nurseries enabling children to play. Few people would resist electricity only because it is, or could be, used for executions. Is nuclear physics amoral in the same sense? Or should we hesitate to produce or acquire knowledge in cases where we worry about its possible applications?

Regardless, a nuclear physicist working on a supercollider may well retort to Trivers's 'I think "bombs"' statement by saying that when they read about Trivers's work in evolutionary biology, they think reactionary and stereotypical gender roles. Similar guilt-oriented comments could be made about most disciplines. When you think about contemporary education in medical school, you could think about how some of the knowledge the students receive was first produced through Nazi experiments. When you think about sociology, you could think of socialist ideology, including communism. Or when you think about economics, you could think of libertarian, laissez-fair ideology. And so on.

In many kinds of knowledge production, some people make such connections. This happens even when the strength and inevitability of these connections are far from evident. Associating knowledge with its background context and possible consequences may reflect fear. People and groups occasionally turn their fears about assumed consequences into worries about the knowledge as such. A lot of knowledge resistance at all levels of society is derived from such worries. However, is this type of knowledge resistance always ungrounded and just plain bad?

This book has so far mainly looked at the negative sides of knowledge resistance. I think this has been appropriate. So much knowledge in the world has been exploited in destructive ways, nuclear physics being one example. Darwinian evolutionary theory is another. Today, evolutionary science is used in a vibrant and socially sensitive way. However, it used to be exploited unscientifically into political perversions. These were manifested as false claims about superior and subordinate races and cultures under the banner of Social Darwinism.

As to cases where knowledge has been applied in devastating ways, the textbook examples include some of Dr Thomas Midgley Jr's inventions. In the late 1920s, there were intensive attempts at developing safe refrigerators for households. A key question was what compounds could be used in them. Several of the previously used compounds had been explosive, toxic, or flammable. Midgley and his team developed the first chlorofluorocarbon (CFC), widely known as freon. They argued that freon would have none of these harmful properties, and thus it began to be used in refrigerators, air conditioners, and aerosol sprays. Whereas Midgley was awarded the Perkin Medal in 1937 by the Society of Chemical Industry (American Section), scientists began to recognise something frightening in the early 1970s. CFC was observed to cause depletion of the ozone layer in the upper atmosphere. Many cases of skin cancer began to be associated with such depletion, as well as adverse effects on plants and marine ecosystems. Luckily, many countries managed to agree on phasing out CFCs under the Montreal Protocol, replacing them with alternatives.[3]

Hearing about such cases, and the possibly adverse consequences of some types of knowledge, leads to a question: is it possible to draw a straight line between bad and good kinds of knowledge resistance that are founded on people's worries about consequences? When writing a draft of this chapter, I was prepared to answer a definite yes to this question. My arguments looked solid, and I was writing with confidence. I looked once more at the comments others had given about this issue, comments that I had casually rejected. Had I deceived myself into doing the same thing that this whole book is problematising? Or had I at least resisted taking some arguments into account, even valid and important ones? Based on these reflections, I realised that the chapter had to be rewritten. It was a bit frustrating, to be sure. At the same time, I started the revision with some excitement. After all, as you are well aware by now, it is relatively rare to recognise one's own knowledge resistance. I guess that's why the recognition of my own resistance felt like a victory. The purpose of this chapter is not only to show how concerns about consequences are a basis for much knowledge resistance. I also hope my personal experiences will give you an idea of how it is possible in certain circumstances to turn knowledge resistance into at least some new openness.

To better understand how to deal with knowledge in light of its possible consequences, I find it very useful to consult a nineteenth-century biologist. His name was Thomas Huxley, but he was nicknamed 'Darwin's bulldog' due to the way he continuously defended Darwin and his find-ings on natural selection. He did so against constructive sceptics as well as deniers and dismissivists. Among his responses, one that concerns the possible societal consequences of Darwin's ideas is particularly interest-ing. It shows three ways to think about knowledge claims and what con-sequences, if any, knowledge should have on our politics, culture, and ethics. This chapter is structured on the basis of Huxley's descriptions of three ways in which society could handle knowledge about evolution. He introduces the three ways in this brilliant quote from 1884:

> Let us understand, once for all, that the ethical progress of society depends, not on *imitating* the cosmic process [evolution by natural selection], still less in *running away* from it – but in *combating* it.[4] (My emphasis)

In short, Huxley's three possible ways of handling knowledge are (i) 'imi-tating', (ii) 'running away' (as in treating some knowledge and natural mechanisms as if they do not exist), and (iii) 'combating' (as in scrutinis-ing and fighting these natural mechanisms through humane policies, regulations, and culture in order to reduce suffering). According to Huxley, the first two strategies are in several parts untenable. The third strategy is the road he argues that society and its members should take: to be knowledge absorbent and learn as much as possible about the natural mechanisms in order to be able to 'combat' the negative implications that nature's processes – such as the suffering of the weak and sick – otherwise entail for society. Below follow further descriptions of the three strategies. In my view, all knowledge – not just that about evolution and natural selection – can be understood through these categories.

Imitating

The imitating strategy contends that knowledge about nature isn't 'neutral' or 'amoral'. This strategy refuses to recognise the amoral charac-ter of knowledge about how life on earth and humans evolve biologically. Instead, knowledge about evolution or other natural things gives us not just a better understanding, proponents of the imitating strategy hold, it also provides us with a moral map, or compass, for how we should create and organise society. This is what Huxley means with 'imitating the cosmic process'. According to the imitating strategy, Darwin's theory of natural selection isn't only factually correct. The insight about how life evolves biologically also sends the one 'right' message to society of what should be done when we organise social, political, and economic life. The imitating strategy entails the embracing – without ethical scrutiny – of what the proponents of that strategy perceived as nature's 'right', normative message.

Neither Darwin, Huxley, today's serious evolutionary scientists, nor myself subscribe to this view. It was the imitating strategy that led to policies and cultural beliefs known as Social Darwinism or social evolution. The notion implied that people in marginal positions – the poor, unhealthy, disabled, particularly challenged, and so forth – shouldn't be helped. Accordingly, people who subscribed to these views felt it was part of 'nature's scheme' to keep these people marginalised. Our gut reactions to learning about this strategy today might be that it's heartless, insensitive, or even sadistic. Still, it was not always so. Many thinkers in the nineteenth century and the first half of the twentieth century promoted the strategy of imitating biological evolution for what they would have called humane reasons. They maintained that the least cruel way to relate to the weak was to leave them to their 'natural' destiny. Herbert Spencer, who coined the term 'survival of the fittest', was a public voice on how to reduce suffering in the world:

> Consumptive patients, with lungs incompetent to perform the duties of lungs … people with defective hearts that break down under excitement of the circulation, people with any constitutional flaw preventing the due fulfilment of the conditions of life, are continually dying out and leaving behind those fit for the climate, food, and habits to which they are born. … And thus is the race kept free from vitiation.[5]

Another aspect of the imitating strategy was the belief that biology shows us how to value groups and cultures. In the same way as organisms may sometimes move from primitive to complex, we can not only categorise but also rank cultures. Savage, barbarian, and civilised cultures used to be standard categorisations. Unsurprisingly, this implied a belief that the white race is superior to other races, and that for the benefit of all cultures and races, white people in 'civilised' cultures were obliged to control and lift the non-white cultures of the world, as discussed in Chapter 4. As a parent, I very much enjoyed reading *The Jungle Book* and *Just So Stories* to my children. It was – to say the least – disappointing to learn that the British author Rudyard Kipling endorsed this view. This is crystal clear in the following poem, written as a response to the Philippine–American War, among several texts:

> Take up the White Man's burden–
> Send forth the best ye breed–
> Go bind your sons to exile
> To serve your captives' need;
> To wait in heavy harness,
> On fluttered folk and wild–
> Your new-caught, sullen peoples,
> Half-devil and half-child.[6]

It's easy to reject the imitating strategy based on today's moral norms. In many of us, the ranking of how 'fit' various people or how 'civilised' different cultures are triggers a feeling of disgust. Yet, since this book has its focus on knowledge resistance, I want to move beyond moral reasoning. Is the imitating strategy not just immoral (from today's perspective) but also false? I would argue that it is, in several ways.

The first thing it gets wrong is that it assumes that any knowledge (in this case about how people evolve genetically) can be translated into how we should organise society, culture, economics, and so forth. Proponents of the imitating strategy try to be more scientific and knowledge embracing than anyone else, to be sure. They do this by suggesting that we should use natural science to govern society. Ironically, the proponents resist knowledge that philosophers have tried to spread at least since the Scottish philosopher David Hume in the eighteenth century. A condition or process that exists in the world, such as genetic evolution (an 'is'), can never be directly or automatically translated into what we should do in society (an 'ought'). To ignore this well-known logical error is to commit 'the naturalistic fallacy'.[7] Darwin, Thomas Huxley, and any (other) respectable human scientist would agree that this type of knowledge resistance is not only morally unacceptable but also logically untenable.

The second problem is that Social Darwinists and others who endorsed the imitating strategy held a belief in biological evolution that is at odds with what most evolutionary scientists believe today. Social Darwinists assumed that biological evolution is a progressive process that turns everything that is primitive, such as simple organisms, into things that are complex. If we ask most evolutionary scientists today, they would tell us the change from simple to complex organisms happens sometimes. Many other times, it doesn't. There are still enormous numbers of simple organisms out there since they can survive, reproduce, and multiply without evolving into complexity. This becomes all too obvious in February each year when millions of people fall ill with winter bugs. These mostly trivial illnesses aside, there are far more life-threatening diseases in the Global South, of course. Pessimists among experts in infectious diseases constantly witness the infamous ingenuity with which a simple organism may adapt to its environment through mutations, leading to frighteningly efficient survival and reproduction. In brief, there doesn't seem to be any clear and linear direction of biological evolution from simple to complex. In turn, there is no such lesson to be learned for society about a progression from simple to sophisticated, let alone from primitive to civilised.

A third error is that Social Darwinists ignored – or resisted – another major insight from Darwin and other serious evolutionary scientists. Surviving and reproducing are about adapting to the natural and social environment in which individuals and groups find themselves. To label another culture as 'primitive' is to ignore the sophistication with which each culture handles the challenges and opportunities in its own natural and social environment.

There are several other shortcomings with the imitating strategy. For our purposes it suffices to mention only one more: drawing any conclusions from historical development in terms of the intellectual and cultural supremacy of people in some cultures over others. To this day it is not uncommon to hear the view that industrialisation, technological advancement, and other modern developments in the white world say something about a superior 'essence' of people in that world. This is a textbook example of self-deception. Westerners who perceive themselves as successful or as winners often fail to recognise one of the most valuable insights from Ancient Greece, the so-called cradle of Western society. That is that there is one 'force' that steers the destiny of people and cultures more than most other forces: luck. By emphasising the high significance of receiving a smile from Eutykhia, the goddess of luck, the ancient Greeks came far closer to a valid explanation of why Western society has enjoyed more progress than many other parts of the world. There is ample evidence, most famously in Jared Diamond's book *Guns, Germs and Steel*, pointing in this direction. Two important reasons for the early success of European societies as colonisers were geographical location and resistance to certain infections – lucky conditions, to be sure.[8]

Is the obsolete strategy of imitating nature worth even spending time confronting today? And is that strategy something that some people still subscribe to beyond the issue of evolution? Yes, it is. Repeatedly, there are claims about letting nature take its course. In our time of globalisation, racially and culturally based distinctions that include value statements are also common. There, one can be sure that the misconceptions and resistance to the insights mentioned above are reproduced. If we move beyond the issue of evolution, the imitation strategy has its sibling in what is perhaps best described using another thought from Ancient Greece: hubris. This is the concept of neglecting or downplaying the gap between what we *can* do with new knowledge and what we *should* do. Thomas Midgley Jr had developed another idea a few years before inventing freon. Knocking was a major problem in internal combustion engines in cars in the early 1920s. Midgley discovered that by adding tetraethyl lead to petrol, the knocking problem was overcome. It would have been difficult for Midgley and his contemporary engineers to realise the hazards freon posed to the ozone layer. Still, terms such as hubris – or knowledge resistance – are probably not unfair concerning the promotion of lead in gasoline. After all, the many risks of lead had been reported ever since the Greek philosopher Nikander of Colophon did so in 250 BC. Moreover, Midgley himself suffered from lead poisoning. That concerns were not raised or acknowledged earlier seems to say something about knowledge resistance. Protests out of fear of the consequences of adding the lead-based compound to petrol would have made the world a much healthier place. If lead exposure had been avoided during several decades of the twentieth century, it would have spared many thousands of people from developing cognitive impairments of various kinds.[9]

It's still common to neglect the need for moral, social, and health-oriented considerations before moving from what we can do to what we should do. Innovators in genetic engineering, geoengineering, or other radical technologies with enormous potential – good or bad – sometimes pressure public agencies and policy-makers in ways similar to the imitation strategy. Accordingly, public agencies and policy-makers should not spend as much time or effort as they do in ensuring that the gap between 'is' (the radical technologies) and 'ought' (whether/how the technologies should be permitted) is understood, and risks are minimised.

For this book, however, there is an even more important reason for bringing up the imitation strategy. Awareness of the imitation strategy has triggered a counter strategy, which I hold is today the most common way of resisting knowledge based on concerns about consequences: it is the strategy of 'running away'.

Running away

'Running away' is to resist producing or gaining knowledge due to worries that the knowledge would have negative consequences in society. On the face of it, running away from knowledge seems to be the opposite of the imitating strategy I mentioned earlier. However, there are similarities between these counter strategies. Neither 'imitators' nor those who favour running away from some kinds of knowledge believe that knowledge is amoral or neutral. What was the stated reason for imitating knowledge about biological evolution, applying it directly to society by 'having nature take its course' also in social activities? Implied in the imitating strategy is the view that nature provides the best normative and ethical tools for organising society. Those who consider running away from particular types of knowledge a valid strategy – whether it concerns the production, learning, or support of the knowledge in question – would agree that knowledge isn't neutral. However, they don't think the norms hidden underneath the knowledge come from nature. Rather, they believe the norms and power hidden in the knowledge produced in society often come from people and groups with special interests.

The evolutionary biologist Robert Trivers claims to see an underlying interest in research on supercolliders that is the whole reason this type of knowledge is produced: an interest in producing more powerful bombs. I don't know if Trivers would conclude that supercollider research should thus be prohibited. Nor do I know if he'd suggest that we shouldn't use tax money for such research. In any case, concerns about possible consequences of some knowledge often generate calls for knowledge resistance, particularly in areas of security, environment, health, or the moral climate. Those who subscribe to the running-away strategy assume that the research and knowledge claims in question are inseparable from special, normative interests. The groups holding these special interests will do all they can to bring about the consequences that the knowledge resisters dislike.

The instinct or calculated strategy of running away from knowledge can be found everywhere – from households to policy-makers, from left to right on the political spectrum. Here's an example of resistance of the political right. In North Carolina in the US, a scientific study predicted that the sea level is likely to rise extensively over a certain period. This change, if it happens, will have very damaging consequences for the coastal areas of North Carolina, the scientists behind the study concluded. In response, the North Carolina legislature barred local and state agencies from developing planning documents and regulations that addressed this issue. As I mentioned in the previous chapter, organisations that exercise knowledge resistance usually do so by obscuring it. Sometimes it takes a comedian to clarify what is happening. In the North

Carolina case, the author and comedian Stephen Colbert commented on the situation: 'This is a brilliant solution. If your science gives you a result that you don't like, pass a law saying the result is illegal. Problem solved.'[10] Colbert put his finger on the reason for the anti-science knowledge resistance of the North Carolina legislature: the state authorities feared that the scientific results, unless they could be hidden or obscured, would have consequences that the state authorities disliked. Such consequences that may have worried them could have included a necessity to place increased pressure on some businesses to halt their most polluting activities. Moreover, there might also have been concerns that they would come under pressure to take resource-demanding measures to mitigate or adapt to the rising sea level.

The consequences climate dismissivists try to avoid by resisting climate data include a need for changes in lifestyles to reduce climate harm. These groups are also concerned that admitting the validity of the climate data would entail a loss of jobs dependent on fossil fuels. In my interview with Rob Bellamy, a social scientist with values around climate change and geoengineering (large-scale projects aimed at tackling the consequences of climate change, described in the Introduction, such as limiting some of the sunlight that reaches the earth or removing climate gases from the air) as his specialism, provided me with additional insights. Geoengineering is highly controversial both in the sciences and among politicians, and has been associated with both great promises and risks. Bellamy referred to an intriguing study done in the US on how the general public – both Republicans and Democrats – perceive climate change and geoengineering.[11] As a background to the study, Bellamy pointed out that Republicans are generally well known – far more so than Democrats – for being dismissive of climate change concerns. Still, something fascinating happened, Bellamy told me, when these climate dismissivists were presented with the possibility of using geoengineering to manage climate change:

> When the study presented Republicans who were sceptical to climate change with the idea of geoengineering the climate, they actually began to accept that climate change existed. The reason was that they liked the

prescribed solution of geoengineering. Geoengineering is a technology that kind of resonates very well with Republican values, which is basically about individualism and innovation an technology and all that kind of stuff.

I found it quite amazing that being provided with a possible tool for solving a problem that people don't believe exists could make them suddenly believe it does exist, simply because they like the tool (in this case geoengineering). The tools that Republican climate change dismissivists usually associate with climate change mitigation include big government and stricter regulations placed on businesses. They have been shown to worry that such strategies stifle innovation, industrial activity, and individual freedom.

In light of these and many other studies about climate change dismissal, Bellamy concludes by making this claim:

> The reason Republicans resisted knowledge about climate change in the past isn't because of the science. More generally, the deficit model is false. It basically says that if you give people more facts, they will change their mind. But that's not true.[12]

However, from the plausible belief that more facts are not sufficient in order to reduce knowledge resistance, it doesn't follow that more knowledge is a necessary part of such a reduction. George Gaskell, a researcher on public perception, expressed this well in our interview by pointing to the fact that most of us find education important:

> I've been at the university for forty years. The university system is based on the idea that it's a good idea for bright students to come here. Look, they didn't get brighter but they learned some things that they didn't know. The fact that we have educational systems [in most countries in the world] seems to me to suggest that there may well be some deficits [that societies find it important to reduce]. Relatively few countries have no education. So the whole thing [of denying that knowledge deficit plays a serious role for people and society] is daft, I think.[13]

So far, we have seen various sub-strategies within the running-away idea. People may sometimes resist the search for knowledge they assume will be true. Research on supercolliders is an example of this. It isn't so much the quality of the knowledge that may worry people here. In other cases, such as in North Carolina, we have the sub-strategy of obscuring or diverting attention from the knowledge that is available. However, one other sub-strategy that we introduced in the previous chapter is at least as common: dismissing knowledge by always questioning its quality and relevance. It is common for conservative newspaper columnists to deny or dismiss the reality of climate change. Far less often they admit that climate change is taking place, although they note the consequences of recognising, mitigating, and adapting to climate change would be too difficult. According to the environmental sociologists Elsasser and Dunlap, the latter type of stance would be interpreted as resignation and weakness. This would raise the issue of whether it wouldn't be reasonable to invest financially in projects that help reduce climate harm.[14]

Climate change is a topic which has turned out to be one where right-wing ideology correlates strongly with knowledge resistance. In other issues, some people that identify with a liberal and left-wing ideology also exercise knowledge resistance out of worries about cultural or political consequences. For example, in the introductory chapter we saw how certain groups keep demanding additional evidence that the measles vaccine is safe, even after scientists have examined this extensively. Some groups will never be satisfied, no matter how much evidence there is. One of the reasons no amount of evidence that the health benefits of vaccines outweigh the risks will be sufficient is not so much connected with health. Instead, the concerns surround a political economy where pharmaceutical corporations are immensely powerful. Digging under the surface of anti-vaccine groups we also find an aversion to authoritarian imperatives delivered by governments. Both these concerns that trigger knowledge resistance about health stem more from frustrations with politics than with the health aspects of vaccination.

When I bring up these examples, the following question comes to my mind: how do we know when people and groups are resisting knowledge due to concerns about the potential cultural and policy-oriented consequences, and not for other reasons? In many of the cases above, people haven't told us so; we have to interpret their claims. Here's an example of how this can be done. The case is a survey that I briefly mentioned in the introductory chapter in which 155 sociologists shared to what extent they agreed with some claims about biological evolution as impacting certain human conditions and practices. When looking at the results, it's easy to see a pattern. In issues where we could expect sociologists not to perceive risks of adverse cultural and political consequences of accepting a significant evolutionary component, the respondents were far more willing to do so. For example, 59.8 per cent of respondents accepted that our taste for sugars and fats has an evolutionary basis. That this is 'natural' was not politically or morally challenging for these sociologists to admit. Nor was it hard for them to admit that fear of spiders and snakes might have an evolutionary basis too: 49.4 per cent accepted this claim. When the issues were moved into power relations between women and men, the acceptance of a biological, evolutionary component was far lower. Merely 32.3 per cent agreed with the statement that the vast differences in violent crime levels worldwide throughout all time might, at least in part, be explained through biological evolution and genetics. That 'the widely observed tendency for men to try to control women's bodies as property' – through virginity cults, veiling, and other gender segregation – could be influenced by genes and biological evolution, albeit in interplay with cultural norms, was a statement with which only 22.7 per cent of the professional sociologists agreed.[15]

The pattern is clear: the respondents were less inclined to agree about genetic influences the more political and culturally sensitive the issue was. The investigators conducted in-depth interviews with some of the respondents to learn more about this. That worries about political and cultural consequences was a reason people resisted accepting knowledge about evolutionary influences (even where this makes up basic knowledge in neighbouring disciplines) was confirmed. For instance, one sociologist said:

> By emphasizing hard wiring due to evolution, there is an implicit acceptance of the behaviour as if there is nothing or very little that can be done to alter the behaviour or as if any such attempts are doomed and misguided. There is no incentive to consider the possibility of altering social envi-

ronments to reduce the likelihood of fighting, or bullying, or raping, or veiling/segregating women, et cetera.[16]

Another respondent expressed their concerns about consequences in this way:

> For me, the more important question is the kind of political possibilities and the ethical imperatives the two oppositional perspectives make available.[17]

Without engaging in a dialogue with these American sociologists, I learned about how they resist well-established knowledge. What I saw made me frustrated. How can so many people, even in my own discipline, compromise with the best available knowledge just because they are worried about its possible consequences? In my daily work, I am fortunate to meet and discuss similar issues with students over time. Such interaction can make all the difference – it can break down our knowledge resistance. Remember that we are equipped with an inclination to confirm our own current knowledge beliefs. One of the good things about discussing and debating with students is that they are not usually stuck with the same knowledge beliefs and values as my colleagues in our field. There is a higher chance of learning something new, and to have one's old beliefs challenged when speaking with students.

At Lund University in Sweden, I give courses in philosophy of science. Many of my students (women and men) have their intellectual background and identity in gender studies. Large parts of this field assume that gender differences can be fully explained as cultural and social products. Everyone in the class is happy when we analyse the vast majority of research papers showing that the similarities in abilities, behaviour, preferences, and so forth by far outweigh the differences between the sexes. Yet we occasionally run into studies that point to small but significant differences between women and men. I routinely make clear that such differences can only be found when researchers compare hundreds or thousands of women and men. Differences can never be found in every individual based on sex. Some studies of linguistic abilities, mathematical skills, or capacities for becoming an effective boss sometimes indicate small but significant sex differences when thousands of women and men are compared.

Without necessarily 'buying' the results of studies pointing to differences between the sexes where genetics and biology play a significant part, I always ask my students: 'What are your reflections and thoughts about these studies?' First, they question the validity of the research, by pointing out possible methodological shortcomings. This makes me pleased. Critical, methodological thinking is one of the course aims. Then I usually cannot help but ask the question again, but differently: 'What are your reflections and thoughts about these studies, if we assume that the studies are correct. Let's just for simplicity assume that the results reflect real differences between women and men.' At least five years in a row, students have formulated their responses as counter-questions: 'Why would the researchers of these studies want to find out about differences between women and men?' 'Why is such research funded in the first place?' I ask them to answer their own questions. They typically posit that the researchers are probably men or reactionary women who wish the results to point at such differences. Or that the scholars might want to go back to a more gender-divided society. Or that the researchers hope to show it's more natural for women to be home with children than to have a paid job. Based on these assumptions, some students conclude that such research, and the knowledge it brings, should be resisted. Some suggest that such research shouldn't be publicly funded. Another view has been that well-respected scientific journals shouldn't accept such studies for publication. Later, when students are asked to evaluate the course, some students – but only a few – have even suggested that such types of findings should be removed from the literature lists of university programmes.

Through the years of giving these courses it has been interesting to note that students problematise both the studies that point to better scores (in linguistic ability, mathematical competence, etc.) among women and girls as well as among men and boys. They have found both results annoying. Our discussions usually get new energy when I show the students studies showing that women on average have a higher ability in certain, traditionally male positions in society. My favourite is a study showing that women more often than men have a combination of skills – not least boldness – that is well suited for having high positions as business executives.[18] Students have reacted to this and similar studies by saying that they think such research results can have positive consequences for society, by puncturing myths about the alpha male leader. Then there are studies, not connected to skills as leaders, showing that women have better social and verbal abilities. The students normally assume that such findings risk societal acceptance of men's sociopathic or arrogant behaviour, arguing it could put more pressure on women to be even more socially flexible, caring, and empathetic, for instance in the workplace.

In my experiences from student discussions, as well as in some of the other examples mentioned throughout this book, there are two levels of knowledge resistance. On the upper, explicit level, people criticise findings and knowledge claims for their lack of validity, shortcomings regarding the research procedure, and so forth. Only when we dig deeper to understand the basis of such knowledge resistance is it possible to find the underlying worries. These – often nonconscious – concerns refer to the possibly dangerous consequences of accepting the findings, as well as concerns that the authorities who are supposed to minimise the risks and hazards are not trustworthy.

When I've discussed these things with students, as above, I've for long periods been confident in my own standpoint: I firmly believed that the running-away strategy, in all its shapes and versions, was plain wrong. In the following section, I will present the position that Huxley endorses in the quote earlier in this chapter. I still share Huxley's position in most parts. However, I will also show how my discussions with students have helped me reduce at least some of my categorical resistance to all aspects of the running-away strategy.

Combating

The 'combating' strategy never involves combat against knowledge as such. On the contrary, this strategy welcomes all systematic knowledge production and learning. Knowledge is amoral and neutral, subscribers of the strategy contend. As long as the knowledge claims are of high quality and validity, produced or at least scrutinised with scientific principles and methods, we should welcome them. However, as regards *applications* of knowledge in society, this strategy is more restrictive. With evolution by natural selection, for instance, Huxley – along with all other serious evolutionary scientists, as well as myself – refuse to translate its knowledge claims (even if they are valid) into societal norms and values. No knowledge about nature, including human nature, provides us with any valid prescription of what *should be done* in policies and culture. In the case of knowledge about evolution by natural selection, it reveals how ecological systems work. Natural selection is a ruthless, amoral process that causes much suffering. As such, we should learn as much as possible about evolution by natural selection. This will help us recognise its enormous, explanatory power about life on earth, including life in human societies. However, a primary reason we should learn about it is to be able to fight and compensate for the pressure it places on people and groups in society. This is what combating is about in this strategy. Combating implies taking continuous measures against the perceived 'natural' order that puts pressure on society to imitate natural selection. Measures include humane policies, regulations, and the fostering of cultural norms of solidarity.

To be sure, one could argue that it is natural for human societies to weave humane traits into its rules and conventions. Compassion has rarely been totally alien to politics throughout history. Archaeologists have found pieces of evidence from many corners of the world revealing that 'the weak' were supported long before the welfare state was invented. Compassion and empathy are natural human traits. In fact, these traits are major reasons for the survival of the human race, it could be argued. The claim about compassion as a human universal has a firm scientific basis, albeit with enormous differences between cultures. Still, the question of what is 'natural' and what is not is beside the point, proponents of the combating strategy maintain. They refuse to use arguments about naturalness as a basis for how society should be organised and regulated. Claims of naturalness can always be interpreted and exploited by groups of any political colour. That women should stay at home, that wars help society get rid of the weak, and that all types of private ownership should be banned are opinions that have all been promoted through claims that they are 'natural'. Instead, what Huxley calls 'the ethical progress of society' requires that we scrutinise the social, health-related, and environmental consequences before applying knowledge to norms and rules in society. In order to avoid the mistake that the imitating strategy does, we need to fill the gap between the knowledge ('is') and its use or prescriptions ('ought') through scrutiny and moral reflection. Nonetheless, we should welcome all knowledge that is of high quality; we should never shy away from any part of reality.

How does the combating strategy work in practice? Let's look at three different cases and assertions. First, social and economic inequality has some of its roots in the unequal abilities and situations that random natural selection creates for various groups of people. Second, diseases also have their roots in random natural selection (e.g. of virus and bacteria) combined with how societies are organised. Although the general process where diseases emerge cannot be removed, social institutions can ensure that their adverse effects are minimised – irrespective of any issue about 'naturalness'. Finally, climate change. The combating strategy does not in fact imply anything different concerning climate change compared to social inequality and diseases. These three cases are very similar, not only because they converge in regions of the world most affected by poverty. They all involve an integrated – inseparable – relationship between natural processes and social organisation. How we organise society makes an immense difference in social inequality. Diseases are also dependent on how society is organised, how close together people live, how much they travel, to what extent they use antibiotics, and so forth. As to climate change, there is a consensus in the relevant scientific communities that human activities have to a significant extent caused the phenomenon (through greenhouse gas emissions).

In none of these three cases would it make any sense to use the running-away strategy – resisting findings and knowledge about these problems, hoping that they can be 'ignored away'. Nor should research results about any of them be treated as directly providing us with any pre-scriptive lesson that could tell us which rules and norms should prevail. Those things should instead be developed through deliberations in the political, market, and civil society realms in close dialogue with science. With climate change, for instance, the combating strategy demands that we obtain as much as possible in terms of scientific findings, followed by extensive deliberation about what should be done to minimise the risks for suffering. It might be less important to what extent climate change is caused by humans. Far more important is how the resultant suffering should be minimised. Findings of climate change should not be seen as direct, normative calls for one measure, whether climate mitiga-tion, adaptation, or on preventing the diseases most likely to follow with climate change. Even in this case, the combating strategy prescribes an unlimited search for knowledge acquisition followed by social, political, and moral debate before deciding what priorities to make.

Annoyed by my dead certainty

My initial position was unequivocal: the first of the three strategies – imitating or applying knowledge without prior reflection in society – isn't only morally wrong, it's also a logical fallacy in the sense that it ignores the gap between 'is' and 'ought'. This fallacy is far more than philosophical hair-splitting. Failing in the face of ethical scrutiny between knowledge and how it's applied has many times had destructive consequences resulting in much suffering. I also held that the second strategy, of running away from knowledge, was also wrong. That strategy is rooted in a failure to separate knowledge as such and its psychological, social, and political contexts. The prescription of running away is noth-ing to do with the quality of the knowledge. Instead it has everything to do with the feelings of those asking us to run away from the knowledge: their background motivations and their worries about how the knowledge might possibly be applied in culture and politics. For instance, we saw how Trivers's 'I think "bombs"' quote at the beginning of the chapter can be reapplied to just about any other discipline. If we avoid every type of knowledge because of its origins or possible consequences, we should probably resist most knowledge. And that would be horrific. This was my thought as I rejected every aspect of the running-away strategy.

In classic, rhetorical style, I knew beforehand that the third strategy, combating, would be my clear favourite. It still is my favourite, to be sure. To repeat the overly apparent example, I – and hopefully most other people – would be absurd to prohibit knowledge about electricity just because it can be applied to torture or execution. Such knowledge resistance would make nurseries and hospitals dark and much medical equipment useless. By the same token, if society institutionalised a resistance to findings in nuclear physics it's humanitarian uses would also be resisted. A good friend of mine in Sweden who is a nuclear physicist runs a company called RaySearch Laboratories. He and his colleagues develop equipment and software for optimising radiation to treat malignant tumours. Their products are used in thousands of clinics worldwide. If the running-away strategy had been applied to his mother discipline, nuclear physics, they wouldn't have been able to develop and spread their lifesaving products. The point of the combating strategy seems to get things right here. No one knows beforehand how new knowledge will be applied. The company my friend took over (through a reverse acquisition) had, prior to his arrival, used partly similar nuclear physics methods but applied them to an entirely different problem area: oil prospecting. When my friend took over, he changed the application to cancer treatment. One type of knowledge may stimulate a palette of applications. All knowledge is welcome, the combat strategy prescribes. Still, extensive ethical deliberations are needed before the knowledge can be translated into practical applications, policies, or cultural norms.

I still evaluate the imitation strategy as bad, the running-away strategy as bad, and the combating strategy as good. Yet a couple of frustrations have stayed with me. The first is based on my puzzlement over having previously been so dead certain in my views. As we learned in Chapter 2, to stick to our own position and knowledge belief can often be associated with knowledge resistance. This includes using most intellectual and emotional energy to find arguments that support our current view. On the positive side, my frustration seemed to be a sign of the uncertainty I think is essential in overcoming the tendency to stick to one's old knowledge beliefs. That uneasy self-reflection could help people see that they don't really allow their own knowledge beliefs and opinions to be profoundly confronted by counter-arguments. The second frustration concerned my specific discussions with my students. I began to sense that I hadn't taken the students' counter-arguments into account thoroughly enough. One could certainly argue that it's unreasonable to resist knowledge as soon as there is a risk that one of its applications might be undesirable, as some students did. It's also untenable to resist knowledge due to 'guilt by association'. A lot of today's knowledge and competence – not least in medicine – albeit valid and useful, has a dubious or overtly horrific origin.

Still, how about situations where we *know* that the knowledge – if produced or spread – will doubtless be exploited in ways destructive to society? Should we never resist producing, learning, or spreading any knowledge? In an open society, it is common to hear that free speech must override other values. Should all knowledge production be there side by side with our freedom of expression? These have been the kinds of questions students have asked me for years. Next time I give one of these courses, I will conclude some of the debates in a different way than before. I will take some pride in including an answer that shows an effort to resist at least some of my own knowledge resistance: 'I don't know, yet.'

8

How to resist knowledge resistance – and when

When something needs to be done

So far, we have learned how and why people in all cultures sometimes resist knowledge. This understanding already exceeds by far the insight gained from merely following the one-sided, common-sense approach in the public debate about 'fact resistance' among 'the others', whoever they might be. Also, we have seen many examples where knowledge resistance doesn't need to be an entirely bad thing. A significant share of the population reports feeling better by resisting some of the genetic health information that is increasingly accessible. Also, building ignorance into schools and workplaces concerning grading and employment procedures could make them fairer. Finally, we have discussed how some knowledge resistance might be best described as 'strategic ignorance' in cases where some underprivileged groups avoid gaining political knowledge in areas where they are in effect excluded from having an influence. One could even argue that it is 'rational' for them to direct their knowledge-seeking somewhere else where they have a more significant chance of making a difference for themselves and their group.

However, gaining an understanding of knowledge resistance, its roots, functions, and versions is not the same as claiming that such resistance is good. Nor should we assume that knowledge resistance is impossible to change. It is true that seemingly problematic knowledge resistance – from climate change dismissal to denial of the possible benefits of genetically modified organisms (GMOs) in food production – usually derives from the overriding social motivation among resistant groups. I have stressed this point throughout the book: the fact that it might be socially rational to resist some knowledge doesn't have to mean that such resistance is acceptable or beneficial, particularly not to others and to society as a whole. Instead, it becomes crucial to ask what we as individuals and groups can do about knowledge resistance in cases where in the long run it is problematic to ourselves and to others – humans, animals, and the environment alike. This chapter will present and examine strategies that either have been proven effective or appear to be promising for reducing or preventing problematic types of knowledge resistance in ourselves and others.

First, however, a question needs to be addressed: how is it even possible to decide to remove the knowledge resistance of ourselves and others where it causes harm?

Can we just decide not to be knowledge resistant?

Saying that people should fight problematic knowledge resistance – including their own – is, to be sure, a well-intended remark frequently made by people seeking a common-sense approach. However, like a New Year's resolution, or suggesting that people avoid trans fats and sugar, it's quite easy to say but much harder to do. We have so far learned that knowledge resistance, like cravings for fat and sugar, under some conditions is deeply rooted in human evolution. Moreover, I have attempted to show how our two mental systems – the ones I call Apollonian (systematic and often slow) and Dionysian (impulsive, highly community-oriented, fast, and impulsive) – are interwoven and never entirely separate from each other. That the two are never entirely separable speaks against the hope that we could simply decide to override our Dionysian system with the Apollonian one in order to be less knowledge resistant.

This also means that the approach of behavioural economists, including the Nobel Memorial Prize laureates Kahneman and Thaler can only take us so far, and not the whole way towards overcoming problematic knowledge resistance. Their approach asserts that humans are to a large extent 'irrational'. Crudely put, all of us are failing computers. Sure, thinking of us as failing computers might be useful if all that matters to us is optimising the knowledge needed to make one highly specific decision at a time. Such decisions could be how to invest for our pensions, whether to decide that our organs can be used once we're dead, and so forth. Kahneman's suggestion is undoubtedly plausible. Computers will soon surpass humans in rational decision-making if we – like he – by 'rational' mean only substantively rational. This is the rationality that is aimed at optimising the satisfaction of specific, explicit goals. Through the years, Kahneman has provided numerous examples where computers and AI with their algorithms outperform human experts. The cases range from predictions of success for new businesses to future prices of wine from specific regions. His conclusion, which seems persuasive, is the following: 'In every case, the accuracy of [human] experts was exceeded by a simple algorithm.'[1]

A central reason why computers outperform humans in such cases is all the cognitive biases – our Dionysian system – that Kahneman perceives as preventing us from making optimal decisions and accurate predictions. The biases are manifested in some of the examples of knowledge resistance that we have explored in previous chapters. Kahneman's analysis is convincing, to be sure. However, his and other behavioural economists' perspective is highly insufficient for understanding what it is to be human. That requires us to focus on the social and evolutionary functions behind knowledge resistance. It's not enough to measure and assess people regarding skills where consumers have been constructed to excel. These skills have not been the most fundamental ones for our survival and reproduction throughout our long human history. These skills – of impartial, unbiased decision-making, strategically selecting the optimal amount of data given one explicit, substantive goal that is well demarcated – are not usually what triggers our strongest emotions and driving forces. (An exception is when we're deeply engaged in trying to solve a maths problem when it would be socially rewarding if we could solve it.)

The ideal of an unbiased computer mind is still very common. For instance, the perspective of behavioural economics subscribes to this ideal by examining the gap between it and how they show through sophisticated research that people actually make decisions. Behavioural economists seek to answer how it is irrational – in the sense described above – to resist knowledge about, say, evidence-based advice concerning how to lead a healthier life. Their research findings typically consist of an identification of biases – myopic bias, optimism bias, and (ideally) 'undiscovered' ones as well. Yet, the broader finding is rarely more than another contribution to the description of humans as faulty computers. At the same time, before I discuss my reverse strategy for managing knowledge resistance, I wish to make sure – of course – that I am not knowledge resistant to the rich findings that have been generated in behavioural economics. To recognise their conclusions helps us identify a set of strategies of how we could make ourselves and others relate to information and knowledge claims in a more Apollonian way.

Apollonian heuristics

There are a set of strategies built on an intuitive hope that is part of the common-sense approach of knowledge resistance: if we become aware of our flaws and biases we can decide to reduce their impact on how we handle information and knowledge. On the face of it, this seems close to simply choosing to be more open to well-grounded knowledge claims and only to resist bad ones. Still, some influential thinkers, not only behavioural economists, believe that it might just work.

I will illustrate this set of strategies through suggestions made by a social thinker, medical doctor, and global health-activist, Hans Rosling. Before he died in 2017 – a significant loss for anyone concerned with global health – he was a leading public intellectual trying to open our minds to real-world conditions concerning issues where we are peculiarly ignorant. Some of his suggestions can be found in his bestselling book *Factfulness*, which Microsoft founder Bill Gates rated so highly he offered a free digital copy to all students graduating from college in the

United States in 2018.[2] Since many of our knowledge beliefs either stem from or are influenced by traditional as well as social media, Rosling's propositions mainly concern how we could best relate to knowledge claims in media. He acknowledges that it is barely possible merely to pull ourselves together into thinking more like Apollo – unbiased, systematic, with statistical rigour, and so forth. At the same time, Rosling finds it crucial that we move a bit more in the Apollonian direction, and provides the readers of his book with tips for how to let the Apollo within borrow the main tool from the principle of the other (Dionysian) mental system, which is characterised by its quickness and shortcuts. The rapid heuristics, shortcuts, mantras, and so forth that Rosling suggests in order for us to gain a more factful understanding of the world are based on the Apollonian goal of truth-seeking combined with the Dionysian way of quick decision-making using limited amounts of information. Nevertheless, Rosling's strategy is intended to help us remove the impulsive, Dionysian claims impregnated by prejudice, stereotypes, and confirmation bias, and replace them with Apollonian, factful ones. This may help us to see reality through less coloured and distorted lenses, Rosling argues.

One distortion that we should try to control in our understanding of the world he calls our 'negativity instinct'. This is the same concept that behavioural economists and psychologists refer to as our universal negativity bias.[3] (Unsurprisingly, research on biases has also identified a positivity bias, also said to be universal – but that's another story.[4]) That many of us are equipped with a negativity bias makes evolutionary sense, surely. It probably helped our ancestors survive and produce offspring. Still, this bias causes us to fail to gain insight into the nuances of the negative and positive that happens in the world. When I teach students about risks and hazards in the fields of health, crime, and environment, I regularly have to face the challenge of the negativity instinct – not only my own but also among the students.

Several books and studies have been published that point to dramatic reductions in various risks globally. Steven Pinker's review of research on violent crime in *The Better Angels of Our Nature* is probably the best-known contribution to this topic.[5] To be sure, Pinker's book has been criticised for only calculating violence that is deadly, for interpreting the Cold War as a sign of increased civilised and peaceful political behaviour, and so forth. Still, given how he defines and studies violence, it is hard to dismiss his conclusion that violence has declined globally. When I've described Pinker's main findings to my students, some of them have found the results upsetting. Their impulse has been to categorise Pinker – as well as me, although I'm mainly the messenger – as ignorers of all the appalling violence that is still taking place in the world. I agree that he speaks far more about how things have got better than about what there is left to do in order to make the world an even nicer place. The former is the central meme that he is most eager to spread. However, it would be very unfair to conclude that Pinker doesn't recognise or doesn't care about the remaining problems with violence in the world.

Rosling makes more laborious effort to deal with this negativity bias, through an 'Apollonian heuristic'. On the one hand, Rosling shows impressive statistics about poverty, women in the workplace, child mortality, and so forth which demonstrate that the world has indeed become a better place. However, he stresses that this doesn't mean that he or anyone else claims that the conditions are good everywhere. Life is still undeniably bad – yes, even appalling – in many places. In sum, the world is both 'bad and better'.[6] Overcoming knowledge resistance about this makes it possible to learn from the places and problem areas where things have become much better than they used to be. It enables us to see how we can generate the same positive mechanisms in other sites and problem areas.

Another of Rosling's Apollonian heuristics is 'expect bad news', along with its sibling 'good news is not news' (in the eyes of media producers).[7] It captures the dual challenge that often leads people to resist solid knowledge about conditions in the world. We have evolved to be far more observant of risks and changes than of situations staying the same or showing gradual improvement. As it did our ancestors, this causes us a lot of worries and anxiety even in some situations that turn out to be harmless. However, it has also helped prepare us to prevent many risks and hazards, in turn increasing our chances for survival and reproduction. On top of our negativity instinct and alertness towards possible risks, there is the media's own bias in favour of reporting news about bad and risky events. These dual challenges are interwoven, of course. Media follows its own negativity instinct since we are genetically hardwired to be more interested in immediate, sensational risks – even if small – than in a grey, eventless status quo or gradual improvements that perhaps better characterises much of life in today's world.

When something negative is reported more actively in traditional and social media, we instinctively get the impression that things have got worse in that problem domain. The increased reporting about sexual harassment, triggered by the #MeToo movement, is easy to misunderstand as a reflection of a dramatic increase in sexual harassment in the mid-2010s. However, as I've shown elsewhere, increased media coverage is more likely to be a sign of the reverse.[8] A more accurate description of the escalated media coverage about sexual harassment is probably that after many years in which sexually harassed women tried in vain to make their voices heard, the cultural climate and social norms have finally recognised the gravity of such abuse to the extent that the media has finally considered it newsworthy.

The last of Rosling's Apollonian heuristics I will share here is most likely highly applicable to sexual harassment: 'Beware of rosy pasts.'[9] It is usually a sign of knowledge resistance to historical facts to believe that things were much better in the 'good old days'. By recognising these heuristics, Rosling hoped that this vicious circle of knowledge resistance about gradual improvements will be reduced in its force. Although it was beyond Rosling's main scope, we should also note that additional heuristics would need to be created to manage our knowledge resistance about the urgency of many problems that rarely emerge in the tabloid press.

The Apollonian heuristics that Rosling provides us with are indeed important. Bill Gates made an excellent decision by all accounts when he offered to give away copies of Rosling's book containing such perfectly accurate recommendations. However, this doesn't mean that Rosling's battery of heuristics is sufficient to manage and prevent knowledge resistance. These heuristics don't deal with people's deeper motivations and rationality: the social. To be sure, there are 'innocent' cases, where you – if you're a middle-class person in the Western world, for instance – have few or no cultural stakes. When considering the increased opportunities for girls to go to school in certain developing countries, for example, it ought to be fairly easy to replace your previously held image of endless misery with a recognition that things have become 'bad and better'. Fair enough. In fact, the heuristic 'bad and better' could be expanded to help us see more clearly the nature of knowledge claims in general. No knowledge claim is perfect in the sense that we can be sure that it may never be revised.

However, there is still an enormous difference in quality and reliability between different knowledge claims. Take systematically generated research findings of climate change, for instance. They are imperfect, to be sure, and may well need to be revised to some extent in the future. At the same time, the research findings are better – more substantial and more likely to be valid – than loose claims that climate change can't be happening since the weather is still cool from time to time. Thus, the best available knowledge is 'imperfect and better'. This is the complicated nature of most evidence-based knowledge about the world. This Apollonian heuristic should repeatedly be taught in schools, I hold. It would be a valuable resource for people when they interpret claims about the world and participate in public debate. Ideally, it would reduce the risk of being deceived by charismatic but unserious claim-makers who constantly appear in traditional and social media

At the same time, we shouldn't expect climate change dismissal, false beliefs about the risks of vaccination, or assumptions about the essential character of people of different ethnicities to go away by introducing people to Apollonian heuristics. Such examples of knowledge resistance have far higher social stakes. For the Apollonian heuristics to be successful in these cases, there seems to be a need for a willingness to reduce one's knowledge resistance in the first place. As we have seen in many examples in this book, such willingness is only likely to be in place once it converges with people's social rationality. Consequently, we need to broaden the battery of strategies. The battery should include strategies that facilitate convergence between the Apollonian goal of seeing the world more clearly and the Dionysian goal of strengthening social bonds.

Dionysian strategies

As we could see above, strategies that emphasise the Apollonian system in our minds are based on the question of how it is substantively irrational to resist the best available knowledge regarding a specific issue, such as how to lead a healthier life. As we move to Dionysian strategies the question will be the reverse: how is it socially rational in specific situations to resist knowledge about how to lead a healthier life? Let's take the case of smoking. Rather than identifying biases, the answer lies in an identification of concrete conditions where it seems to be socially rewarding to smoke. The short breaks at the workplace or college might be structured in ways that make it awkward to start conversations and get to know people. To share the habit of smoking during breaks might be a way of overcoming this challenge. Strengthening social bonds is often more emotionally rewarding to us than making every effort possible to maximise our longevity. This means that it ought to be possible to replace smoking by providing one or several other social icebreakers: perhaps a ping-pong or pool table.

Stated differently, instead of just trying to decide to reduce the knowledge resistance of ourselves and others, or of merely identifying biases, we should search for the social rationality behind the skewed handling of knowledge and information. How is the knowledge resistance tied to conscious or nonconscious assumptions about how the knowledge resistance will help the person or group maintain or strengthen its social bonds, esteem, and so forth? This approach is typically ignored in the simplistic complaints about knowledge resistance where all its instances are categorised as 'irrational' – as if getting the facts right in the world were the essential goal of humans. However, once we are familiar with these challenges it becomes possible to develop evidence-based ways of managing harmful knowledge resistance.

Here I will briefly mention three types of Dionysian strategy. By this I mean strategies that have been shown to resonate particularly well with our Dionysian system, while at the same time converging with more accurate handling of knowledge. These strategies have been introduced in various parts of this book already, but deserve to be repeated in a concentrated form here. The strategies and their different versions can be summarised as problem reframing, employing cognitive role models, and deliberative knowledge collaboration.

Problem reframing

One of the few issues where the human science disciplines covered in this book agree at least to some extent concerns the importance of problem framing. How problems are framed matters immensely for whether people from different groups will resist or recognise the validity of knowledge claims about the problem. To refresh our memory, framing is, roughly formulated, the organisation of complex and multifaceted issues into a meaningful, coherent, and manageable message or position – a frame. Crudely put, knowledge disputes come in two forms. The first is disagreements, which occur among people and groups that share a common frame for how to understand the problem. If we take a health example, a disagreement might concern how many glasses of wine (if any) are safe for pregnant women to drink in a week without harming the foetus. Mainstream science and the informed public share here one common problem frame, which is their fundamental knowledge belief: alcohol in more than minimal amounts is hazardous to unborn children. There is a cultural, Dionysian component in disputes in alcohol-related cases, to be sure. And that's not only because Dionysus is also the god of wine. Countries with a rich wine culture tend to be less restrictive in their recommendations to pregnant women of how much is safe to drink. At the same time, the case is Apollonian in the sense that scientific data can be expected to be recognised and taken seriously. If overwhelming evidence shows that two glasses is likely to be harmful to the foetus, we can expect it to be translated into revised recommendations to pregnant women in several countries. Essential to disagreements within a common frame is that knowledge quality is taken seriously. Knowledge resistance does not usually operate here. Instead, there can be some scepticism to specific knowledge claims, which can generally be resolved by showing more substantial scientific evidence.

In controversies, the second type of frame disputes, knowledge resistance is far more common. Controversies take place between two separate frames of understanding regarding the issue in question. An example can be found in the controversy over genetic modification in agriculture. On the surface, studies have shown that people in Europe, who have in general been more sceptical on this issue than people in the US, had a slightly lower understanding than Americans about GMOs. A striking finding was that more Europeans believed that non-GMO tomatoes had no genes, and that only GMO tomatoes had genes.[10] However, in my interview with George Gaskell, an expert on risk perception, he maintained that this difference in knowledge was in itself not very important for the different attitudes in the controversy:

> The crucial thing is not the absence of an understanding of genetics, but what that signifies is that they think of a genetically modified foodstuff as adulterated. There's something strange about that foodstuff.[11]

Stated differently, it was the differences in framings in this controversy that created an obstacle to a resolution. Since one side thought of GMO food as adulterated and the other didn't, it turned out to be very difficult to reach a resolution without reframing the issue entirely.

Why is knowledge resistance more often tied to controversies (between two different frames) than to disagreements (within one and the same frame)? The reason is that separate frames for how to understand the issue are usually held by people from different groups, cultures, ideologies, disciplines, and so forth. Examples of controversies include the death penalty, gun ownership, genetic research towards new cures of human diseases, evolution, and climate change. The Dionysian dimension is strongly tied to knowledge beliefs. When facts appear that support the knowledge claim of the frame other than our own, we have the impulse to resist such claims. Denial, dismissal, and diversion – strategies explained earlier in the book – are three kinds of knowledge resistance used in controversies. Our Apollonian dimension comes in after the instinctive resistance with the function of finding the most convincing ways of rejecting the other frame.

Sometimes seemingly subtle differences in framings may strongly impact how significant a proportion of people resist the knowledge claim in question. A study conducted by Schuldt and colleagues showed that significantly more people accept the assertion that climate change is taking place if it is reframed from global warming to climate change, the gap between believers and non-believers shrinking by 30 per cent. How could this be? To be sure, the term 'climate change' better captures what mainstream science agrees is happening. Still, the main difference between the framing of global warming and of climate change is that people conceive of the term 'global warming' as (even) more politicised than climate change. Conservatives, in particular, perceive global warming as something that belongs to a liberal-progressive belief system. Therefore, it is socially rational for many conservatives to resist claims about global warming.[12]

Based on what we've learned so far in the book, the following prediction is plausible: if the ideology-related polarisation in beliefs about climate change is to be reduced or removed, it will *not* happen by simply providing climate change dismissivists or worriers with huge volumes of substantial evidence showing that climate change is or isn't taking place. Instead, a reduced polarisation is far more likely to happen by reframing solutions to climate change, either as explicit goals or as positive side effects of other social, economic, and technological efforts. The following case concerning environmental pros and cons is one I prefer to remain agnostic about. Still, it is an illustrative example of such reframing. A number of pro-nuclear advocacy groups of environmentalists with names like Mothers for Nuclear, describing themselves in terms such as 'atomic humanists', have held a 'Nuclear Pride Fest' and other campaigns in Germany and beyond.[13] Such a reframing of nuclear power from a massive environmental hazard into a significant solution to the threat of climate change might make groups of various ideologies – including some traditional greens – reconsider which energy sources are preferable. More intriguingly, it may also cause some of the climate sceptics with preferences for large-scale technological systems to change their knowledge beliefs towards climate concern.[14]

I have argued in previous chapters that people and groups are often too quick in treating disputes as controversies between 'values', even when clear facts are available that the two sides have not become familiar with. If, for instance, people who are in favour of the death penalty learned that its application doesn't prevent crime but might even increase it, at least a few of these proponents might shift sides, I hold. At the same time, I admit concerning this case and many other controversies that the polarised views of either side seem immune to challenging facts. Consequently, to resolve controversies, there is a need for something other than merely better and more facts. Reframing can sometimes generate such resolutions.[15] To reframe an issue is to redefine it, giving people new associations of the issue and its meaning. We hear about reframings all the time in media and the public debate. At one point in time, a group might argue that there should be more women or people of colour on corporate boards. If reactionary groups are powerful enough in their opposition to incorporating diversity into the rules of corporations, the issue might be reframed into one that says nothing about fairness, but instead maintains that gender- and ethnically diverse boards make companies more innovative and productive. This reframing – if sufficiently supported by data – might resonate among shareholders to the extent that they pressure the company into enforcing diversity through a quota or the like.

Reframings can be particularly powerful if they are based on careful consideration of the differing 'moral foundations' of the groups that represent the separate framings in question. In Chapter 3 we discussed the view of moral psychologist Jonathan Haidt that leftists/liberals and conservatives often base their reasoning and convictions on different 'moral foundations'. I showed in that chapter how recognition of differences between the moral foundations – for instance about care, fairness, sanctity/purity, and authority – makes it possible to reframe several controversies into problem descriptions that better resonate with additional ideologies than before. Topics where this might be useful include climate change, vaccination, evolution, energy sources, immigration, and animal welfare.

Employing cognitive role models

Another Dionysian strategy is to use and spread information via what I call cognitive role models. Evolutionary psychologist and anthropologist Robin Dunbar is particularly well known for 'Dunbar's number', his calculation of how many friends we can develop trusting relationships with. Dunbar's perspective is strongly based on Darwinian evolution. In an interview for this book, he told me about an episode when he spoke to a large number of people who were very critical of the notion that humans had evolved through natural selection:

> I learned this a long, long time ago when I was in social anthropology in London. I was giving some first-year lectures, and I was going to introduce them to evolutionary biology and sociobiology, as it might have been called then. I made the mistake of thinking: 'The way to convince them is to just show them the evidence, just overwhelm them with evidence from all these studies.' It was completely the wrong thing to do. They just refused to believe it. All their discussion wanted to be at the conceptual, ideological level. So I started to think: 'I see what the problem is; I should not have presented any facts at all, and maybe we would have done much better.'[16]

Dunbar might have succeeded in making people aware of the fundamental principles of evolution. However, given his goal was to make people less knowledge resistant about evolution, his lecture was probably a failure. Why didn't it work? Because he only addressed the Apollonian dimension of people's minds while neglecting the Dionysian. Facts, logic, and elegant reasoning are often insufficient to make people lower their guard. Dunbar's delivery of facts and logical arguments would have made it substantively rational for the audience to recognise his knowledge claim as valid if their only goal was to gain more valid knowledge. However, such recognition wouldn't have been socially rational. When substantive and social rationality are in conflict, we tend to prioritise social rationality. This usually means sticking to the knowledge beliefs of the group that we identify ourselves as members of. Dunbar's audience were young social anthropologists who dismissed the knowledge claim that there is a genetic component behind social life. One way to manage their knowledge resistance would have been to reframe the argument in terms that resonated with this specific audience. In this case, he could have emphasised that people's genetics alone almost never determine their specific behaviour but rather prepare them for social and cultural learning, in turn generating behaviour. Moreover, he could have stressed, as I often do with my students with their solid basis in gender studies, that we should never accept as 'natural' the evolved genetic traits that make men on average far more violent than women, for example.

Another context with a similar challenge would be addressing people with a firm religious conviction that makes them identify more with a group that denies claims that we humans are the product of evolution by natural selection. To manage their knowledge resistance, you could frame the evolutionary process as an invisible hand (similar to what Adam Smith, the founder of classical economics, did concerning the dynamics of supply and demand). You could also reflect on the universality among humans in holding a spiritual belief. Finally, you could also admit that the issue of where evolutionary processes 'come from' is beyond science, and that this question might be better discussed by theologians or philosophers interested in metaphysics – and so forth.

There is another way that would further increase the chances of reducing the audiences' knowledge resistance: employing cognitive role models. As previously discussed, the actual identity of the person making a knowledge claim is irrelevant from the Apollonian perspective of logic and best available evidence. However, the question of who is making the claim makes an immense difference to the Dionysian dimension of our minds. Many groups of people tend to trust and accept challenging knowledge claims not just because the spokesperson is skilled at reframing the issue in a way that resonates better with the group. The individual who makes the challenging claim should ideally be a highly respected person in the group's community, sharing as many traits as possible with the rest of the group. Thus, Dunbar could have invited to his lecture a well-respected anthropologist who shared ideas and concerns with Dunbar's group of social anthropology students, but who recognised how valid and vital the evolutionary perspective is for understanding human and social life. To address our group of religious people, on the other hand, we could invite an open dialogue with a religious person who is well respected within the group, and who has incorporated the evolutionary perspective into her or his belief system.

There are numerous examples of cognitive role models that may help alleviate knowledge resistance. This could be particularly useful in problem areas where there is an assumption that only people of a specific ideology, faith, discipline, gender, or ethnicity can hold a particular knowledge belief. For instance, there is a movement of conservatives in the US who strongly endorse actions to mitigate and adapt to climate change. Jerry Taylor, the conservative vice-president of the free-market think tank the Cato Institute, is one such person. After many years rejecting the reality of climate change, Taylor has now become an outspoken, cognitive role model favouring climate action. 'How is that [climate change denial] conservative?' Taylor asks rhetorically.[17]

The role of a cognitive role model who has changed her or his mind from the conventional view in the group to the opposite view turns out to be particularly compelling. It assures others in the group that the person truly belongs there. Role models might play a role behind the fact that in the US, millennials – people born between 1981 and 1996 – who consider themselves Republican are twice as likely as older Republicans (36 per cent compared to 18 per cent) to recognise climate change as being caused by human activity. A hypothesis could be that these young conservatives are influenced by cognitive role models from wider circles than are older party affiliates.[18]

On the issue of whether humans have evolved through natural selection or by God's creation of Adam and Eve, there are also cognitive role models who try to manage knowledge resistance. For instance, there are evangelical Christians who give talks sharing their experiences of how they have come to recognise the basics of the Darwinian theory of evolution. They become cognitive role models showing others in the religious community that it is possible to accept evolutionary theory while at the same time remaining part of that community and holding the Bible sacred.[19] To show this cultural possibility is probably more crucial than showing a perfect coherence between evolutionary science and one's Christian convictions.

Similar efforts are made by people and groups who identify as environmentalists and greens but who have moved from strong opposition to endorsement of GMO use in agriculture.[20] Although being 'green' is often assumed to require rejection of GMOs, some people within communities of greens and environmentalists nevertheless seek to discuss the scientific findings regarding the risks and opportunities offered by GMOs in a way that moves beyond community-oriented, categorical opposition into an informed knowledge sharing. A major theme for discussion is what future we should envision for food security in light of various risks and uncertainties that involve all types of food production.[21]

Knowledge collaboration

Both the strategies of reframing and employing cognitive role models make use of our Dionysian dimension aimed at social bonding more than optimising the quality of knowledge. The last Dionysian strategy that we'll discuss is that of deliberative knowledge collaboration. Why include people from various backgrounds and competencies to create knowledge in collaboration? One reason is that diverse groups are, under certain conditions and in the face of some types of problems, better at producing knowledge than are single isolated individuals. I should make clear that it is not always that way, and the science about how to organise the production of knowledge in different problem areas is multifaceted and far from internally coherent in its recommendations.[22]

Still, some research has shown examples of how the quality of findings and problem-solving can be better with collaboration between people from various backgrounds.[23] I myself am working on a research project together with Anna Jonsson and Maria Grafström on why and how people from multiple organisations unite in so-called transdisciplinary research projects.[24] The term indicates that cooperation transcends academics. Individuals from industries, public authorities, nongovernmental organisations, and sometimes 'ordinary citizens' might also participate. Transdisciplinary knowledge collaboration takes place, for instance, in projects aimed at understanding and improving the quality of a particular lake or river. Other aims could be to learn how consumers could be persuaded to take environmental factors into account more when they make their purchases.

It's common in knowledge collaboration that the topics demand that many different types of information be collected and analysed. A lake or river project will need everything from water quality tests to interviews with the local population about what the lake or river means to them. Typically, the issues that these diverse constellations are studying are loaded with much uncertainty and controversies between separate problem framings. In the case of the quality of a river or lake, the following questions are likely to emerge: what is quality? Should lakes be free from any human activities – housing nearby, windmills, motor boats, recreation? How important is the water quality compared to permitting a wide range of human activities to take place there?

Sometimes in the project that I'm working on together with Jonsson and Grafström, an overwhelming number of issues have emerged in our interviews with various groups who are involved in collaborative knowledge production. This makes it difficult for participants in those collaborations to agree on what should count as 'successful' knowledge collaboration. Is it that the knowledge that is generated helps to solve a specific local conflict, such as a conflict about a lake? Or is it to make policy-makers more aware of dilemmas for making consumption more sustainable?

Another transdisciplinary research project that I've had the privilege of participating in concerned a different topic – sustainable consumption.[25] There, issues included the question of what should count as environmental impact from consumption in a country in the Global North. Should it only be the harmful emissions that it causes in that country, from its own factories, car emissions, and unrecycled waste? Or should environmental harm caused in the producing country – often located in the Global South – also be counted as a responsibility of the northern country where the product is consumed? These are issues that can't be solved by simple fact checking. They are interwoven with politics, economics, and cultural values in ways such that they are best resolved in knowledge collaboration far broader than only academic circles.[26]

More to the point of this book, luckily, we can with some certainty say that there are several signs that participation between people from diverse backgrounds can be a way of reducing knowledge resistance. At its core, this is a democratic issue. In nineteenth-century England, quite a few people – not just men and not only conservatives – were dismissive of the idea of allowing women to vote in political elections. Along with moralistic arguments about how women's pure souls would be soiled by being introduced to the filthy game of politics, there was an argument about knowledge. Opponents of women's suffrage might not have been entirely wrong when they complained that women on average didn't know much about the significant political issues out there in the world. (Few of these critics realised that people's private sphere also includes important political issues – for instance concerning liberty, equality, and justice.) The political philosopher John Stewart Mill was solidly in favour of introducing voting rights for women. His main argument was precisely the one that the critics had asserted: women were remarkably ignorant about significant political issues, and that was exactly the reason why they should have the right to vote. He – probably along with many women – realised that knowledge presupposes that people are included and are allowed to participate. By being allowed to vote there would be a motivation for women to become knowledgeable about issues related to voting and beyond. One reason for women's ignorance (if we allow ourselves to assume they were less familiar with big politics than men) was particularly apparent. How could they, after all, have been knowledgeable about political issues discussed in pubs, gentlemen's clubs, and political meetings, realms from which women were largely excluded? The exclusion of women was systematic and built into the structure of society. The other possible reason comes close to what we learned in Chapter 5, with its telling title question of 'what's in it for me?' Women, at least working-class women, probably had more urgent matters to concern themselves with than learning about the world of politics in which they didn't have a say anyway. To summarise, social inclusion and collaboration in knowledge production between different 'types' of people reduce the risk of ignorance and knowledge resistance, not least in areas where they are harmful to society.

A second reason why collaboration when producing knowledge may reduce knowledge resistance relates to another Dionysian aspect that was discussed in Chapter 3. It concerns how we as isolated individuals or highly homogeneous groups handle knowledge claims stemming from ourselves or others. When we are alone or only collaborate with others who are similar to ourselves, we tend to search too much for arguments and people who support and confirm our knowledge belief.[27] But knowledge needs to be continuously re-scrutinised and revised. The way for that to happen is to meet others whom we allow to scrutinise our claims. The research is clear here. We are far better at finding flaws in other people's knowledge claims than in our own. By opening up to others and identifying the weaknesses – and strengths, if our pride allows it – in the other person's reasoning, there can be a constructive pressure for us to reduce some of our knowledge resistance-challenging claims. Of course, whether such collaboration would benefit most from people with similar expertise and experiences or with very different ones has to be assessed from case to case.

A third reason why collaboration can reduce knowledge resistance ties to the theme of Chapter 7. There, we saw how some of our knowledge resistance can be derived from our concerns about cultural and political consequences if we recognise certain knowledge claims as valid. What happens if we accept assertions that women on average differ from men – albeit marginally and far less than two individuals – in specific patterns of behaviour and interests? If we give credence to the assertion that women are less active in arguing in favour of higher salaries, does this mean that we must accept the ongoing situation in which women often have lower salaries than men for the same type of work? If we accept the suggestion that climate change is created by humans, does this mean that we must also accept all the policies suggested by liberal-progressives? Although I hope and believe that the answers are no to both questions, such matters indeed demand open debate and collaboration to remove misunderstandings and conspiracy theories about the true motivations of academics with all their findings.

It is not unlikely that such misunderstandings about the necessary cultural consequences of some factual knowledge claims resulted in Ronald Reagan's both brilliant and opaque statement that we saw in Chapter 1 about liberals knowing 'so much that isn't so'.[28] A study shows that the general public perceives social scientific research as a search for evidence that favours these scientists' own ideology.[29] Conservatives, on average, hold this view more strongly than liberal-progressives. This difference is not difficult to understand. As Georg Lukianoff and Jonathan Haidt convincingly show in their book *The Coddling of the American Mind*, only a tiny minority of academic researchers in the human sciences, including the social sciences, are conservative.[30] Consequently, increased collaboration in knowledge production between people of different ideologies would possibly reduce the knowledge resistance that is rooted in suspicions of what hidden intentions might lie behind scholars' research.

Handling knowledge resistance requires joint effort

To summarise this chapter, let's repeat the question posed at its beginning. Can we just decide not to be knowledge resistant? If 'we' and 'decide' refers to a single individual who out of their own free will decides to be open to claims that challenge their own beliefs, I would be very hesitant to answer yes. One possible exception would be what in this chapter has been called 'Apollonian heuristics'. These are short and accurate phrases that may direct us towards a more balanced view of events in a world where media has a bias towards reporting negative and sensational events. Such heuristics include the recognition that the world is 'bad and better' and that we should 'expect bad news' since 'good news is not news'. Apollonian heuristics have the highest chance of reducing our knowledge resistance to positive developments in the world concerning issues where we don't have direct and strong social stakes. Getting a more balanced and nuanced understanding of world poverty and global health statistics could be such issues.

Such topics aside, we will usually need to use strategies that make use of our Dionysian dimension. This dimension is more geared towards social bonding and esteem than calibrating our own assumptions about the world perfectly with reality. One such strategy is to test our own assumptions with other individuals or groups ideally with different perspectives than ourselves. Our Dionysian dimension makes us – as individuals – far better at finding flaws in other people's reasoning than in their own. This is because the social, Dionysian function of argumentation is for the individual to win the knowledge dispute, not necessarily to generate the most valid knowledge. Thus, by debating with others and having others comment on our claims, this might force us to reduce some of our resistance to knowledge claims that challenge our previous assumptions.

The rest of the strategies presented in this chapter demand joint and organised efforts to reduce or manage knowledge resistance. This can be done by enriching knowledge disputes in the public debate with new types of problem framings. By making sure that the reframings include moral foundations that resonate with all groups involved – conservative, progressive, women, men, and other relevant categories – chances are that resistance to the best available facts is reduced. Bringing in cognitive role models who challenge their own group's knowledge resistance may additionally increase such chances.

Finally, as we will discuss more in the next and final chapter, we all live in social institutions that have a significant impact on what is socially rational for us to do – to be open to alternative knowledge claims or to resist them. Consequently, we need to address and revise the structural arrangements and incentive systems that seem to push us towards knowledge resistance in harmful ways.

9

On whether knowledge resistance is always bad, and other questions

We've covered a lot of themes throughout this book. Here I review and summarise its main findings. I do this by posing some questions about the book, followed by brief answers.

What's the most important reason we resist knowledge?

The most important reason we resist knowledge is that humans haven't evolved by being truth-seeking machines in our core. To be sure, we might sometimes wish that it would always have been in the most profound interest of humans to acquire the most valid knowledge. However, such an alternative 'human nature' would probably have made it impossible for our ancestors to survive and reproduce throughout hundreds of generations in hunter-gatherer societies. Instead, those generations of humans that have survived and reproduced from prehistory until today have been able to do so since they have been social to their core. When the goal of searching for the most valid knowledge has been in conflict with the purpose of maintaining or strengthening social bonds and esteem within our community, our social rationality often dictates – nonconsciously or consciously – that we should prioritise social bonds and esteem. This is where knowledge resistance comes in. Evolution even allows us to sometimes deceive ourselves in order to convincingly signal to others in our group that we are loyal to the dominant knowledge beliefs in the group.

What's the difference between sound scepticism and knowledge resistance?

Scepticism and knowledge resistance might at first glance seem like degrees of the same concept. If this were true, scepticism would have been mild and knowledge resistance more stubborn. However, they are in fact opposites. Scepticism implies the sound approach of demanding evidence, proof, or solid arguments before we are ready to accept a knowledge claim. This is how science should ideally work. To be sceptical is also often a good approach outside of science. In my interview with the evolutionary psychologist Robin Dunbar, he noted a similarity between ideas in society and genetic mutations (random changes in genetic information) that occur in the physical world all the time:

> If you look at the nature of evolution, 90 per cent of mutations are deleterious. What you're looking for is the 10 per cent or even only 5 per cent that are actually beneficial. It's the same with ideas. Scepticism to new ideas kind of makes sense. It's very frustrating when you know what the answer is, but it's probably wise.[1]

Knowledge resistance, in contrast, is almost immune to evidence, proof, or solid arguments. We still resist the knowledge that challenges our old beliefs. That scepticism and knowledge resistance are opposites is perhaps most apparent if we look at that close sibling of knowledge resistance: blind faith in certain descriptions about the world. Superstition is an example of blind faith where people are immune to counter-arguments that challenge their superstitious explanations. Scepticism is also the opposite of blind faith.

Is knowledge resistance always bad?

To the question of whether knowledge resistance is always a negative thing, the answer must be a clear *no*. This is something that unfortunately gets missed in the public debate and in many previous writings about fact resistance. To some people it might be good to resist specific health information through genetic screening or the like. Some people have been shown to prefer to avoid learning about genetically based prognoses relating to their lives. This could be a preference for some individuals in cases where they cannot reduce their risk of contracting a disease or would have to make immensely tricky decisions under additional uncertainty if they were given such information. It can also be beneficial in organisations – schools, universities, and other workplaces – to institutionalise ignorance about the ethnicity, gender, social class, sexual orientation, and so forth of students doing exams or of people applying for jobs. Finally, although it is terrible for society as a whole, it is hard to blame groups of people who are excluded from having influence in politics and planning when they avoid gaining insights into these areas. In a sense, they are rationally ignorant on such matters.

Can ignorance increase our freedom?

Ignorance is in some organisational settings seen as an asset that makes people think in novel ways. Some argue that people who are new to a field can be both more innovative and more scientifically path-breaking than those who have worked long in the field. To be 'ignorant' here seems to imply that people who are new to a field are the opposite of knowledge resistant: open-minded. In this sense, ignorance might increase our freedom. Moreover, we should recognise that the reverse is also essential: that freedom is needed in order to turn our ignorance into something valuable to society. This view of ignorance is found both in the research area called 'ignorance studies' and in studies on how best to organise research. To appreciate and make use of ignorance – naivety – where no questions are too foolish is here often presented as a recipe for novelty. On my colleague's office door ten metres from mine is a sign that reads: 'A safe space for stupidity'.

Ignorance comes in two forms relevant to this book. The first concerns things that we are aware that we don't know or understand. This is the favourite ignorance among many funding agencies supporting research and innovation. The reason that they like it is that being aware of what the world doesn't know increases the chances that their funding will generate research results. The other type of ignorance concerns things that we are not aware that we don't know. For researchers or innovators to explore such areas of 'double ignorance', they need more extensive freedom – time, money, and few directives. Funding agencies are often cautious here since the risk is much higher that their funding will not generate valid research results. But when it does, the findings can be novel and path-breaking. The examples in Chapter 6 about penicillin and the microwave oven illustrate this. These two cases point to the importance of giving people room and freedom to explore things that they aren't aware they don't know. To avoid giving researchers and innovators a degree of this type of freedom is, in fact, a way of exercising knowledge resistance.

The other side of the coin of freedom is responsibility. We have seen several examples of where people and groups exercise 'strategic ignorance' to avoid responsibility. From an egotistical perspective of individuals and organisations, certain ignorance makes it possible to avoid uncomfortable liability. By not knowing the harm that others suffer due to our own activities or how the work of one division of an organisation ties into that of our division it is sometimes possible to free ourselves from responsibility.

Are we more prone to resist certain types of knowledge?

Some evidence suggest that we are prone to resist certain types of knowledge. I'd like to argue that three factors operate in any knowledge claim in issues where we can't check the validity of the facts independently. These three factors determine whether the likelihood is high or low that the claim will be resisted or if it will be recognised as valid.

The first factor is the 'nature' of the claim. We saw earlier that it is particularly difficult for people to accept knowledge claims of long-term processes, such as climate change or evolution by natural selection. We are better prepared genetically to believe that things are fixed and static. Moreover, we are extremely good – too good – at accepting knowledge claims about two sides – good and evil, us and them, black and white –

and about what we should include or exclude in our lives. For example, we are inclined to divide substances into those that are absolutely bad and others that are absolutely good (for health, environment, and so forth). The 'bad' substances we perceive as poison. Some of us might include 'artificial substances' in that category, perceiving any amount of the 'bad' substances as hazardous. However, the fact is that which substances are healthy or unhealthy largely depends on the amount to which we are exposed, hence the strict instructions on medicines about the proper dosage. 'Natural' substances such as herbal remedies and supplements from the health store are often erroneously perceived as 'the more the better'. This misconception leads some people to consume overly high doses of these health supplements, which can actually cause various health problems such as liver and kidney damage.

The second factor is the way the issue is framed. If a problem, say risks of reduced biodiversity in the local region, is framed in such a way that the moral foundations resonate well among conservatives, chances are higher that conservatives will find the problem important. Such moral foundations concern purity, authenticity, a risk of contamination, sacredness, and the sense of regional identity. If we add a framing that connects risks of reduced biodiversity with increased harm, reduced care, and lack of fairness in terms of insufficient reciprocity with other cultural groups dependent on that biodiversity, this will resonate better with political liberals.

The third factor is which people and groups we associate with certain knowledge beliefs. If you identify yourself as a green or an environmentalist, you will probably be more likely to resist knowledge claims from science that indicate low or non-existent levels of risk to health or the environment from genetically modified agriculture. However, if you see that others who you identify as greens or environmentalists begin to accept such results as valid, chances are that you will be prepared to challenge your old belief that such agricultural methods are hazardous.

Again, these three factors interact. The second and third factors are mainly about culture and social context. Still, the first factor – about the essential character of an issue – also seems to play an important role.

What's the most effective way of reducing knowledge resistance?

The best way of reducing knowledge resistance has actually been implied in almost all chapters of this book. As we have come to the end of the book, it deserves to be spelled out more clearly. I'm thinking about adjustments of structures – both formal rules and informal norms – that make it socially rational to resist knowledge. Debates and analyses that use the term 'fact resistance' are typically limited to a focus on how individuals and groups act out of free will. However, when people and groups resist knowledge, they don't do it as independent actors making free and active choices. These and other recent lessons from the human sciences need to be incorporated into an update of Enlightenment thinking in order to handle society's problematic knowledge resistance in comprehensive and more informed ways. Single individuals often don't have the power to overcome knowledge resistance. Instead, social structures and incentive systems typically have a substantial influence over what knowledge people find accessible and relevant. Therefore, we all need to look behind – and around – the individual and group: at the social norms, structures, and social contexts that people and groups live through.

Differences in individuals – for instance between scientists and non-scientists – are often secondary to differences in structures and norms, for example between a religious and scientific community. Ideally, scientific communities have a strong norm (at least verbally) that prescribes openness towards new and challenging data. However, in a scientific environment where such a normative basis is absent, scientists – as the human beings they are – are likely to deviate from this norm. They might gear themselves towards knowledge resistance not just by ignoring rival disciplines but also by compromising scientific rigour in their own.

A definite threat to open knowledge exchange and scepticism can be found in the field of psychology. In 2012 a survey of the 100 most high-ranking journals in psychology showed that only 1 per cent of their published papers were aimed at re-testing (replicating) previous knowledge claims in psychology to see if they were valid.[2] To scrutinise other scientists' research – something that we have learned is crucial given our universal confirmation bias – is a task that is unfortunately given fairly low status in the research community. This means it is not socially rational for a research psychologist to scrutinise the claims of others in this deep way of trying to assess if it's possible to replicate their findings. Scientific journals, research foundations, and universities should make conscious and strategic efforts to raise the status of such unappreciated research efforts of testing the replicability of past studies.

Another structural measure to reduce knowledge uncertainty is to favour and reward collaboration in knowledge production between people of different ideologies, perspectives, and disciplines. This book has particularly shown how disciplines resist the knowledge of others. Debates are becoming increasingly widespread about the pervasive problem that universities are too ideologically homogeneous. Most university professors in the Western world are liberals or liberal-progressives (in the US sense). Critics see how this homogeneity reduces the acceptance of open debate between people with conflicting knowledge claims. The one-sidedness can be seen in many sectors of society. By one-sidedness I don't mean liberal-progressive one-sidedness in particular, but a tendency to only repeat and recycle knowledge and ideas among people who are like ourselves – whether liberal-progressive, conservative, orthodox religious, and so on.

This book has shed some new light on how and why we resist the knowledge of others in many realms of life. Hopefully, this light will help you identify dark spots between the circles of your community and others where you can contribute to bolder knowledge exchange. I'll try to do the same.

Notes

Introduction

1 Roald Dahl, 'Death of Olivia', on Roald Dahl's official website, accessed 13 February 2019, www.roalddahl.com/roald-dahl/timeline/1960s/november-1962.

2 A. J. Wakefield *et al.*, 'RETRACTED: Ileal-Lymphoid-Nodular Hyperplasia, Non-Specific Colitis, and Pervasive Developmental Disorder in Children', *Lancet* 351, no. 9103 (28 February 1998): 637–41, https://doi.org/10.1016/S0140-6736(97)11096-0.

3 Lindzi Wessel, 'Four Vaccine Myths and Where They Came From', *Science*, 27 April 2017, https://doi.org/10.1126/science.aal1110.

4 Stanley Plotkin, Jeffrey S. Gerber, and Paul A. Offit, 'Vaccines and Autism: A Tale of Shifting Hypotheses', *Clinical Infectious Diseases* 48, no. 4 (15 February 2009): 456–61, https://doi.org/10.1086/596476.

5 Centers for Disease Control and Prevention, 'Measles Vaccination', last updated 22 November 2016, www.cdc.gov/measles/vaccination.html.

6 Heidi J. Larson *et al.*, 'The State of Vaccine Confidence 2016: Global Insights Through a 67-Country Survey', *EBioMedicine* 12 (13 September 2016): 295–301, https://doi.org/10.1016/j.ebiom.2016.08.042.

7 Kai Kupferschmidt, 'Can Skeptical Parents Be Persuaded to Vaccinate?', *Science*, 27 April 2017, https://doi.org/10.1126/science.aal1108.

8 Hans Rosling, Anna Rosling Rönnlund, and Ola Rosling, *Factfulness: Ten Reasons We're Wrong About the World – and Why Things Are Better Than You Think* (New York: Sceptre, 2018).

9 D. J. Flynn, Brendan Nyhan, and Jason Reifler, 'The Nature and Origins of Misperceptions: Understanding False and Unsupported Beliefs About Politics', *Political Psychology* 38 (February 2017): 127–50.

10 Mark Horowitz, William Yaworsky, and Kenneth Kickham, 'Whither the Blank Slate? A Report on the Reception of Evolutionary Biological Ideas among Sociological Theorists', *Sociological Spectrum* 34, no. 6 (2 November

2014): 489–509, https://doi.org/10.1080/02732173.2014.947451; also Chris Mooney, 'Liberals Deny Science, Too', *Washington Post*, 28 October 2014, Wonkblog, www.washingtonpost.com/news/wonk/wp/2014/10/28/liberals-deny-science-too/.

11 David M. Buss, *The Dangerous Passion: Why Jealousy Is as Necessary as Love and Sex*, 1st printed edn (New York: Free Press, 2000), 5.

12 Mikael Klintman, Thomas Lunderquist, and Andreas Olsson, *Gruppens grepp: Hur vi fördomsfulla flockvarelser kan lära oss leva tillsammans* (Stockholm: Natur & Kultur, 2018).

13 Horowitz, Yaworsky, and Kickham, 'Whither the Blank Slate?', 506; see also Mooney, 'Liberals Deny Science, Too'.

14 Frank Newport and Andrew Dugan, 'College-Educated Republicans Most Skeptical of Global Warming', Gallup, 26 March 2015, http://news.gallup.com/poll/182159/college-educated-republicans-skeptical-global-warming.aspx; Frank Newport, 'Where Americans Stand on the Environment, Energy', Gallup, 22 March 2018, http://news.gallup.com/opinion/gallup/231386/new-series-americans-stand-environment-energy.aspx.

15 This study can be found in Dan M. Kahan *et al.*, 'Geoengineering and Climate Change Polarization: Testing a Two-Channel Model of Science Communication', *Annals of the American Academy of Political and Social Science* 658, no. 1 (March 2015): 192–222.

16 Nicole A. Cooke, *Fake News and Alternative Facts: Information Literacy in a Post-Truth Era* (Chicago: American Library Association, 2018); Lee McIntyre, *Post-Truth* (Cambridge, MA: MIT Press, 2018).

17 Daniel Levitin, *A Field Guide to Lies and Statistics: A Neuroscientist on How to Make Sense of a Complex World* (New York: Penguin, 2018); Rosling, Rönnlund, and Rosling, *Factfulness*.

18 Pierre L. van den Berghe, 'Why Most Sociologists Don't (and Won't) Think Evolutionarily', *Sociological Forum* 5, no. 2 (June 1990): 173–85; see also McIntyre, *Post-Truth*; Cooke, *Fake News and Alternative Facts*.

19 See, for example, Steven Sloman, *The Knowledge Illusion: Why We Never Think Alone* (New York: Riverhead Books, 2017), on cognitive science; Carol Tavris and Elliot Aronson, *Mistakes Were Made (but Not by Me): Why We Justify Foolish Beliefs, Bad Decisions, and Hurtful Acts* (Boston: Mariner Books, 2015), on cognitive psychology; Richard H. Thaler, *Misbehaving: The Making of Behavioral Economics*, 1st edn (New York: W. W. Norton and Company, 2015); Levitin, *A Field Guide to Lies and Statistics*; Rosling, Rönnlund, and Rosling, *Factfulness*.

20 Carlo Prato and Stephane Wolton, 'Rational Ignorance, Populism, and Reform', *European Journal of Political Economy* 55 (December 2017), 119–35, https://doi.org/10.1016/j.ejpoleco.2017.11.006.

21 cf. Erin B. Godfrey, Carlos E. Santos, and Esther Burson, 'For Better or Worse? System-Justifying Beliefs in Sixth-Grade Predict Trajectories of

Self-Esteem and Behavior Across Early Adolescence', *Child Development* 90, no. 1 (19 June 2017): 180–95, https://doi.org/10.1111/cdev.12854.

22   Richard H. Thaler and Prof. Cass R. Sunstein, *Nudge: Improving Decisions About Health, Wealth, and Happiness,* 1st edn (New Haven: Yale University Press, 2008); Daniel Kahneman, *Thinking, Fast and Slow,* reprint edition (New York: Farrar, Straus and Giroux, 2011).

23   Omer Shubert, 'Bloody Backlash: While Veganism Thrives, Meat Lovers Are Establishing a Hardcore Carnivore Underground in Israel', *Haaretz,* 13 March 2018, www.haaretz.com/israel-news/.premium.MAGAZINE-backlash-to-veganism-israel-s-hardcore-carnivore-underground-1.5896025; for the latter issue of vegan–carnivore dynamics, see, for example, Dominique Lestel, 'The Carnivore's Ethics', *Angelaki: Journal of the Theoretical Humanities* 19, no. 3 (September 2014): 161–7, https://doi.org/10.1080/0969725X.2014.976066.

24   Pilita Clark, 'Chronic Unease Is a Fine State of Mind', *Financial Times,* 20 May 2018, www.ft.com/content/354ea53c-59bb-11e8-bdb7-f6677d2e1ce8; L. S. Fruhen, R. H. Flin, and R. McLeod, 'Chronic Unease for Safety in Managers: A Conceptualisation', *Journal of Risk Research* 17, no. 8 (14 September 2014): 969–79, https://doi.org/10.1080/13669877.2013.822924.

1   What knowledge resistance isn't and a hint at what it is

1   Søren Kierkegaard, *Kierkegaard's Writings, XVI, Volume 16: Works of Love* (Princeton: Princeton University Press, [1847] 2013), 9.

2   Ted Scheinman, 'What Lies Beneath: Why Do Archaeological Fraudsters Work So Hard to Deceive Us?', *Aeon,* 28 July 2015, Essays, https://aeon.co/essays/why-do-archaeological-fraudsters-work-so-hard-to-deceive-us.

3   Carol A. Heimer, 'Inert Facts and the Illusion of Knowledge: Strategic Uses of Ignorance in HIV Clinics', *Economy and Society* 41, no. 1 (February 2012): 17–41, https://doi.org/10.1080/03085147.2011.637332; Scheinman, 'What Lies Beneath'; Miles Russell, *Piltdown Man: The Secret Life of Charles Dawson* (Stroud: Tempus, 2004).

4   Doug Parr, 'Greenpeace: This Is Why We Stand Against GM Crops', *New Scientist,* 23 October 2014, www.newscientist.com/article/dn26445-greenpeace-this-is-why-we-stand-against-gm-crops/; Edward Royzman, Corey Cusimano, and Robert F. Leeman, 'What Lies Beneath? Fear vs. Disgust as Affective Predictors of Absolutist Opposition to Genetically Modified Food and Other New Technologies', *Judgment and Decision Making* 12, no. 5 (September 2017): 466–80.

5   Chen Zhang, R. Wohlhueter, and Han Zhang, 'Genetically Modified Foods: A Critical Review of Their Promise and Problems', *Food Science and Human Wellness* 5, no. 3 (1 January 2016): 116–23; Parr, 'Greenpeace: This Is Why We Stand against GM Crops'; Royzman, Cusimano, and Leeman, 'What Lies Beneath?'.

6   Karl Raimund Popper, *The Logic of Scientific Discovery* (London: Psychology Press, 1959); William A. Gorton, *Karl Popper and the Social Sciences*, SUNY Series in the Philosophy of the Social Sciences (Albany: State University of New York Press, 2006).

7   Christian Pfeiffer, Dirk Baier, and Soeren Kliem, 'Zur Entwicklung der Gewalt in Deutschland. Schwerpunkte: Jugendliche und Flüchtlinge Als Täter und Opfer' ('Teenagers as Perpetrators and Victims'), research report (Zürich: Zürcher Hochschule für Angewandte Wissenschaften, January 2018.

8   John Archer, 'Does Sexual Selection Explain Human Sex Differences in Aggression?', *Behavioral and Brain Sciences* 32, no. 3–4 (August 2009): 249, https://doi.org/10.1017/S0140525X09990951; Anne Campbell, 'The Evolutionary Psychology of Women's Aggression', *Philosophical Transactions of the Royal Society B: Biological Sciences* 368, no. 1631 (5 December 2013), https://doi.org/10.1098/rstb.2013.0078; Martin Daly and Margo Wilson, *Homicide: Foundations of Human Behavior* (London: Routledge, 2017).

9   Kahneman, *Thinking, Fast and Slow*.

10 Friedrich Nietzsche, *The Birth Of Tragedy* (Whitefish: Kessinger Publishing, [1872] 2010).

11 S. Jouffre and J.-C. Croizet, 'Empowering and Legitimizing the Fundamental Attribution Error: Power and Legitimization Exacerbate the Translation of Role-Constrained Behaviors into Ability Differences', *European Journal of Social Psychology* 46, no. 5 (August 2016): 621–31, https://doi.org/10.1002/ejsp.2191.

12 George A. Kourvetaris, 'The Dionysian and Apollonian Dimensions of Ethnicity: A Convergence Model', *International Review of Sociology* 7, no. 2 (July 1997): 229–37.

13 Hugo Mercier and Christophe Heintz, 'Scientists' Argumentative Reasoning', *Topoi* 33, no. 2 (October 2014): 513–24, https://doi.org/10.1007/s11245-013-9217-4.

14 Mikael Klintman, *Human Sciences and Human Interests: Integrating the Social, Economic, and Evolutionary Sciences* (London: Routledge, 2017); cf. Antonio Damasio, *Descartes' Error: Emotion, Reason and the Human Brain* (London: Vintage, 2006).

15 Hardcore and softcore relativism are my less technical formulations of what the philosopher Roy Bhaskar calls judgmental and epistemic relativism; Roy Bhaskar, *Scientific Realism and Human Emancipation*, 1st edn (London: Routledge, 1986), 72.

16 Javier Lezaun, interview with the author, 5 February 2018.

17 James A. Heathcote, 'Why Do Old Men Have Big Ears?', *British Medical Journal*, no. 7021 (1995): 1668.

18 Juan M. Toro, Josep B. Trobalon, and Núria Sebastián-Gallés, 'Effects of

Backward Speech and Speaker Variability in Language Discrimination by Rats', *Journal of Experimental Psychology. Animal Behavior Processes* 31, no. 1 (January 2005): 95–100.

19 R. A. J. Matthews, 'Tumbling Toast, Murphy's Law and the Fundamental Constants', *European Journal of Physics* 16, no. 4 (18 July 1995): 172–6, https://doi.org/10.1088/0143-0807/16/4/005.

20 cf. Alice H. Eagly and Shelly Chaiken, *The Psychology of Attitudes* (Fort Worth: Harcourt Brace Jovanovich, 1993); Elizabeth Shove, 'Beyond the ABC: Climate Change Policy and Theories of Social Change', *Environment and Planning A* 42, no. 6 (2010): 1273–85, https://doi.org/10.1068/a42282.

21 Lorraine Whitmarsh, Gill Seyfang, and Saffron O'Neill, 'Public Engagement with Carbon and Climate Change: To What Extent Is the Public "Carbon Capable"?', *Global Environmental Change* 21, no. 1 (February 2011): 56–65, https://doi.org/10.1016/j.gloenvcha.2010.07.011.

22 Gaston Godin, Mark Conner, and Paschal Sheeran, 'Bridging the Intention–Behaviour Gap: The Role of Moral Norm', *British Journal of Social Psychology* 44, no. 4 (1 December 2005): 497–512, https://doi.org/10.1348/014466604X17452; Whitmarsh, Seyfang, and O'Neill, 'Public Engagement with Carbon and Climate Change'.

23 Mikael Klintman, *Citizen-Consumers and Evolution: Reducing Environmental Harm through Our Social Motivation* (Basingstoke: Palgrave Pivot, 2012); Magnus Boström and Mikael Klintman, 'Can We Rely on "Climate-Friendly" Consumption?', *Journal of Consumer Culture*, 12 July 2017, 1–20, https://doi.org/doi.org/10.1177/1469540517717782.

24 Leon Festinger, *A Theory of Cognitive Dissonance*, 1st edn (Stanford: Stanford University Press, 1957).

25 Pew Research Center, 'Americans, Politics and Science Issues', published on the Pew Research Center website, 1 July 2015, www.pewinternet.org/2015/07/01/americans-politics-and-science-issues/; Matthews, 'Tumbling Toast'.

26 Andy Borowitz, 'Scientists: Earth Endangered by New Strain of Fact-Resistant Humans', *New Yorker*, 12 May 2015, www.newyorker.com/humor/borowitz-report/scientists-earth-endangered-by-new-strain-of-fact-resistant-humans; Tiziano Gomiero, David Pimentel, and Maurizio G. Paoletti, 'Environmental Impact of Different Agricultural Management Practices: Conventional vs. Organic Agriculture', *Critical Reviews in Plant Sciences* 30, no. 1–2 (2011): 95–124, https://doi.org/10.1080/07352689.2011.554355.

27 Mike Pence, 'Theory of the Origin of Man', *Congressional Record: Proceedings and Debates of the US Congress*, 11 July 2002, www.congress.gov/congressional-record/2002/7/11/house-section/article/h4527-1; Kahneman, *Thinking, Fast and Slow*; Thaler and Sunstein, *Nudge*.

28 Charles Darwin, *On the Origin of Species: By Means of Natural Selection*, Dover Giant Thrift edn (Mineola: Dover Publications, [1859] 2012).

29 Ronald Reagan, 'A Time for Choosing' (speech, 27 October 1964), *The Constitution Reader*, accessed 13 February 2019, http://cdn.constitution reader.com/files/pdf/constitution/ch123.pdf.

30 Jeremy A. Frimer, Linda J. Skitka, and Matt Motyl, 'Liberals and Conservatives Are Similarly Motivated to Avoid Exposure to One Another's Opinions', *Journal of Experimental Social Psychology* 72 (1 September 2017): 1–12, https://doi.org/10.1016/j.jesp.2017.04.003.

31 Raymond S. Nickerson, 'Confirmation Bias: A Ubiquitous Phenomenon in Many Guises', *Review of General Psychology* 2, no. 2 (1998): 175–220, https://doi.org/10.1037/1089-2680.2.2.175.

32 Mercier and Heintz, 'Scientists' Argumentative Reasoning'.

33 Michael Shermer, *Why People Believe Weird Things: Pseudoscience, Superstition, and Other Confusions of Our Time* (New York: Souvenir, 2007).

34 Stewart Elliott Guthrie, *Faces in the Clouds: A New Theory of Religion*, 1st edn (Oxford: Oxford University Press, 1995).

35 To give Shermer his dues, he later made some remarks along these lines elsewhere; see Michael Shermer, 'How to Convince Someone When Facts Fail', *Scientific American*, 1 January 2017, https://doi.org/10.1038/scientifi-american0117-69.

36 Klintman, *Human Sciences and Human Interests*.

37 I have examined such issues within a large Swedish research programme, MISTRA Sustainable Consumption, which is due to run from 2017 to 2021. The programme leaders are Åsa Svenfelt and Karin Bradley.

2 If you're with us, don't believe them

1 Frimer, Skitka, and Motyl, 'Liberals and Conservatives Are Similarly Motivated'.

2 Gordon Gauchat, 'Politicization of Science in the Public Sphere: A Study of Public Trust in the United States, 1974 to 2010', *American Sociological Review* 77, no. 2 (April 2012): 167–87, https://doi.org/10.1177/0003122412438225.

3 Stephanie Hanes, 'To Spank or Not to Spank: Corporal Punishment in the US', *Christian Science Monitor*, 19 October 2014, www.csmonitor.com/USA/Society/2014/1019/To-spank-or-not-to-spank-Corporal-punishment-in-the-US; E. T. Gershoff and A. Grogan-Kaylor, 'Spanking and Child Outcomes: Old Controversies and New Meta-Analyses', *Journal of Family Psychology* 30, no. 4 (June 2016): 453–69, https://doi.org/10.1037/fam0000191.

4 Bastiaan T. Rutjens, Robbie M. Sutton, and Romy van der Lee, 'Not All Skepticism Is Equal: Exploring the Ideological Antecedents of Science Acceptance and Rejection', *Personality and Social Psychology Bulletin* 44, no. 3 (2018): 384–405.

5 Timur Kuran, *Private Truths, Public Lies: The Social Consequences of Preference Falsification* (Cambridge, MA: Harvard University Press, 1998).

Notes

6   A. Shtulman, 'Qualitative Differences between Naïve and Scientific Theories of Evolution', *Cognitive Psychology* 52, no. 2 (March 2006): 170–94, https://doi.org/10.1016/j.cogpsych.2005.10.001.

7   Paul Bloom and Deena Skolnick Weisberg, 'Childhood Origins of Adult Resistance to Science', *Science* 316, no. 5827 (2007): 996–7.

8   Stephan Lewandowsky, Gilles E. Gignac, and Klaus Oberauer, 'The Role of Conspiracist Ideation and Worldviews in Predicting Rejection of Science', *PLOS ONE* 8, no. 10 (October 2013): e75637, https://doi.org/10.1371/journal.pone.0075637.

9   Patrick Kingsley, 'Turkey Drops Evolution from Curriculum, Angering Secularists', *New York Times*, 23 June 2017, Europe, www.nytimes.com/2017/06/23/world/europe/turkey-evolution-high-school-curriculum.html.

10 Jon D. Miller, Eugenie C. Scott, and Shinji Okamoto, 'Public Acceptance of Evolution', *Science* 313, no. 5788 (11 August 2006): 765–6. https://doi.org/10.1126/science.1126746.

11 See Kevin Simler and Robin Hanson, *The Elephant in the Brain: Hidden Motives in Everyday Life*. (Oxford: Oxford University Press, 2017).

12 Allan Dafoe, interview with the author, 26 April 2018.

13 P. Diethelm and M. McKee, 'Denialism: What Is It and How Should Scientists Respond?', *European Journal of Public Health* 19, no. 1 (January 2009): 2–4; cf. Simler and Hanson, *The Elephant in the Brain*.

14 Robert Merton, 'The Normative Structure of Science', in *The Sociology of Science: Theoretical and Empirical Investigations* (Chicago: University of Chicago Press, 1942), 267–78.

15 Boström and Klintman, 'Can We Rely on "Climate-Friendly" Consumption?'.

16 Simon Jenkins, 'It's Not Only the Queen. We're All Screaming for an Answer', *Guardian*, 12 November 2008, Opinion, www.theguardian.com/commentisfree/2008/nov/12/queen-economy-recession-lse.

17 Walter Houston, *Purity and Monotheism: Clean and Unclean Animals in Biblical Law* (Sheffield: Sheffield Academic Press, 2009).

18 Mary Douglas, *Purity and Danger: An Analysis of the Concepts of Pollution and Taboo* (London: Routledge and Kegan Paul, 1978); Peter L. Berger, *The Many Altars of Modernity: Toward a Paradigm for Religion in a Pluralist Age* (Boston: De Gruyter Mouton, 2014).

19 Thomas S. Kuhn, *The Structure of Scientific Revolutions*, 50th anniversary edn (Chicago: University of Chicago Press, [1962] 2012); Douglas, *Purity and Danger*; Berger, *The Many Altars of Modernity*.

20 Stephanie Solomon, 'Kuhn's Alternative Path: Science and the Social Resistance to Criticism', *Perspectives on Science*, no. 3 (2010): 352.

21 Kuhn, *The Structure of Scientific Revolutions*.

22 Robin Dunbar, interview with the author, 13 February 2018.

23 Mary Douglas, *How Institutions Think* (New York: Syracuse University Press, 1986).

24 Douglas, *How Institutions Think*, 76.

25 Linsey McGoey, 'The Logic of Strategic Ignorance', *British Journal of Sociology* 63, no. 3 (1 September 2012): 533–76, https://doi.org/10.1111/j.1468-4446.2012.01424.x.

26 Dan M. Kahan *et al.*, 'The Polarizing Impact of Science Literacy and Numeracy on Perceived Climate Change Risks', *Nature Climate Change* 2, no. 10 (27 May 2012): 732–5, https://doi.org/10.1038/nclimate1547.

27 Mike Thelwall, 'Homophily in MySpace', *Journal of the American Society for Information Science and Technology* 60, no. 2 (February 2009): 219–31, https://doi.org/10.1002/asi.20978.

28 Joshua Greene, *Moral Tribes: Emotion, Reason and the Gap between Us and Them* (London: Atlantic Books, 2015).

29 Angelique Chrisafis, '"France Is 50 Years Behind": The "State Scandal" of French Autism Treatment', *Guardian*, 8 February 2018, www.theguardian.com/world/2018/feb/08/france-is-50-years-behind-the-state-scandal-of-french-autism-treatment.

3 Why invalid claims can be valuable

1   Bob McCathy, 'Four Audio Myths', *Sound and Video Contractor* 29, no. 6 (June 2011): 44–9.

2   C. Edwards, 'Believe in Better [Audio Technology Myths]', *Engineering and Technology* 6, no. 11 (December 2011): 54–7.

3   M. Perlman, 'Golden Ears and Meter Readers: The Contest for Epistemic Authority in Audiophilia', *Social Studies of Science* 34, no. 5 (1 December 2004): 783–807, https://doi.org/10.1177/0306312704047613.

4   Malcolm Steward, 'The Original SATA Cable Post', *Malcolm Steward: Audio Journalist*, 15 June 2011, http://web.archive.org/web/20110615192300/http://www.malcolmsteward.co.uk/?p=2534.

5   A. Gat, 'The Human Motivational Complex: Evolutionary Theory and the Causes of Hunter-Gatherer Fighting, Part II. Proximate, Subordinate, and Derivative Causes', *Anthropological Quarterly* 73, no. 2 (April 2000), 74–88.

6   Jaime C. Confer *et al.*, 'Evolutionary Psychology: Controversies, Questions, Prospects, and Limitations', *American Psychologist* 65, no. 2 (2010): 110–26, https://doi.org/10.1037/a0018413.

7   Robin Dunbar, 'Social Networks and Their Implications for Community Living for People with a Learning Disability', *International Journal of Developmental Disabilities* 61, no. 2 (April 2015): 101–6, https://doi.org/10.1179/2047386914Z.00000000093.

8   For a critical appraisal of the notion of 'The Original Affluent Society', see David Kaplan, 'The Darker Side of the "Original Affluent Society"', *Journal of Anthropological Research* 56, no. 3 (Autumn 2000): 301–24.

Notes

9 Steven A. LeBlanc, with Katherine E. Register, *Constant Battles: The Myth of the Peaceful, Noble Savage*, 1st edn (New York: St Martin's Press, 2003).

10 Anne Campbell, 'Mothers Matter Most: Women and Parental Investment', in *A Mind of Her Own: The Evolutionary Psychology of Women* (Oxford: Oxford University Press, 2013).

11 John T. Cacioppo, Stephanie Cacioppo, and Dorret I. Boomsma, 'Evolutionary Mechanisms for Loneliness', *Cognition and Emotion* 28, no. 1 (January 2014): 3–21, https://doi.org/10.1080/02699931.2013.837379.

12 David F. Bjorklund and Anthony D. Pellegrini, 'Classifying Cognition', in *The Origins of Human Nature: Evolutionary Developmental Psychology* (Washington DC: American Psychological Association, 2002), 113–45.

13 Bella M. DePaulo *et al.*, 'Verbal and Nonverbal Dynamics of Privacy, Secrecy, and Deceit', *Journal of Social Issues* 59, no. 2 (July 2003): 391–410, https://doi.org/10.1111/1540-4560.00070; William von Hippel and Robert Trivers, 'The Evolution and Psychology of Self-Deception', *Behavioral and Brain Sciences* 34, no. 1 (2011): 1–16, https://doi.org/10.1017/S0140525X10001354.

14 Jill M. Mateo, 'Perspectives: Hamilton's Legacy: Mechanisms of Kin Recognition in Humans', *Ethology* 121, no. 5 (May 2015): 419–27, https://doi.org/10.1111/eth.12358.

15 Robert Trivers, 'Reciprocal Altruism: 30 Years Later', in *Cooperation in Primates and Humans: Mechanisms and Evolution*, ed. Peter Kappeler and Carel P. van Schaik (Berlin: Springer, 2006), 67–83.

16 Greene, *Moral Tribes*.

17 Dominic D. P. Johnson and James H. Fowler, 'The Evolution of Overconfidence', *Nature* 477, no. 7364 (14 September 2011): 317–20, https://doi.org/10.1038/nature10384.

18 Jonathan Haidt, 'Morality', *Perspectives on Psychological Science* 3, no. 1 (2008): 65–72; Jonathan Haidt, *The Righteous Mind: Why Good People Are Divided by Politics and Religion* (New York: Knopf Doubleday Publishing Group, 2012).

19 Mikael Klintman and Magnus Boström, 'Framings of Science and Ideology: Organic Food Labelling in the US and Sweden', *Environmental Politics* 13, no. 3 (2004): 612–34.

20 Proverbs 3:12 *(New International Version)*.

21 Eva Bergenlöv, *Drabbade barn: aga och barnmisshandel i Sverige från reformationen till nutid* (Stockholm: Nordic Academic Press, 2009); 'SOU (Statens Offentliga Utredningar)', governmental report, National Library of Sweden (Stockholm: Swedish Department of Justice, 1978).

22 Alan Kazdin, 'Disciplining Children Effectively', 24 September 2014, in *Speaking of Psychology* (podcast), American Psychological Association, www.apa.org/research/action/speaking-of-psychology/disciplining-children.aspx; Bergenlöv, *Drabbade barn: aga och barnmisshandel i Sverige från reformationen till nutid*; SOU, 'SOU (Statens Offentliga Utredningar)'.

23   Gershoff and Grogan-Kaylor, 'Spanking and Child Outcomes'.

24   Kazdin, 'Disciplining Children Effectively'.

25   Child Trends, 'Attitudes toward Spanking: Indicators of Child and Youth Well-Being', Child Trends Databank, accessed 21 February 2018, www. childtrends.org/indicators/attitudes-toward-spanking/ (article no longer on website).

26   Haidt, *The Righteous Mind*.

27   Christopher Wolsko, Hector Ariceaga, and Jesse Seiden, 'Red, White, and Blue Enough to Be Green: Effects of Moral Framing on Climate Change Attitudes and Conservation Behaviors', *Journal of Experimental Social Psychology* 65 (July 2016): 7–19, https://doi.org/10.1016/j.jesp.2016. 02.005.

28   J. Graham, J. Haidt, and B. A. Nosek, 'Liberals and Conservatives Rely on Different Sets of Moral Foundations', *Journal of Personality and Social Psychology* 96, no. 5 (May 2009): 1029–46, https://doi.org/10.1037/a0015141; Yoel Inbar, David A. Pizarro, and Paul Bloom, 'Conservatives Are More Easily Disgusted than Liberals', *Cognition and Emotion* 23, no. 4 (June 2009): 714–25, https://doi.org/10.1080/02699930802110007.

29   Pope Francis, 'Laudato Sì of the Holy Father Francis on Care for Our Common Home', Encyclical Letter, The Holy See, 24 May 2015, http:// w2.vatican.va/content/francesco/en/encyclicals/documents/papa-francesco_20150524_enciclica-laudato-si.html.

30   Stanley G. Payne, *A History of Fascism 1914–1945* (Madison: University of Wisconsin Press, 1996), 56.

31   Years later it turned out that Ted himself, outside of his marriage, had practised his own bisexuality, something that he discussed on *The Oprah Winfrey Show*. 'Ted Haggard Talks', on Oprah Winfrey's official website, 30 June 2009, www.oprah.com/oprahshow/ted-haggard-and-his-wife-talk-about-the-gay-sex-scandal/1.

32   Von Hippel and Trivers, 'The Evolution and Psychology of Self-Deception'.

33   Kahneman, *Thinking, Fast and Slow*; Thaler and Sunstein, *Nudge*.

34   Klintman, *Citizen-Consumers and Evolution*; Klintman, *Human Sciences and Human Interests*.

35   Solomon E. Asch, 'Studies of Independence and Conformity: I. A Minority of One against a Unanimous Majority', *Psychological Monographs: General and Applied* 70, no. 9 (1956): 1–70, https://doi.org/10.1037/h0093718.

36   Rebecca Mead, Momna Hejmadi, and Laurence D. Hurst, 'Scientific Aptitude Better Explains Poor Responses to Teaching of Evolution than Psychological Conflicts', *Nature Ecology and Evolution* 2 (8 January 2018): 388–94, https://doi.org/10.1038/s41559-017-0442-x.

37   See Simler and Hanson, *The Elephant in the Brain*.

38   Emilie Buchwald, Pamela Fletcher, and Martha Roth, eds, *Transforming a Rape Culture*, revised edn (Minneapolis: Milkweed, 2005); Griet

Vandermassen, 'A Tale of Male Bias and Feminist Denial', *European Journal of Women's Studies* 11, no. 1 (February 2004): 9–26.

39 Tina Uys, 'Rational Loyalty and Whistleblowing: The South African Context', *Current Sociology* 56, no. 6 (1 November 2008): 904–21, https://doi.org/10.1177/0011392108095345; Griet Vandermassen, 'Evolution and Rape: A Feminist Darwinian Perspective', *Sex Roles* 64, no. 9–10 (May 2011): 732–47, https://doi.org/10.1007/s11199-010-9895-y; Buchwald, Fletcher, and Roth, *Transforming a Rape Culture*.

40 Andi Hoxhaj, 'Anti-Corruption Policy in the EU and Reflexive Governance' (PhD thesis, University of Warwick, 2019).

41 Tenzin Gyatso (the fourteenth Dalai Lama), 'Our Faith in Science', *New York Times*, 12 November 2005, Opinion, www.nytimes.com/2005/11/12/opinion/our-faith-in-science.html.

4 Knowledge belief first, confirming evidence second

1 Robert Bellah *et al.*, *The Good Society* (New York: Random House, 2011).

2 H. L. Tuomisto *et al.*, 'Does Organic Farming Reduce Environmental Impacts? – A Meta-Analysis of European Research', *Journal of Environmental Management* 112 (15 December 2012): 309–20, https://doi.org/10.1016/j.jenvman.2012.08.018.

3 Bent Flyvbjerg, interview with the author, 22 January 2018.

4 Tobias Greitemeyer, 'I Am Right, You Are Wrong: How Biased Assimilation Increases the Perceived Gap between Believers and Skeptics of Violent Video Game Effects', *PLoS ONE* 9, no. 4 (10 April 2014): e93440, https://doi.org/10.1371/journal.pone.0093440.

5 Kahneman, *Thinking, Fast and Slow*.

6 Klintman, *Citizen-Consumers and Evolution*; Mikael Klintman, Kjell Mårtensson, and Magnus Johansson, 'Bioenergi För Uppvärmning – Hushållens Perspektiv' (research report, Lund University, Department of Sociology, 2003).

7 Steven Pinker, *The Blank Slate: The Modern Denial of Human Nature*, 1st edn (New York: Viking Press, 2002).

8 J. Henrich *et al.*, '"Economic Man" in Cross-Cultural Perspective: Behavioral Experiments in 15 Small-Scale Societies', *Behavioral and Brain Sciences* 28, no. 6 (2005): 795–815.

9 J. Henrich, S. J. Heine, and A. Norenzayan, 'The Weirdest People in the World?', *Behavioral and Brain Sciences* 33, no. 2–3 (June 2010): 61–83.

10 Max Weber, *The Protestant Ethic and the Spirit of Capitalism: And Other Writings* (New York: Penguin, [1905] 2002).

11 Alexis de Tocqueville, *Democracy in America: The Complete and Unabridged Volumes I and II* (New York: Bantam Classics, [1835] 2000), 625–6; Henrich *et al.*, '"Economic Man" in Cross-Cultural Perspective'.

12 See John Bargh, *Before You Know It: The Unconscious Reasons We Do What We Do* (New York: Penguin, 2017).

13 C. G. Lord, L. Ross, and M. R. Lepper, 'Biased Assimilation and Attitude Polarization: The Effects of Prior Theories on Subsequently Considered Evidence', *Journal of Personality and Social Psychology* 37, no. 11 (1979): 2098–109, https://doi.org/10.1037//0022-3514.37.11.2098; de Tocqueville, *Democracy in America*, 625–6.

14 Scott Plous, 'Biases in the Assimilation of Technological Breakdowns: Do Accidents Make Us Safer?', *Journal of Applied Social Psychology* 21, no. 13 (1991): 1058–82; cf. Bargh, *Before You Know It*; Henrich, Heine, and Norenzayan, 'The Weirdest People in the World?'.

15 Xiaoli Nan and Kelly Daily, 'Biased Assimilation and Need for Closure: Examining the Effects of Mixed Blogs on Vaccine-Related Beliefs', *Journal of Health Communication* 20, no. 4 (3 April 2015): 462–71.

16 Festinger, *A Theory of Cognitive Dissonance*.

17 Tavris and Aronson, *Mistakes Were Made*.

18 C. Leor Harris, *Evolution, Genesis and Revelations* (Albany: State University of New York Press, 1981).

19 Xiang Chen and Peter Barker, 'Process Concepts and Cognitive Obstacles to Change: Perspectives on the History of Science and Science Policy', *Centaurus* 51, no. 4 (November 2009): 314–20, https://doi.org/10.1111/j.1600-0498.2009.00155.x.

20 Lezaun, interview.

21 Julian Baggini, 'Dan Dennett and the New Atheism', *Philosophers' Magazine*, 8 May 2017, www.philosophersmag.com/interviews/31-dan-dennett-and-the-new-atheism.

22 George Gaskell, interview with the author, 27 February 2018.

23 Deborah Kelemen, 'The Scope of Teleological Thinking in Preschool Children', *Cognition* 70, no. 3 (April 1999): 241–72, https://doi.org/10.1016/S0010-0277(99)00010-4.

24 Guy de Maupassant, 'In the Moonlight' (n.p.: CreateSpace Independent Publishing Platform, 2014).

25 Charles Darwin, *The Descent of Man* (London: Penguin Classics, [1879] 2004), 612.

26 Allen MacNeill, 'The Capacity for Religious Experience Is an Evolutionary Adaptation to Warfare', in *The Psychology of Resolving Global Conflicts: From War to Peace*, ed. F. A. Stout (Westport: Praeger Security International, 2006), 257–84.

27 Dominic Johnson, *God Is Watching You: How the Fear of God Makes Us Human* (Oxford: Oxford University Press, 2016).

28 Jared M. Diamond, *Guns, Germs and Steel: The Fates of Human Societies*, 20th anniversary edn (New York: Norton, 2017).

29 Johnson and Fowler, 'The Evolution of Overconfidence'.

30 Johnson, *God Is Watching You*.

31 Chen and Barker, 'Process Concepts and Cognitive Obstacles to Change'.

32 J. Bohr, 'Is It Hot in Here or Is It Just Me? Temperature Anomalies and Political Polarization over Global Warming in the American Public', *Climatic Change* 142, no. 1–2 (May 2017): 271–85, https://doi.org/10.1007/s10584-017-1934-z.

33 Matthew A. Cronin, Cleotilde Gonzalez, and John D. Sterman, 'Why Don't Well-Educated Adults Understand Accumulation? A Challenge to Researchers, Educators, and Citizens', *Organizational Behavior and Human Decision Processes* 108, no. 1 (January 2009): 116–30, https://doi.org/10.1016/j.obhdp.2008.03.003.

34 Bloom and Weisberg, 'Childhood Origins of Adult Resistance to Science'; Cronin, Gonzalez, and Sterman, 'Why Don't Well-Educated Adults Understand Accumulation?'.

35 Frank C. Keil, *Semantic and Conceptual Development: An Ontological Perspective*, reprint edn (Cambridge, MA: Harvard University Press, 2014).

36 Xiang Chen, 'The Object Bias and the Study of Scientific Revolutions: Lessons from Developmental Psychology', *Philosophical Psychology* 20, no. 4 (1 August 2007): 479–503.

37 Avnika B. Amin *et al.*, 'Association of Moral Values with Vaccine Hesitancy', *Nature Human Behaviour* 1, no. 12 (December 2017): 873, https://doi.org/10.1038/s41562-017-0256-5.

38 Gavin I. Clark and Adam J. Rock, 'Processes Contributing to the Maintenance of Flying Phobia: A Narrative Review', *Frontiers in Psychology* 7 (1 June 2016), https://doi.org/10.3389/fpsyg.2016.00754.

39 Marianna Masiero, Claudio Lucchiari, and Gabriella Pravettoni, 'Personal Fable: Optimistic Bias in Cigarette Smokers', *International Journal of High Risk Behaviors and Addiction* 4, no. 1 (20 March 2015), https://doi.org/10.5812/ijhrba.20939.

40 E. Scott Fruehwald, *Overcoming Cognitive Biases: Thinking More Clearly and Avoiding Manipulation by Others* (n.p.: CreateSpace Independent Publishing Platform, 2017); D. Kahneman, J. L. Knetsch, and R. H. Thaler, 'Anomalies: The Endowment Effect, Loss Aversion, and Status Quo Bias', *Journal of Economic Perspectives* 5, no. 1 (1991): 193–206; Masiero, Lucchiari, and Pravettoni, 'Personal Fable: Optimistic Bias in Cigarette Smokers'.

41 Steven Pinker, *Enlightenment Now: The Case for Reason, Science, Humanism, and Progress* (New York: Viking, 2018).

42 Gaskell, interview.

43 See Noel T. Brewer and William K. Hallman, 'Subjective and Objective Risk as Predictors of Influenza Vaccination during the Vaccine Shortage of 2004–2005', *Clinical Infectious Diseases* 43, no. 11 (2006): 1379–86.

44 Bloom and Weisberg, 'Childhood Origins of Adult Resistance to Science'.

45 Max Tegmark, *Life 3.0: Being Human in the Age of Artificial Intelligence* (London: Allen Lane, 2017), chapter 2.

46 Tegmark, *Life 3.0*, chap. 2.

47 Klintman, *Human Sciences and Human Interests*, 30.

48 Bargh, *Before You Know It*.

49 Mercier and Heintz, 'Scientists' Argumentative Reasoning', 514.

50 Mercier and Heintz, 'Scientists' Argumentative Reasoning', 514.

51 See Hugo Mercier and Helene E. Landemore, 'Reasoning Is for Arguing: Understanding the Successes and Failures of Deliberation', *Political Psychology* 33, no. 2 (April 2012): 243–58, https://doi.org/10.1111/j.1467-9221.2012.00873.x.

52 Daniel Kahneman, 'A Perspective on Judgment and Choice: Mapping Bounded Rationality', *American Psychologist* 58, no. 9 (September 2003): 699, https://doi.org/10.1037/0003-066X.58.9.697.

53 Hugo Mercier, 'Using Evolutionary Thinking to Cut Across Disciplines', in *Comparative Decision Making*, ed. Thomas R. Zentall and Philip H. Crowley (Oxford: Oxford University Press, 2013), 279–304.

54 James R. Flynn, *What Is Intelligence?: Beyond the Flynn Effect*, 1st edn (Cambridge and New York: Cambridge University Press, 2007).

55 Geir Kirkebøen, Erik Vasaasen, and Karl Halvor Teigen, 'Revisions and Regret: The Cost of Changing Your Mind', *Journal of Behavioral Decision Making* 26, no. 1 (January 2013): 1–12, https://doi.org/10.1002/bdm.756.

5 Knowledge: what's in it for me?

1 See Michael J. Sandel, *What Money Can't Buy: The Moral Limits of Markets*, reprint edn (New York: Farrar, Straus and Giroux, 2013).

2 Milton Friedman, *There's No Such Thing as a Free Lunch* (LaSalle: Open Court Publishing, 1977), 178–80.

3 Tegmark, *Life 3.0*, chap. 2.

4 George Stigler, 'The Economics of Information', *Journal of Political Economy*, no. 3 (1961): 213.

5 Bryan Caplan, 'Rational Ignorance versus Rational Irrationality', *Kyklos* 54, no. 1 (1 February 2001): 3–26, https://doi.org/10.1111/1467-6435.00138.

6 Senja Post, 'Communicating Science in Public Controversies: Strategic Considerations of the German Climate Scientists', *Public Understanding of Science* 25, no. 1 (2016): 61–70.

7 Alexander Elbittar et al., 'Ignorance and Bias in Collective Decisions', *Journal of Economic Behavior and Organization*, 27 December 2016, https://doi.org/10.1016/j.jebo.2016.12.011.

8 Ilya Somin, *Democracy and Political Ignorance: Why Smaller Government Is Smarter*, 1st edn (Stanford: Stanford Law Books, 2013), 61.

9 Somin, *Democracy and Political Ignorance*, 64.

Notes

10 Somin, *Democracy and Political Ignorance*, 65; see also Tom Hoffman, 'Rational Choice and Political Irrationality in the New Millennium', *Critical Review* 27, no. 3–4 (2 October 2015): 299–315, https://doi.org/10.1080/089138 11.2015.1111679.

11 Garrett Hardin, 'The Tragedy of the Commons', *Science*, New Series, 162, no. 3859 (13 December 1968): 1243–8.

12 Anthony J. Evans and Jeffrey Friedman, '"Search" vs. "Browse": A Theory of Error Grounded in Radical (Not Rational) Ignorance', *Critical Review* 23, no. 1–2 (March 2011): 73–104, https://doi.org/10.1080/08913811.2011.574471.

13 Evans and Friedman, '"Search" vs. "Browse"', 75.

14 Martha Augoustinos, 'Ideology, False Consciousness and Psychology', *Theory and Psychology* 9, no. 3 (1999): 295–312.

15 Wilbert E. Moore and Melvin M. Tumin, 'Some Social Functions of Ignorance', *American Sociological Review* 14, no. 6 (December 1949): 787–95.

16 Øistein Anmarkrud, Ivar Bråten, and Helge I. Strømsø, 'Multiple-Documents Literacy: Strategic Processing, Source Awareness, and Argumentation When Reading Multiple Conflicting Documents', *Learning and Individual Differences* 30 (February 2014): 64–76, https://doi.org/10.1016/j.lindif.2013.01.007.

17 'Interesting Facts about Sydney Opera House', on the Sydney Opera House official website, accessed 18 July 2018, www.sydneyoperahouse.com/content/soh/our-story/sydney-opera-house-facts.html.

18 Flyvbjerg, interview.

19 Evans and Friedman, '"Search" vs. "Browse"', 78; Stephen Earl Bennett and Jeffrey Friedman, 'The Irrelevance of Economic Theory to Understanding Economic Ignorance', *Critical Review: An Interdisciplinary Journal of Politics and Society* 20, no. 3 (1 January 2008): 195–258.

20 'DoD News Briefing – Secretary Rumsfeld and Gen. Myers', Transcript, DoD News Briefing (Washington, DC: US Department of Defense, 12 February 2002), http://archive.defense.gov/Transcripts/Transcript.aspx?TranscriptID=2636.

21 Juan D. Carrillo and Thomas Mariotti, 'Strategic Ignorance as a Self-Disciplining Device', *Review of Economic Studies* 67, no. 3 (July 2000): 529; Jonathan Haidt, 'The Age of Outrage', *City Journal*, 17 December 2017, www.city-journal.org/html/age-outrage-15608.html.

22 W. Kip Viscusi, 'Do Smokers Underestimate Risks?', *Journal of Political Economy* 98, no. 6 (1990): 1253–69; cf. Joan Costa-Font and Joan Rovira, 'When Do Smokers "Underestimate" Smoking Related Mortality Risks?', *Applied Economics Letters* 12, no. 13 (20 October 2005): 789–94, https://doi.org/10.1080/13504850500190279.

23 Carrillo and Mariotti, 'Strategic Ignorance as a Self-Disciplining Device', 529–30.

24 James M. Griffin, ed., *Global Climate Change: The Science, Economics*

and Politics, Bush School Series in the Economics of Public Policy, vol. 4 (Cheltenham and Northampton, MA: Edward Elgar, 2003); William Nordhaus, 'Critical Assumptions in the Stern Review on Climate Change', *Science* 317, no. 5835 (2007): 201–2.

25 Flyvbjerg, interview.

26 Magnus Boström and Mikael Klintman, *Eco-Standards, Product Labelling and Green Consumerism* (Basingstoke: Palgrave Macmillan, 2008).

27 Pierre Lemieux, 'Following the Herd', *Regulation* 26, no. 4 (Winter 2003–4): 16–21.

28 Robert Trivers, *Deceit and Self-Deception: Fooling Yourself the Better to Fool Others* (New York: Penguin, 2011).

29 'Sincere Deceivers', *The Economist*, 15 July 2004, Leaders, www.economist.com/node/2921794.

30 Haidt, 'The Age of Outrage'.

31 Dunbar, interview.

32 Dunbar, interview.

6 When knowledge is responsibility and ignorance freedom

1 J. Ely, A. Frankel, and E. Kamenica, 'Suspense and Surprise', *Journal of Political Economy* 123, no. 1 (2015): 215–60. https://doi.org/10.1086/677350.

2 A. J. A. Kooper *et al*, 'Why do parents prefer to know the fetal sex as part of invasive prenatal testing?' *Obstetrics and Gynecology* (2012). http://dx.doi.org/10.5402/2012/524537.

3 Ralph Hertwig and Christoph Engel, 'Homo Ignorans: Deliberately Choosing Not to Know.' *Perspectives on Psychological Science* 11, no. 3 (May 2016): 359–72. https://doi.org/10.1177/1745691616663559.

4 Christina Leuker and Wouter Van Den Bos, 'We Need to Save Ignorance From AI.' *Nautilus Magazine*, 14 June 2018.

5 Abraham H. Maslow, 'The Need to Know and the Fear of Knowing', in *Toward a Psychology of Being*. (Princeton, NJ, US: D Van Nostrand, 1962), 62, https://doi.org/10.1037/10793–005.

6 G. Gigerenzer and R. Garcia-Retamero. 'Cassandra's Regret: The Psychology of Not Wanting to Know', *Psychological Review* 124, no. 2 (January 2017): 179–96, https://doi.org/10.1037/rev0000055.

7 John Brockman, ed., *This Will Make You Smarter: New Scientific Concepts to Improve Your Thinking*, 1st edn (New York: Harper Perennial, 2012).

8 Pamela J. McKenzie, 'Justifying Cognitive Authority Decisions: Discursive Strategies of Information Seekers', *Library Quarterly* 73, no. 3 (July 2003): 261; Hann *et al.*, 'Awareness, Knowledge, Perceptions, and Attitudes towards Genetic Testing'.

9 Donald O. Case *et al.*, 'Avoiding versus Seeking: The Relationship of Information Seeking to Avoidance, Blunting, Coping, Dissonance, and

Related Concepts', *Journal of the Medical Library Association* 93, no. 3 (July 2005): 353–62; Brockman, ed., *This Will Make You Smarter*.

10   Karine Nyborg, 'I Don't Want to Hear about It: Rational Ignorance among Duty-Oriented Consumers', *Journal of Economic Behavior and Organization* 79, no. 3 (August 2011): 263–74, https://doi.org/10.1016/j.jebo.2011.02.004.

11   Festinger, *A Theory of Cognitive Dissonance*.

12   Nyborg, 'I Don't Want to Hear about It', 268.

13   Dr Steven Garber, 'The Politics of Self-Deception', Washington Institute for Faith, Vocation and Culture, 15 April 2013, www.washingtoninst.org/4138/the-politics-of-self-deception-2/.

14   Bent Flyvbjerg, 'How Planners Deal with Uncomfortable Knowledge: The Dubious Ethics of the American Planning Association', *Cities* 32 (June 2013): 157–63, https://doi.org/10.1016/j.cities.2012.10.016.

15   Flyvbjerg, interview.

16   Flyvbjerg, interview.

17   Steve Rayner, 'Uncomfortable Knowledge: The Social Construction of Ignorance in Science and Environmental Policy Discourses', *Economy and Society* 41, no. 1 (1 February 2012): 107–25, https://doi.org/10.1080/03085147.2011.637335.

18   Rachael Revesz, 'MPs Voted That Animals Cannot Feel Pain or Emotions', *Independent*, 20 November 2017, www.independent.co.uk/news/uk/home-news/brexit-bill-latest-animal-sentience-cannot-feel-pain-emotion-vote-mps-agree-eu-withdrawal-bill- a8064676.html.

19   Rayner, 'Uncomfortable Knowledge'.

20   McGoey, 'The Logic of Strategic Ignorance'.

21   cf. Sissela Bok, *Lying: Moral Choice in Public and Private Life*, updated edn (New York: Vintage, 1999).

22   cf. Kenneth Dauber, 'Bureaucratizing the Ethnographer's Magic', *Current Anthropology* 36, no. 1 (1995): 75–95.

23   Heimer, 'Inert Facts and the Illusion of Knowledge'.

24   Matthias Gross and Alena Bleicher, '"It's Always Dark in Front of the Pickaxe": Organizing Ignorance in the Long-Term Remediation of Contaminated Land', *Time and Society* 22, no. 3 (1 November 2013): 316–34, https://doi.org/10.1177/0961463X12444059; Matthias Gross, '"Objective Culture" and the Development of Nonknowledge: Georg Simmel and the Reverse Side of Knowing', *Cultural Sociology* 6, no. 4 (2012): 422–37.

25   Gross and Bleicher, '"It's Always Dark in Front of the Pickaxe"', 318.

26   Popper, *The Logic of Scientific Discovery*.

27   Piet Hein, *Grooks* (London: Hodder and Stoughton, 1969).

28   Robert K. Merton, 'Three Fragments from a Sociologist's Notebooks: Establishing the Phenomenon, Specified Ignorance, and Strategic Research Materials', *Annual Review of Sociology* 13, no. 1 (August 1987): 1–29, https://doi.org/10.1146/annurev.so.13.080187.000245.

29 Samira Shackle, 'Science and Serendipity: Famous Accidental Discoveries', *New Humanist (Online)*, 2 April 2015, https://newhumanist.org.uk/4852/science-and-serendipity-famous-accidental-discoveries.

30 Kuhn, *The Structure of Scientific Revolutions*, 89–90.

31 John Rawls, *A Theory of Justice* (Cambridge, MA: Harvard University Press, 1971).

32 Paul Matthews and Rob Stephens, 'Sociable Knowledge Sharing Online: Philosophy, Patterns and Intervention', *Aslib Proceedings* 62, no. 6 (23 November 2010): 539–53, https://doi.org/10.1108/00012531011089667.

33 Niklas Arevik *et al.*, 'Pojkar missgynnas i betygsättningen', *Lärarnas tidning* (Swedish teachers' magazine), 9 February 2011, https://lararnastidning.se/pojkar-missgynnas-i-betygsattningen/.

34 Lin Bian *et al.*, 'Messages about Brilliance Undermine Women's Interest in Educational and Professional Opportunities', *Journal of Experimental Social Psychology* 76 (May 2018), https://doi.org/10.1016/j.jesp.2017.11.006.

35 Thomas Hobbes, *Leviathan* (Harmondsworth: Penguin Classics, [1651] 1982); Francis Bacon, *Meditationes Sacrae and Human Philosophy* (Whitefish: Kessinger Publishing, [1597] 1996).

36 Klintman, *Citizen-Consumers and Evolution*.

37 Boström and Klintman, *Eco-Standards*.

38 Greene, *Moral Tribes*.

39 Peter Singer, 'The Man Who Didn't Save the World', *Project Syndicate*, 12 December 2017, www.project-syndicate.org/commentary/salvator-mundi-purchase-price-world-s-poor-by-peter-singer-2017-12.

7 What if the earth is round? Concerns about cultural consequences

1 Paul Raeburn, 'Lying to Yourself Helps You Lie to Others', *Discover Magazine*, 17 December 2013, http://discovermagazine.com/2013/june/01-lying-to-yourself-helps-you-lie-to-others.

2 Trivers, *Deceit and Self-Deception*, 307.

3 Lynn L. Bergeson, 'The Montreal Protocol Is Amended and Strengthened', *Environmental Quality Management* 26, no. 3 (Spring 2017): 137–41, https://doi.org/10.1002/tqem.21496.

4 Thomas Huxley, 'Evolution and Ethics', in *The Essays of Thomas Henry Huxley* (New York: Appleton-Century-Crofts, [1893] 1948), 81–3.

5 Herbert Spencer and J. D. Y. Peel, *On Social Evolution: Selected Writings* (Chicago: University of Chicago Press, 1983).

6 Rudyard Kipling, *Kipling: Poems* (London: Knopf Doubleday Publishing Group, 2013), 96. The poem 'The White Man's Burden' was written in 1899.

7 David Hume, *A Treatise of Human Nature: Being an Attempt to Introduce*

the Experimental Method of Reasoning into Mor (London: Penguin Classics, [1739] 1986).

8   Diamond, *Guns, Germs and Steel.*

9   Gagan Flora, Deepesh Gupta, and Archana Tiwari, 'Toxicity of Lead: A Review with Recent Updates', *Interdisciplinary Toxicology* 5, no. 2 (June 2012): 47–58, https://doi.org/10.2478/v10102-012-0009-2.

10 George Yancy and Noam Chomsky, 'Noam Chomsky: On Trump and the State of the Union', *New York Times*, 5 July 2017, Opinion, www.nytimes.com/2017/07/05/opinion/noam-chomsky-on-trump-and-the-state-of-the-union.html.

11 This study can be found in Kahan *et al.*, 'Geoengineering and Climate Change Polarization'.

12 Rob Bellamy, interview with the author, 25 January 2018.

13 Gaskell, interview.

14 Shaun W. Elsasser and Riley E. Dunlap, 'Leading Voices in the Denier Choir: Conservative Columnists' Dismissal of Global Warming and Denigration of Climate Science', *American Behavioral Scientist* 57, no. 6 (2013): 754–76.

15 Horowitz, Yaworsky, and Kickham, 'Whither the Blank Slate?'

16 Horowitz, Yaworsky, and Kickham, 'Whither the Blank Slate?', 499; also in Klintman, *Human Sciences and Human Interests.*

17 Horowitz, Yaworsky, and Kickham, 'Whither the Blank Slate?', 499.

18 Jack Zenger and Joseph Folkman, 'Are Women Better Leaders Than Men?', *Harvard Business Review*, 15 March 2012, https://hbr.org/2012/03/a-study-in-leadership-women-do.

8   How to resist knowledge resistance – and when

1   Kahneman, *Thinking, Fast and Slow.*

2   Alison Flood, 'Bill Gates Gives a Book to Every US Student Graduating in 2018', *Guardian*, 8 June 2018, www.theguardian.com/books/2018/jun/08/bill-gates-gives-a-book-to-every-us-student-graduating-in-2018.

3   J. R. Keene *et al.*, 'The Biological Roots of Political Extremism: Negativity Bias, Political Ideology, and Preferences for Political News', *Politics and the Life Sciences* 36, no. 2 (Fall 2017): 37–48, https://doi.org/10.1017/pls.2017.16.

4   D. Bahn *et al.*, 'Age-Dependent Positivity-Bias in Children's Processing of Emotion Terms', *Frontiers in Psychology* 8 (26 July 2017), https://doi.org/10.3389/fpsyg.2017.01268.

5   Steven Pinker, *The Better Angels of Our Nature: Why Violence Has Declined*, 1st edn (New York: Viking Adult, 2011); Pinker, *Enlightenment Now.*

6   Rosling, Rönnlund, and Rosling, *Factfulness.*

7   Rosling, Rönnlund, and Rosling, *Factfulness.*

8   Klintman, *Human Sciences and Human Interests.*

9   Rosling, Rönnlund, and Rosling, *Factfulness.*

10   George Gaskell *et al.*, 'GM Foods and the Misperception of Risk Perception', *Risk Analysis* 24, no. 1 (February 2004): 185–94, https://doi.org/10.1111/j.0272-4332.2004.00421.x.

11   Gaskell, interview.

12   Jonathon P. Schuldt, Peter K. Enns, and Victoria Cavaliere, 'Does the Label Really Matter? Evidence That the US Public Continues to Doubt "Global Warming" More Than "Climate Change"', *Climatic Change* 143, no. 1–2 (July 2017): 271–80, https://doi.org/10.1007/s10584-017-1993-1.

13   Michael Shellenberger, 'In Wake of Terrifying Climate Report, German Environmentalists Will, in a Twist, Rally for Nuclear', *Forbes*, 15 October 2018, www.forbes.com/sites/michaelshellenberger/2018/10/15/in-wake-of-terrifying-climate-report-german-environmentalists-will-in-a-twist-rally-for-nuclear/.

14   Shellenberger, 'In Wake of Terrifying Climate Report'.

15   See Martin Rein, 'Reframing Problematic Policies', in *The Oxford Handbook of Public Policy*, ed. Michael Moran, Martin Rein, and Robert E. Goodin (Oxford: Oxford University Press, 2006), 389–408; K. Bickerstaff *et al.*, 'Reframing Nuclear Power in the UK Energy Debate: Nuclear Power, Climate Change Mitigation and Radioactive Waste', *Public Understanding of Science* 17, no. 2 (April 2008): 145–69, https://doi.org/10.1177/0963662506066719.

16   Dunbar, interview.

17   Bud Ward, 'The Evolution of a One-Time Climate Skeptic', *Yale Climate Connections* (blog), 20 February 2018, www.yaleclimateconnections.org/2018/02/the-evolution-of-a-one-time-climate-skeptic/.

18   Cary Funk and Meg Hefferon, 'Many Republican Millennials Differ with Older Party Members on Climate Change and Energy Issues', Pew Research Center, 14 May 2018, www.pewresearch.org/fact-tank/2018/05/14/many-republican-millennials-differ-with-older-party-members-on-climate-change-and-energy-issues/.

19   Kathryn Applegate and J. B. Stump, eds, *How I Changed My Mind About Evolution: Evangelicals Reflect on Faith and Science* (Downers Grove: IVP Academic, 2016).

20   Michael Specter, 'An Environmentalist's Conversion', *New Yorker*, 7 January 2013, www.newyorker.com/news/daily-comment/an-environmentalists-conversion.

21   Omri Ben-Shahar, 'The Environmentalist Case in Favor of GMO Food', *Forbes*, 26 February 2018, www.forbes.com/sites/omribenshahar/2018/02/26/the-environmentalist-case-in-favor-of-gmo-food/.

22   Joaquin Navajas *et al.*, 'Aggregated Knowledge from a Small Number of Debates Outperforms the Wisdom of Large Crowds', *Nature Human Behaviour* 2 (2018): 126–32, https://doi.org/10.1038/s41562-017-0273-4.

23   Hélène Landemore and Jon Elster, *Collective Wisdom: Principles and Mechanisms* (New York: Cambridge University Press, 2012); Dražen Prelec,

H. Sebastian Seung, and John McCoy, 'A Solution to the Single-Question Crowd Wisdom Problem', *Nature* 541, no. 7638 (January 2017): 532–5, https://doi.org/10.1038/nature21054.

24 The project is called 'Beyond the market stalls and ivory towers: A study on integrated science for sustainable provision of knowledge'. It is supported financially by the Swedish Foundation for Humanities and the Social Sciences (RJ). The project is part of a larger programme called 'Framtidens kunskapsförsörjning' (Knowledge supply for the future).

25 This research project is part of the MISTRA Sustainable Consumption research programme.

26 Nazli Choucri, *Cyberpolitics in International Relations* (Cambridge, MA: MIT Press, 2012).

27 Nickerson, 'Confirmation Bias'.

28 Reagan, 'A Time for Choosing'.

29 Ivar R. Hannikainen, 'Ideology between the Lines: Lay Inferences about Scientists' Values and Motives', *Social Psychological and Personality Science*, 25 July 2018, https://doi.org/10.1177/1948550618790230.

30 Greg Lukianoff and Jonathan Haidt, *The Coddling of the American Mind: How Good Intentions and Bad Ideas Are Setting Up a Generation for Failure* (New York: Penguin Press, 2018).

9 On whether knowledge resistance is always bad, and other questions

1 Dunbar, interview.

2 Michelle N. Meyer and Christopher Chabris, 'Why Psychologists' Food Fight Matters', *Slate*, 31 July 2014, www.slate.com/articles/health_and_sci ence/science/2014/07/replication_controversy_in_psychology_bullying_file _drawer_effect_blog_posts.html.

Select bibliography

Amin, Avnika B., Robert A. Bednarczyk, Cara E. Ray, Kala J. Melchiori, Jesse Graham, Jeffrey R. Huntsinger, and Saad B. Omer. 'Association of Moral Values with Vaccine Hesitancy'. *Nature Human Behaviour* 1, no. 12 (December 2017): 873–80. https://doi.org/10.1038/s41562-017-0256-5.

Anmarkrud, Øistein, Ivar Bråten, and Helge I. Strømsø. 'Multiple-Documents Literacy: Strategic Processing, Source Awareness, and Argumentation When Reading Multiple Conflicting Documents'. *Learning and Individual Differences* 30 (February 2014): 64–76. https://doi.org/10.1016/j.lindif.2013.01.007.

Applegate, Kathryn, and J. B. Stump, eds. *How I Changed My Mind About Evolution: Evangelicals Reflect on Faith and Science.* Downers Grove: IVP Academic, 2016.

Arevik, Niklas, Stanley Plotkin, Jeffrey S. Gerber, and Paul A. Offit. 'Pojkar missgynnas i betygsättningen'. *Lärarnas tidning* (Swedish teachers' magazine), 9 February 2011. https://lararnastidning.se/pojkar-missgynnas-i-betyg sattningen/.

Asch, Solomon E. 'Studies of Independence and Conformity: I. A Minority of One against a Unanimous Majority'. *Psychological Monographs: General and Applied* 70, no. 9 (1956): 1–70. https://doi.org/10.1037/h0093718.

Augoustinos, Martha. 'Ideology, False Consciousness and Psychology'. *Theory and Psychology* 9, no. 3 (1999): 295–312.

Bacon, Francis. *Meditationes Sacrae and Human Philosophy.* Whitefish: Kessinger Publishing, [1597] 1996.

Bellah, Robert, Richard Madsen, Steve Tipton, William Sullivan, and Ann Swidler. *The Good Society.* New York: Random House, 2011.

Bennett, Stephen Earl, and Jeffrey Friedman. 'The Irrelevance of Economic Theory to Understanding Economic Ignorance'. *Critical Review: An Interdisciplinary Journal of Politics and Society* 20, no. 3 (1 January 2008): 195–258.

Berger, Peter L. *The Many Altars of Modernity: Toward a Paradigm for Religion in a Pluralist Age.* Boston: De Gruyter Mouton, 2014.

Select bibliography

Bergeson, Lynn L. 'The Montreal Protocol Is Amended and Strengthened'. *Environmental Quality Management* 26, no. 3 (Spring 2017): 137–41. https://doi.org/10.1002/tqem.21496.

Bhaskar, Roy. *Scientific Realism and Human Emancipation*. 1st edn. London: Routledge, 1986.

Bian, Lin, Sarah-Jane Leslie, Mary C. Murphy, and Andrei Cimpian. 'Messages about Brilliance Undermine Women's Interest in Educational and Professional Opportunities'. *Journal of Experimental Social Psychology* 76 (May 2018). https://doi.org/10.1016/j.jesp.2017.11.006.

Bloom, Paul, and Deena Skolnick Weisberg. 'Childhood Origins of Adult Resistance to Science'. *Science* 316, no. 5827 (2007): 996–7.

Bohr, J. 'Is It Hot in Here or Is It Just Me? Temperature Anomalies and Political Polarization over Global Warming in the American Public'. *Climatic Change* 142, no. 1–2 (May 2017): 271–85. https://doi.org/10.1007/s10584-017-1934-z.

Bok, Sissela. *Lying: Moral Choice in Public and Private Life*. Updated edn. New York: Vintage, 1999.

Borowitz, Andy. 'Scientists: Earth Endangered by New Strain of Fact-Resistant Humans'. *New Yorker*, 12 May 2015. www.newyorker.com/humor/borowitz-report/scientists-earth-endangered-by-new-strain-of-fact-resistant-humans.

Boström, Magnus, and Mikael Klintman. *Eco-Standards, Product Labelling and Green Consumerism*. Basingstoke: Palgrave Macmillan, 2008.

Brewer, Noel T., and William K. Hallman. 'Subjective and Objective Risk as Predictors of Influenza Vaccination during the Vaccine Shortage of 2004–2005'. *Clinical Infectious Diseases* 43, no. 11 (2006): 1379–86.

Buchwald, Emilie, Pamela Fletcher, and Martha Roth, eds. *Transforming a Rape Culture*. Revised edn. Minneapolis: Milkweed, 2005.

Buss, David M. *The Dangerous Passion: Why Jealousy Is as Necessary as Love and Sex*. 1st printed edn. New York: Free Press, 2000.

Campbell, Anne. *A Mind of Her Own: The Evolutionary Psychology of Women*. Oxford: Oxford University Press, 2013.

Caplan, Bryan. 'Rational Ignorance versus Rational Irrationality'. *Kyklos* 54, no. 1 (1 February 2001): 3–26. https://doi.org/10.1111/1467-6435.00138.

Carrillo, Juan D., and Thomas Mariotti. 'Strategic Ignorance as a Self-Disciplining Device'. *Review of Economic Studies* 67, no. 3 (July 2000): 529.

Case, Donald O., James E. Andrews, J. David Johnson, and Suzanne L. Allard. 'Avoiding versus Seeking: The Relationship of Information Seeking to Avoidance, Blunting, Coping, Dissonance, and Related Concepts'. *Journal of the Medical Library Association* 93, no. 3 (July 2005): 353–62.

Centers for Disease Control and Prevention. 'Measles Vaccination'. Last updated 22 November 2016. www.cdc.gov/measles/vaccination.html.

Chen, Xiang. 'The Object Bias and the Study of Scientific Revolutions: Lessons from Developmental Psychology'. *Philosophical Psychology* 20, no. 4 (1 August 2007): 479–503.

Chen, Xiang, and Peter Barker. 'Process Concepts and Cognitive Obstacles to Change: Perspectives on the History of Science and Science Policy'. *Centaurus* 51, no. 4 (November 2009): 314–20. https://doi.org/10.1111/j.1600-0498.2009.00155.x.

Choucri, Nazli. *Cyberpolitics in International Relations.* Cambridge, MA: MIT Press, 2012.

Clark, Gavin I., and Adam J. Rock. 'Processes Contributing to the Maintenance of Flying Phobia: A Narrative Review'. *Frontiers in Psychology* 7 (1 June 2016).

Cohen, Stanley. *States of Denial: Knowing about Atrocities and Suffering.* Cambridge: Polity, 2001.

Confer, Jaime C., Judith A. Easton, Diana S. Fleischman, Cari D. Goetz, David M. G. Lewis, Carin Perilloux, and David M. Buss. 'Evolutionary Psychology: Controversies, Questions, Prospects, and Limitations'. *American Psychologist* 65, no. 2 (2010): 110–26. https://doi.org/10.1037/a0018413.

Cooke, Nicole A. *Fake News and Alternative Facts: Information Literacy in a Post-Truth Era.* Chicago: American Library Association, 2018.

Costa-Font, Joan, and Joan Rovira. 'When Do Smokers "Underestimate" Smoking Related Mortality Risks?' *Applied Economics Letters* 12, no. 13 (20 October 2005): 789–94. https://doi.org/10.1080/13504850500190279.

Cronin, Matthew A., Cleotilde Gonzalez, and John D. Sterman. 'Why Don't Well-Educated Adults Understand Accumulation? A Challenge to Researchers, Educators, and Citizens'. *Organizational Behavior and Human Decision Processes* 108, no. 1 (January 2009): 116–30. https://doi.org/10.1016/j.obhdp.2008.03.003.

Dahl, Roald. 'Death of Olivia'. Roald Dahl's official website, accessed 13 February 2019. www.roalddahl.com/roald-dahl/timeline/1960s/november-1962.

Darwin, Charles. *On the Origin of Species: By Means of Natural Selection.* Dover Giant Thrift edn. Mineola: Dover Publications, [1859] 2012.

Dauber, Kenneth. 'Bureaucratizing the Ethnographer's Magic'. *Current Anthropology* 36, no. 1 (1995): 75–95.

Diamond, Jared M. *Guns, Germs and Steel: The Fates of Human Societies.* 20th anniversary edn. New York: Norton, 2017.

Diethelm, P., and M. McKee. 'Denialism: What Is It and How Should Scientists Respond?'. *European Journal of Public Health* 19, no. 1 (January 2009): 2–4.

Douglas, Mary. *How Institutions Think.* New York: Syracuse University Press, 1986.

Dunbar, Robin. 'Social Networks and Their Implications for Community Living for People with a Learning Disability'. *International Journal of Developmental Disabilities* 61, no. 2 (April 2015): 101–6. https://doi.org/10.1179/20473869 14Z.00000000093.

Edwards, C. 'Believe in Better [Audio Technology Myths]'. *Engineering and Technology* 6, no. 11 (December 2011): 54–7.

Elbittar, Alexander, Andrei Gomberg, César Martinelli, and Thomas R. Palfrey. 'Ignorance and Bias in Collective Decisions'. *Journal of Economic Behavior and Organization*, 27 December 2016. https://doi.org/10.1016/j.jebo.2016.12.011.

Elsasser, Shaun W., and Riley E. Dunlap. 'Leading Voices in the Denier Choir: Conservative Columnists' Dismissal of Global Warming and Denigration of Climate Science'. *American Behavioral Scientist* 57, no. 6 (2013): 754–76.

Ely, J., A. Frankel, and E. Kamenica. "Suspense and Surprise." *Journal of Political Economy* 123, no. 1 (2015): 215–60. https://doi.org/10.1086/677350.

Evans, Anthony J., and Jeffrey Friedman. '"Search" vs. "Browse": A Theory of Error Grounded in Radical (Not Rational) Ignorance'. *Critical Review* 23, no. 1–2 (March 2011): 73–104. https://doi.org/10.1080/08913811.2011.574 471.

Festinger, Leon. *A Theory of Cognitive Dissonance*. 1st edn. Stanford: Stanford University Press, 1957.

Flood, Alison. 'Bill Gates Gives a Book to Every US Student Graduating in 2018'. *Guardian*, 8 June 2018. www.theguardian.com/books/2018/jun/08/bill-gates-gives-a-book-to-every-us-student-graduating-in-2018.

Flora, Gagan, Deepesh Gupta, and Archana Tiwari. 'Toxicity of Lead: A Review with Recent Updates'. *Interdisciplinary Toxicology* 5, no. 2 (June 2012): 47–58. https://doi.org/10.2478/v10102-012-0009-2.

Flynn, D. J., Brendan Nyhan, and Jason Reifler. 'The Nature and Origins of Misperceptions: Understanding False and Unsupported Beliefs About Politics'. *Political Psychology* 38 (February 2017): 127–50.

Flynn, James R. *What Is Intelligence?: Beyond the Flynn Effect*. 1st edn. Cambridge and New York: Cambridge University Press, 2007.

Friedman, Milton. *There's No Such Thing as a Free Lunch*. LaSalle: Open Court Publishing, 1977.

Frimer, Jeremy A., Linda J. Skitka, and Matt Motyl. 'Liberals and Conservatives Are Similarly Motivated to Avoid Exposure to One Another's Opinions'. *Journal of Experimental Social Psychology* 72 (1 September 2017): 1–12. https://doi.org/10.1016/j.jesp.2017.04.003.

Fruehwald, E. Scott. *Overcoming Cognitive Biases: Thinking More Clearly and Avoiding Manipulation by Others*. N.p.: CreateSpace Independent Publishing Platform, 2017.

Fruhen, L. S., R. H. Flin, and R. McLeod. 'Chronic Unease for Safety in Managers: A Conceptualisation'. *Journal of Risk Research* 17, no. 8 (14 September 2014): 969–79. https://doi.org/10.1080/13669877.2013.822924.

Garber, Dr Steven. 'The Politics of Self-Deception'. Washington Institute for Faith, Vocation and Culture, 15 April 2013. www.washingtoninst.org/4138/the-politics-of-self-deception-2/.

Gat, A. 'The Human Motivational Complex: Evolutionary Theory and the Causes of Hunter-Gatherer Fighting, Part II. Proximate, Subordinate, and Derivative Causes', *Anthropological Quarterly* 73, no. 2 (April 2000), 74–88.

Gauchat, Gordon. 'Politicization of Science in the Public Sphere: A Study of Public Trust in the United States, 1974 to 2010'. *American Sociological Review* 77, no. 2 (April 2012): 167–87. https://doi.org/10.1177/0003122412438225.

Gershoff, E. T., and A. Grogan-Kaylor. 'Spanking and Child Outcomes: Old Controversies and New Meta-Analyses'. *Journal of Family Psychology* 30, no. 4 (June 2016): 453–69. https://doi.org/10.1037/fam0000191.

Gigerenzer, G., and R. Garcia-Retamero. "Cassandra's Regret: The Psychology of Not Wanting to Know." *Psychological Review* 124, no. 2 (01 2017): 179–96. https://doi.org/10.1037/rev0000055.

Godfrey, Erin B., Carlos E. Santos, and Esther Burson. 'For Better or Worse? System-Justifying Beliefs in Sixth-Grade Predict Trajectories of Self-Esteem and Behavior Across Early Adolescence'. *Child Development* 90, no. 1 (19 June 2017): 180–95. https://doi.org/10.1111/cdev.12854.

Godin, Gaston, Mark Conner, and Paschal Sheeran. 'Bridging the Intention–Behaviour Gap: The Role of Moral Norm'. *British Journal of Social Psychology* 44, no. 4 (1 December 2005): 497–512. https://doi.org/10.1348/014466604X17452.

Graham, J., J. Haidt, and B. A. Nosek. 'Liberals and Conservatives Rely on Different Sets of Moral Foundations'. *Journal of Personality and Social Psychology* 96, no. 5 (May 2009): 1029–46. https://doi.org/10.1037/a0015141.

Greene, Joshua. *Moral Tribes: Emotion, Reason and the Gap between Us and Them*. London: Atlantic Books, 2015.

Greitemeyer, Tobias. 'I Am Right, You Are Wrong: How Biased Assimilation Increases the Perceived Gap between Believers and Skeptics of Violent Video Game Effects'. *PLoS ONE* 9, no. 4 (10 April 2014): e93440. https://doi.org/10.1371/journal.pone.0093440.

Griffin, James M., ed. *Global Climate Change: The Science, Economics and Politics*. Bush School Series in the Economics of Public Policy, vol. 4. Cheltenham and Northampton, MA: Edward Elgar, 2003.

Gross, Matthias. '"Objective Culture" and the Development of Nonknowledge: Georg Simmel and the Reverse Side of Knowing'. *Cultural Sociology* 6, no. 4 (2012): 422–37.

Gross, Matthias, and Alena Bleicher. '"It's Always Dark in Front of the Pickaxe": Organizing Ignorance in the Long-Term Remediation of Contaminated Land'. *Time and Society* 22, no. 3 (1 November 2013): 316–34. https://doi.org/10.1177/0961463X12444059.

Gyatso, Tenzin (the fourteenth Dalai Lama). 'Our Faith in Science'. *New York Times*, 12 November 2005, Opinion. www.nytimes.com/2005/11/12/opinion/our-faith-in-science.html.

Haidt, Jonathan. 'Morality'. *Perspectives on Psychological Science* 3, no. 1 (2008): 65–72.

———. *The Righteous Mind: Why Good People Are Divided by Politics and Religion*. New York: Knopf Doubleday Publishing Group, 2012.

Hann, Katie E. J., Madeleine Freeman, Lindsay Fraser, Jo Waller, Saskia C. Sanderson, Belinda Rahman, Lucy Side, Sue Gessler, and Anne Lanceley. 'Awareness, Knowledge, Perceptions, and Attitudes towards Genetic Testing for Cancer Risk among Ethnic Minority Groups: A Systematic Review'. *BMC Public Health* 17, no. 503 (25 May 2017). https://doi.org/10.1186/s12889-017-4375-8.

Hannikainen, Ivar R. 'Ideology between the Lines: Lay Inferences about Scientists' Values and Motives'. *Social Psychological and Personality Science*, 25 July 2018. https://doi.org/10.1177/1948550618790230.

Hardin, Garrett. 'The Tragedy of the Commons'. *Science*, New Series, 162, no. 3859 (13 December 1968): 1243–8.

Harris, C. Leor. *Evolution, Genesis and Revelations*. Albany: State University of New York Press, 1981.

Heathcote, James A. 'Why Do Old Men Have Big Ears?'. *British Medical Journal*, no. 7021 (1995): 1668.

Heimer, Carol A. 'Inert Facts and the Illusion of Knowledge: Strategic Uses of Ignorance in HIV Clinics'. *Economy and Society* 41, no. 1 (February 2012): 17–41. https://doi.org/10.1080/03085147.2011.637332.

Hein, Piet. *Grooks* (London: Hodder and Stoughton, 1969).

Hertwig, Ralph, and Christoph Engel. "Homo Ignorans: Deliberately Choosing Not to Know." Perspectives on Psychological Science 11, no. 3 (May 2016): 359–72. https://doi.org/10.1177/1745691616635594.

Hippel, William von, and Robert Trivers. 'The Evolution and Psychology of Self-Deception'. *Behavioral and Brain Sciences* 34, no. 1 (2011): 1–16. https://doi.org/10.1017/S0140525X10001354.

Hobbes, Thomas. *Leviathan*. Harmondsworth: Penguin Classics, [1651] 1982.

Hoffman, Tom. 'Rational Choice and Political Irrationality in the New Millennium'. *Critical Review* 27, no. 3–4 (2 October 2015): 299–315. https://doi.org/10.1080/08913811.2015.1111679.

Horowitz, Mark, William Yaworsky, and Kenneth Kickham. 'Whither the Blank Slate? A Report on the Reception of Evolutionary Biological Ideas among Sociological Theorists'. *Sociological Spectrum* 34, no. 6 (2 November 2014): 489–509. https://doi.org/10.1080/02732173.2014.947451.

Inbar, Yoel, David A. Pizarro, and Paul Bloom. 'Conservatives Are More Easily Disgusted than Liberals'. *Cognition and Emotion* 23, no. 4 (June 2009): 714–25. https://doi.org/10.1080/02699930802110007.

Johnson, Dominic. *God Is Watching You: How the Fear of God Makes Us Human*. Oxford: Oxford University Press, 2016.

Johnson, Dominic D. P., and James H. Fowler. 'The Evolution of Overconfidence'. *Nature* 477, no. 7364 (14 September 2011): 317–20. https://doi.org/10.1038/nature10384.

Kahan, Dan M., Hank Jenkins-Smith, Carol L. Silva, Tor Tarantola, and Donald Braman. 'Geoengineering and Climate Change Polarization: Testing a Two-

Channel Model of Science Communication', *Annals of the American Academy of Political and Social Science* 658, no. 1 (March 2015): 192–222.

Kahan, Dan M., Ellen Peters, Maggie Wittlin, Paul Slovic, Lisa Larrimore Ouellette, Donald Braman, and Gregory Mandel. 'The Polarizing Impact of Science Literacy and Numeracy on Perceived Climate Change Risks'. *Nature Climate Change* 2, no. 10 (27 May 2012): 732–5. https://doi.org/10.1038/nclimate1547.

Kahneman, Daniel. 'A Perspective on Judgment and Choice: Mapping Bounded Rationality'. *American Psychologist* 58, no. 9 (September 2003): 697–720. https://doi.org/10.1037/0003-066X.58.9.697.

———. *Thinking, Fast and Slow.* Reprint edition. New York: Farrar, Straus and Giroux, 2011.

Kahneman, D., J. L. Knetsch, and R. H. Thaler. 'Anomalies: The Endowment Effect, Loss Aversion, and Status Quo Bias'. *Journal of Economic Perspectives* 5, no. 1 (1991): 193–206.

Kaplan, David. 'The Darker Side of the "Original Affluent Society"'. *Journal of Anthropological Research* 56, no. 3 (Autumn 2000): 301–24.

Keene, J. R., P. D. Bolls, H. Shoenberger, and C. K. Berke. 'The Biological Roots of Political Extremism: Negativity Bias, Political Ideology, and Preferences for Political News'. *Politics and the Life Sciences* 36, no. 2 (Fall 2017): 37–48. https://doi.org/10.1017/pls.2017.16.

Keil, Frank C. *Semantic and Conceptual Development: An Ontological Perspective.* Reprint edn. Cambridge, MA: Harvard University Press, 2014.

Kelemen, Deborah. 'The Scope of Teleological Thinking in Preschool Children'. *Cognition* 70, no. 3 (April 1999): 241–72. https://doi.org/10.1016/S0010-0277(99)00010-4.

Kierkegaard, Søren. *Kierkegaard's Writings, XVI, Volume 16: Works of Love.* Princeton: Princeton University Press, [1847] 2013.

Kingsley, Patrick. 'Turkey Drops Evolution from Curriculum, Angering Secularists'. *New York Times*, 23 June 2017, Europe. www.nytimes.com/2017/06/23/world/europe/turkey-evolution-high-school-curriculum.html.

Kipling, Rudyard. *Kipling: Poems.* London: Knopf Doubleday Publishing Group, 2013.

Kirkebøen, Geir, Erik Vasaasen, and Karl Halvor Teigen. 'Revisions and Regret: The Cost of Changing Your Mind'. *Journal of Behavioral Decision Making* 26, no. 1 (January 2013): 1–12. https://doi.org/10.1002/bdm.756.

Klintman, Mikael. *Citizen-Consumers and Evolution: Reducing Environmental Harm through Our Social Motivation.* Basingstoke: Palgrave Pivot, 2012.

———. *Human Sciences and Human Interests: Integrating the Social, Economic, and Evolutionary Sciences.* London: Routledge, 2017.

Klintman, Mikael, Thomas Lunderquist, and Andreas Olsson. *Gruppens grepp: Hur vi fördomsfulla flockvarelser kan lära oss leva tillsammans.* Stockholm: Natur & Kultur, 2018.

Klintman, Mikael, Kjell Mårtensson, and Magnus Johansson. 'Bioenergi För Uppvärmning – Hushållens Perspektiv'. Research report. Lund University, Department of Sociology, 2003.

Kuhn, Thomas S. *The Structure of Scientific Revolutions.* 50th anniversary edn. Chicago: University of Chicago Press, [1962] 2012.

Kupferschmidt, Kai. 'Can Skeptical Parents Be Persuaded to Vaccinate?' *Science,* 27 April 2017. https://doi.org/10.1126/science.aal1108.

Kuran, Timur. *Private Truths, Public Lies: The Social Consequences of Preference Falsification.* Cambridge, MA: Harvard University Press, 1998.

Larson, Heidi J., Alexandre de Figueiredo, Zhao Xiahong, William S. Schulz, Pierre Verger, Iain G. Johnston, Alex R. Cook, and Nick S. Jones. 'The State of Vaccine Confidence 2016: Global Insights Through a 67-Country Survey'. *EBioMedicine* 12 (13 September 2016): 295–301. https://doi.org/10.1016/j.ebiom.2016.08.042.

LeBlanc, Steven A., with Katherine E. Register. *Constant Battles: The Myth of the Peaceful, Noble Savage.* 1st edn. New York: St Martin's Press, 2003.

Lemieux, Pierre. 'Following the Herd'. *Regulation* 26, no. 4 (Winter 2003–4): 16–21.

Lestel, Dominique. 'The Carnivore's Ethics'. *Angelaki: Journal of the Theoretical Humanities* 19, no. 3 (September 2014): 161–7. https://doi.org/10.1080/0969725X.2014.976066.

Levitin, Daniel. *A Field Guide to Lies and Statistics: A Neuroscientist on How to Make Sense of a Complex World.* New York: Penguin, 2018.

Lewandowsky, Stephan, Gilles E. Gignac, and Klaus Oberauer. 'The Role of Conspiracist Ideation and Worldviews in Predicting Rejection of Science'. *PLOS ONE* 8, no. 10 (October 2013): e75637. https://doi.org/10.1371/journal.pone.0075637.

Lord, C. G., L. Ross, and M. R. Lepper. 'Biased Assimilation and Attitude Polarization: The Effects of Prior Theories on Subsequently Considered Evidence'. *Journal of Personality and Social Psychology* 37, no. 11 (1979): 2098–109. https://doi.org/10.1037//0022-3514.37.11.2098.

Lukianoff, Greg, and Jonathan Haidt. *The Coddling of the American Mind: How Good Intentions and Bad Ideas Are Setting Up a Generation for Failure.* New York: Penguin Press, 2018.

MacNeill, Allen. 'The Capacity for Religious Experience Is an Evolutionary Adaptation to Warfare'. In *The Psychology of Resolving Global Conflicts: From War to Peace,* edited by F. A. Stout, 257–84. Westport: Praeger Security International, 2006.

Masiero, Marianna, Claudio Lucchiari, and Gabriella Pravettoni, 'Personal Fable: Optimistic Bias in Cigarette Smokers'. *International Journal of High Risk Behaviors and Addiction* 4, no. 1 (20 March 2015). https://doi.org/10.5812/ijhrba.20939.

Maslow, Abraham H. 'The Need to Know and the Fear of Knowing'. In *Toward a Psychology of Being*, 57–64. Princeton: D. Van Nostrand, 1962. https://doi.org/10.1037/10793-005.

Mateo, Jill M. 'Perspectives: Hamilton's Legacy: Mechanisms of Kin Recognition in Humans'. *Ethology* 121, no. 5 (May 2015): 419–27. https://doi.org/10.1111/eth.12358.

Matthews, Paul, and Rob Stephens. 'Sociable Knowledge Sharing Online: Philosophy, Patterns and Intervention'. *Aslib Proceedings* 62, no. 6 (23 November 2010): 539–53. https://doi.org/10.1108/000125310110896 67.

Matthews, R. A. J. 'Tumbling Toast, Murphy's Law and the Fundamental Constants'. *European Journal of Physics* 16, no. 4 (18 July 1995): 172–6. https://doi.org/10.1088/0143-0807/16/4/005.

Maupassant, Guy de. 'In the Moonlight'. N.p.: CreateSpace Independent Publishing Platform, 2014.

McCathy, Bob. 'Four Audio Myths'. *Sound and Video Contractor* 29, no. 6 (June 2011): 44–9.

McGoey, Linsey. 'The Logic of Strategic Ignorance'. *British Journal of Sociology* 63, no. 3 (1 September 2012): 533–76. https://doi.org/10.1111/j.1468-4446.2012.01424.x.

McIntyre, Lee. *Post-Truth*. Cambridge, MA: MIT Press, 2018.

McKenzie, Pamela J. 'Justifying Cognitive Authority Decisions: Discursive Strategies of Information Seekers'. *Library Quarterly* 73, no. 3 (July 2003): 261–88.

Mead, Rebecca, Momna Hejmadi, and Laurence D. Hurst. 'Scientific Aptitude Better Explains Poor Responses to Teaching of Evolution than Psychological Conflicts'. *Nature Ecology and Evolution* 2 (8 January 2018): 388–94. https://doi.org/10.1038/s41559-017-0442-x.

Mercier, Hugo. 'Using Evolutionary Thinking to Cut Across Disciplines'. In *Comparative Decision Making*, edited by Thomas R. Zentall and Philip H. Crowley, 279–304. Oxford: Oxford University Press, 2013.

Mercier, Hugo, and Christophe Heintz. 'Scientists' Argumentative Reasoning'. *Topoi* 33, no. 2 (October 2014): 513–24. https://doi.org/10.1007/s11245-013-9217-4.

Mercier, Hugo, and Helene E. Landemore. 'Reasoning Is for Arguing: Understanding the Successes and Failures of Deliberation'. *Political Psychology* 33, no. 2 (April 2012): 243–58. https://doi.org/10.1111/j.1467-9221.2012.00873.x.

Merton, Robert K. 'Three Fragments from a Sociologist's Notebooks: Establishing the Phenomenon, Specified Ignorance, and Strategic Research Materials'. *Annual Review of Sociology* 13, no. 1 (August 1987): 1–29. https://doi.org/10.1146/annurev.so.13.080187.000245.

Meyer, Michelle N., and Christopher Chabris, 'Why Psychologists' Food Fight Matters', *Slate*, 31 July 2014, www.slate.com/articles/health_and_science/

science/2014/07/replication_controversy_in_psychology_bullying_file_draw er_effect_blog_posts.html.

Miller, Jon D., Eugenie C. Scott, and Shinji Okamoto. 'Public Acceptance of Evolution'. *Science* 313, no. 5788 (11 August 2006): 765–6. https://doi. org/10.1126/science.1126746.

Moore, Wilbert E., and Melvin M. Tumin. 'Some Social Functions of Ignorance'. *American Sociological Review* 14, no. 6 (December 1949): 787–95.

Nan, Xiaoli, and Kelly Daily. 'Biased Assimilation and Need for Closure: Examining the Effects of Mixed Blogs on Vaccine-Related Beliefs'. *Journal of Health Communication* 20, no. 4 (3 April 2015): 462–71.

Nietzsche, Friedrich. *The Birth of Tragedy*. Whitefish: Kessinger Publishing, [1872] 2010.

Nordhaus, William. 'Critical Assumptions in the Stern Review on Climate Change'. *Science* 317, no. 5835 (2007): 201–2.

Nyborg, Karine. 'I Don't Want to Hear about It: Rational Ignorance among Duty-Oriented Consumers'. *Journal of Economic Behavior and Organization* 79, no. 3 (August 2011): 263–74.

Payne, Stanley G. *A History of Fascism 1914–1945*. Madison: University of Wisconsin Press, 1996.

Pence, Mike. 'Theory of the Origin of Man'. *Congressional Record: Proceedings and Debates of the US Congress*, 11 July 2002. www.congress.gov/congressional-record/2002/7/11/house-section/article/h4527-1.

Perlman, M. 'Golden Ears and Meter Readers: The Contest for Epistemic Authority in Audiophilia'. *Social Studies of Science* 34, no. 5 (1 December 2004): 783–807. https://doi.org/10.1177/0306312704047613.

Pfeiffer, Christian, Dirk Baier, and Soeren Kliem. 'Zur Entwicklung der Gewalt in Deutschland. Schwerpunkte: Jugendliche und Flüchtlinge Als Täter und Opfer' ('Teenagers as Perpetrators and Victims'). Research report. Zürich: Zürcher Hochschule für Angewandte Wissenschaften, January 2018.

Pinker, Steven. *The Blank Slate: The Modern Denial of Human Nature*. 1st edn. New York: Viking Press, 2002.

_____. *Enlightenment Now: The Case for Reason, Science, Humanism, and Progress*. New York: Viking, 2018.

Plotkin, Stanley, Jeffrey S. Gerber, and Paul A. Offit. 'Vaccines and Autism: A Tale of Shifting Hypotheses'. *Clinical Infectious Diseases* 48, no. 4 (15 February 2009): 456–61. https://doi.org/10.1086/596476.

Plous, Scott. 'Biases in the Assimilation of Technological Breakdowns: Do Accidents Make Us Safer?' *Journal of Applied Social Psychology* 21, no. 13 (1991): 1058–82.

Pope Francis. 'Laudato Sì of the Holy Father Francis on Care for Our Common Home'. Encyclical Letter, The Holy See, 24 May 2015. http://w2.vatican.va/content/francesco/en/encyclicals/documents/papa-francesco_20150524_enc iclica-laudato-si.html.

Popper, Karl Raimund. *The Logic of Scientific Discovery*. London: Psychology Press, 1959.

Post, Senja. 'Communicating Science in Public Controversies: Strategic Considerations of the German Climate Scientists'. *Public Understanding of Science* 25, no. 1 (2016): 61–70.

Prato, Carlo, and Stephane Wolton. 'Rational Ignorance, Populism, and Reform'. *European Journal of Political Economy* 55 (December 2017), 119–35. https://doi.org/10.1016/j.ejpoleco.2017.11.006.

Prelec, Dražen, H. Sebastian Seung, and John McCoy, 'A Solution to the Single-Question Crowd Wisdom Problem'. *Nature* 541, no. 7638 (January 2017): 532–5. https://doi.org/10.1038/nature21054.

Rawls, John. *A Theory of Justice*. Cambridge, MA: Harvard University Press, 1971.

Rayner, Steve. 'Uncomfortable Knowledge: The Social Construction of Ignorance in Science and Environmental Policy Discourses'. *Economy and Society* 41, no. 1 (1 February 2012): 107–25. https://doi.org/10.1080/03085147.2011.637335.

Reagan, Ronald. 'A Time for Choosing' (speech, 27 October 1964). *The Constitution Reader*, accessed 13 February 2019. http://cdn.constitutionreader.com/files/pdf/constitution/ch123.pdf.

Revesz, Rachael. 'MPs Voted That Animals Cannot Feel Pain or Emotions'. *Independent*, 20 November 2017. www.independent.co.uk/news/uk/home-news/brexit-bill-latest-animal-sentience-cannot-feel-pain-emotion-vote-mps-agree-eu-withdrawal-bill-a8064676.html.

Rosling, Hans, Anna Rosling Rönnlund, and Ola Rosling. *Factfulness: Ten Reasons We're Wrong About the World – and Why Things Are Better Than You Think*. New York: Sceptre, 2018.

Royzman, Edward, Corey Cusimano, and Robert F. Leeman. 'What Lies Beneath? Fear vs. Disgust as Affective Predictors of Absolutist Opposition to Genetically Modified Food and Other New Technologies'. *Judgment and Decision Making* 12, no. 5 (September 2017): 466–80.

Russell, Miles. *Piltdown Man: The Secret Life of Charles Dawson*. Stroud: Tempus, 2004.

Rutjens, Bastiaan T., Robbie M. Sutton, and Romy van der Lee. 'Not All Skepticism Is Equal: Exploring the Ideological Antecedents of Science Acceptance and Rejection'. *Personality and Social Psychology Bulletin* 44, no. 3 (2018): 384–405.

Sandel, Michael J. *What Money Can't Buy: The Moral Limits of Markets*. Reprint edn. New York: Farrar, Straus and Giroux, 2013.

Scheinman, Ted. 'What Lies Beneath: Why Do Archaeological Fraudsters Work So Hard to Deceive Us?'. *Aeon*, 28 July 2015, Essays. https://aeon.co/essays/why-do-archaeological-fraudsters-work-so-hard-to-deceive-us.

Shtulman, A. 'Qualitative Differences between Naive and Scientific Theories of

Evolution'. *Cognitive Psychology* 52, no. 2 (March 2006): 170–94. https://doi. org/10.1016/j.cogpsych.2005.10.001.

Singer, Peter. 'The Man Who Didn't Save the World'. *Project Syndicate*, 12 December 2017. www.project-syndicate.org/commentary/salvator-mun di-purchase-price-world-s-poor-by-peter-singer-2017-12.

Somin, Ilya. *Democracy and Political Ignorance: Why Smaller Government Is Smarter*. 1st edn. Stanford: Stanford Law Books, 2013.

Steward, Malcolm. 'The Original SATA Cable Post'. *Malcolm Steward: Audio Journalist*, 15 June 2011. http://web.archive.org/web/20110615192300/http:// www.malcolmsteward.co.uk/?p=2534.

Stigler, George. 'The Economics of Information'. *Journal of Political Economy*, no. 3 (1961): 213.

Tavris, Carol, and Elliot Aronson. *Mistakes Were Made (but Not by Me): Why We Justify Foolish Beliefs, Bad Decisions, and Hurtful Acts*. Boston: Mariner Books, 2015.

Tegmark, Max. *Life 3.0: Being Human in the Age of Artificial Intelligence*. London: Allen Lane, 2017.

Thaler, Richard H., and Prof. Cass R. Sunstein. *Nudge: Improving Decisions About Health, Wealth, and Happiness*. 1st edn. New Haven: Yale University Press, 2008.

The Economist. 'Sincere Deceivers'. Leaders, 15 July 2004. www.economist.com/ node/2921794.

Tocqueville, Alexis de. *Democracy in America: The Complete and Unabridged Volumes I and II*. New York: Bantam Classics, [1835] 2000.

Trivers, Robert. 'Reciprocal Altruism: 30 Years Later'. In *Cooperation in Primates and Humans: Mechanisms and Evolution*, edited by Peter Kappeler and Carel P. van Schaik, 67–83. Berlin: Springer, 2006.

_____. *Deceit and Self-Deception: Fooling Yourself the Better to Fool Others*. New York: Penguin, 2011.

Tuomisto, H. L., I. D. Hodge, P. Riordan, and D. W. Macdonald. 'Does Organic Farming Reduce Environmental Impacts? – A Meta-Analysis of European Research'. *Journal of Environmental Management* 112 (15 December 2012): 309–20. https://doi.org/10.1016/j.jenvman.2012.08.018.

Vandermassen, Griet. 'Evolution and Rape: A Feminist Darwinian Perspective'. *Sex Roles* 64, no. 9–10 (May 2011): 732–47. https://doi.org/10.1007/s11199- 010-9895-y.

Viscusi, W. Kip. 'Do Smokers Underestimate Risks?' *Journal of Political Economy* 98, no. 6 (1990): 1253–69.

Wakefield, A. J., S. H. Murch, A. Anthony, J. Linnell, D. M. Casson, M. Malik, M. Berelowitz, *et al.* 'RETRACTED: Ileal-Lymphoid-Nodular Hyperplasia, Non-Specific Colitis, and Pervasive Developmental Disorder in Children'. *Lancet* 351, no. 9103 (28 February 1998): 637–41. https://doi.org/10.1016/ S0140-6736(97)11096-0.

Weber, Max. *The Protestant Ethic and the Spirit of Capitalism: And Other Writings*. New York: Penguin, [1905] 2002.

Wessel, Lindzi. 'Four Vaccine Myths and Where They Came From'. *Science*, 27 April 2017. https://doi.org/10.1126/science.aal1110.

Wolsko, Christopher, Hector Ariceaga, and Jesse Seiden. 'Red, White, and Blue Enough to Be Green: Effects of Moral Framing on Climate Change Attitudes and Conservation Behaviors'. *Journal of Experimental Social Psychology* 65 (July 2016): 7–19. https://doi.org/10.1016/j.jesp.2016.02.005.

Yancy, George, and Noam Chomsky. 'Noam Chomsky: On Trump and the State of the Union'. *New York Times*, 5 July 2017, Opinion. www.nytimes.com/2017/07/05/opinion/noam-chomsky-on-trump-and-the-state-of-the-union.html.

Zenger, Jack, and Joseph Folkman. 'Are Women Better Leaders Than Men?'. *Harvard Business Review*, 15 March 2012. https://hbr.org/2012/03/a-study-in-leadership-women-do.

Zhang, Chen, R. Wohlhueter, and Han Zhang, 'Genetically Modified Foods: A Critical Review of Their Promise and Problems'. *Food Science and Human Wellness* 5, no. 3 (1 January 2016): 116–23.

Index

Index